Caterer, cookery teacher and author of *Hot & Spicy*, Marlena Spieler is truly innovative in her field. Well respected by experts on both sides of the Atlantic, she contributes to all the major food publications, including *Taste*, in this country.

D1375420

By the same author

Sun-drenched Cuisine
Hot & Spicy

MARLENA
SPIELER

Flavours of Mexico

Grafton Books

A Division of HarperCollinsPublishers

GraftonBooks
A Division of HarperCollins*Publishers*
77–85 Fulham Palace Road,
Hammersmith, London W6 8JB

A GraftonBooks Paperback Original 1991
9 8 7 6 5 4 3 2 1

A CIP catalogue record for this book
is available from the British Library

ISBN 0-586-21043-1

Printed in Great Britain by
HarperCollinsManufacturing Glasgow

Set in Janson Text

Flavours of Mexico

ACKNOWLEDGEMENTS

To: Leah, as always,

To: Thirty-Seven, with love,

To: Jane Middleton, extremely understanding and patient editor; Teresa Chris, literary agent, whose enthusiasm for my Mexican feasts resulted in this book; Leslie Forbes, for tales of Oaxaca and a shoulder to cry or laugh on as the need came up; editor Paul Richardson, for sending me off to exotic places like Provence, Ireland or Bulgaria, each time I became insufferable on the subject of Mexican food.

To: Gretchen Spieler for her transatlantic wishful-tasting; Fred and Mary Barclay, Alex Bratell, Jacqueline Jones, Paula Levine, Jo McAllister, Alan McLaughlan, Robin and Hélène Simpson and family for their tasting time and talents; David Aspin for his tortilla press; Joan and Malcolm Key for their assistance in locating resources; Andrew Barr for Mexican beer information.

To: my grandmother, Sophia 'Bachi' Dubowsky; my parents, Caroline and Izzy Smith; and my computer 'angels', Estelle and Sy Opper.

CONTENTS

◄◄◄◄◄◄◄◄◄◄◄◄◄◄◄◄◄◄◄◄◄◄◄◄◄◄◄◄◄◄◄<>►►►►►►►►►►►►►►►►►►►►►►►►►►►►►►

PREFACE

I grew up in California, in a neighbourhood that bordered on a large Mexican population. I revelled in the cross-cultural richness this provided: at school it meant learning bits of Spanish and teaching English to the new arrivals, delighting in their different lifestyle, holidays and fiestas. I knew nothing of the economic hardships of their own country that brought these people to my neighbourhood, nor did I know of the problems they faced once they arrived. I was a child, and was innocently, though selfishly, delighted that their lives enriched mine.

Mexican culture exerted other influences on my childhood as well. At one time California, as well as much of America's Southwest, was a part of New Spain, then Mexico, and contemporary California reflects this. Everyday life was, and is, constantly coloured by our shared heritage, especially in architecture and food.

Ah, the food. Weekly outings to our local Mexican restaurant, *tacos* for school dinners, a big cauldron of *chile con carne* as a special treat, *tamales* homemade by our neighbours at fiesta times. It was food that made eating fun, unlike the ordinary, three-square meat and potato meals. This was spicy food, full of flavours so vibrant I was surprised we children were actually allowed to eat it. In my young mind it surpassed mere physical nourishment and represented something more than food. No doubt it kindled my interest in food and travel.

Yet the Mexican food I grew up eating was but a small regional variation of an ancient, complex cuisine. As a teenager I visited Mexico for the first time and thrilled at the sophistication and variety of the country and its cuisine. I emerged from the train in Guadalajara after a forty-eight-hour journey and was immediately captivated. Everything was wildly different from whatever I had come to expect from life: here were tropical aromas in the air, mariachis serenading café-goers, parrots resting on perches lining the path through the park. Schoolgirls walked arm-in-arm, as did mothers and daughters; it was more like the Mediterranean than a short distance from my US home. And the food was scarcely the delicious but not terribly delicate fried minced-meat *tacos*, sloppy chilli stews and red chilli *enchiladas* I grew up with. First of all, food was everywhere: in the market-place cafés known as *fondas*, which displayed row upon row of *cazuelitas* filled with an endless variety of fragrantly sauced dishes; food stalls lined up along the streets, each one with its own special offering; outdoor restaurants with their umbrella-topped tables emitted the aroma of savoury grilled foods; street vendors offered vividly coloured fruit ices – it all appeared as a bright mosaic of colours and flavours that beckoned to me.

I dipped into bowls of pungent *salsa*, freshly cooked tortillas wrapped around tasty shreds of meat, cocktails of seafood in pristine freshness and variety. I sampled grilled turtle meat slathered with *salsa*, funny little worms that tasted crisp, rather than offensive as I had expected, *quesadillas* filled with cheese or with soft brains, lightly cooked eggs splashed with *salsa* and scattered with enough chillies to intimidate even the most macho.

I remained undaunted, ever eager, admittedly greedy. I could not be restrained, and tasted my way eagerly through the republic of Mexico. There were bad moments, to be sure – the unexpected tuft of fur that peered out of my *taco* somewhere in a desolate patch of Baja, or the several days of 'Montezuma's revenge' visited on me after a particularly enjoyable bout of market-place feasting. But mostly I thrived, both in body and mind. It was a time of discovery, filled with images of landscape and flavoured with foods that have coloured the way I have lived my adult life.

I have since visited often, but not nearly enough. I have learned and cooked, yet the more I feel I have mastered the language of Mexico's cuisines, the more I feel it slip away. It has a richness of culture and cuisine that one lifetime is far too short for.

In this book I have tried to communicate my enthusiasm and joy through a collection of vibrant and exciting dishes. There are so many dishes not represented at all: the variety of regional

◁◁◁◁◁◁◁◁◁◁◁◁◁◁◁◁◁◁◁◁◁◁◁◁◁◁◁◁◁◁▷▷▷▷▷▷▷▷▷▷▷▷▷▷▷▷▷▷▷▷▷▷▷▷▷▷▷▷▷▷

dishes is far too extensive for even the most dedicated cook to research and catalogue. I have tried to offer a balance of traditional regional and national dishes, as well as contemporary interpretations and ideas. I have also included a selection of recipes from America's Southwest, because they are familiar to the British diner; too often, however, Mexican and Southwestern dishes are lumped together in England, without any explanations.

I offer my apologies for any omissions of the reader's favourites; a number of Mexican specialities can also be found in my other Grafton book, *Hot & Spicy*.

I urge the reader to read the eloquent writers on Mexican food, most notably Diana Kennedy, Elizabeth Lambert Ortiz, and Patricia Quintara, as well as such travel writers as Kate Simon and Sybil Bedford, all of whom offer further glimpses into life in a land of great complexity and richness.

A note of practicality: all recipes serve four, approximately, unless otherwise specified.

INTRODUCTION

Cocina Mexicana is in my opinion one of the world's greatest cuisines. For a nation that in many ways seems quite primitive to North Americans and Europeans, Mexico offers a cuisine that is staggering in its complexity and range.

It has a culinary history that speaks of antiquity, with dishes as old as civilization itself. Layers of foreign influence have contributed to its national character, but in the end Mexican cooking is distinct from all other cuisines and is as eloquent an expression of Mexico as its music, dance and painting. The food is tied up not only with Mexico's religious, cultural and political history but with the landscape itself. Just being in Mexico makes everything taste different. Take a deep breath: in Mexico the air has as much flavour as the food (D. H. Lawrence likened Mexico's distinctive scent to the individual smell each person has).

Mexico is a land of greatly differing climates and regions, each with its own distinctive landscape, culture and cuisine. The northern reaches are great expanses of endless desert, broken up only by tumbleweeds and cacti. At times this austere desert glides right down to the sea, but soon the coast grows lush again, with small villages and tourist resorts juxtaposed against each other. Away from the coast the desert is transformed into tropical jungle, with moist, verdant smells and exotic wildlife, then come the mountains, capped breathtakingly with snow and dotted with myriad lakes. The Yucatán Peninsula is flat and so densely covered with jungle that until the relatively recent motorway was completed, the peninsula was not connected with the rest of Mexico, except by air or sea. The Maya, the inhabitants of the Yucatán, were never completely conquered by the Spanish; their pride remains undiminished.

The landscape is exotically beautiful, even the arid desert, and so too are the cities. Even in industrial decay, they shimmer with a vitality and complexity.

Mexico City, once the Aztec city of Tenochtitlán, is one of the largest cities ever built. Contemporary Mexico City is a startling place where well-dressed cosmopolites walk next to serape-draped *campesinos*, and cars share the roads with donkeys, sometimes the latter moving faster due to the horrendous traffic congestion. Pollution hangs in the air, covering all in its ominous cloak. Modern office blocks are built alongside Spanish colonial mansions and the ruins of Aztec palaces; an Indian vendor spreads his or her humble offerings on a cloth laid out in the street, outside the door of a huge, ultra-sleek shopping centre.

One can sit in a café and watch as young trendsetters swing down the street, looking as glam as in Paris; an old Indian man might try to sell you a snake; a group of schoolgirls giggle down the street, in starched white shirts, black hair in tight plaits down their backs, hugging their books to their chests as they window shop and enjoy their group outing; black-coated, fur-hatted Chassidim hurry past, lost in discussion and contemplation of life's mysteries. You dip your *churro* or croissant into your *café de olla*, and continue to watch the parade of life outside the window.

While none compares in variety or size with Mexico (as the natives call it) there are so many cities, towns and villages, each with widely differing architecture, ethnic make-up, historical influences, geography and so on. Guadalajara, Mexico's second largest city, is eminently hospitable. Founded in 1539, its architecture reflects the period: there are beautiful plazas, and it is scattered with trees, monuments and fountains. Then there is Oaxaca, the rugged mountain city that is descended from the Zapotecs rather than the Aztecs, and nearby Teotihuacán, with its matriarchal tribe of very tall, very strong women. San Luis Potosí, the Spanish mining town founded on the site of the Cimichimec Indian town of Tanga-Manga, grew very rich as the Spanish discovered the great veins of silver that ran beneath the region. The buildings remain today, beautiful and lavish. Pátzcuaro is also an old colonial town, quiet and charming, built on Tarascan Indian land and enjoying pleasant weather, lush surroundings and secure peace. Southeast is the Caribbean port city

◁◁▷▷▷▷▷▷▷▷▷▷▷▷▷▷▷▷▷▷▷▷▷▷▷▷▷▷▷▷▷▷▷▷

of Veracruz, as raucous and wild as Marseilles, with its European and Afro-Caribbean flavour apparent in everything: the language, the music, the beat of the city. Housefronts form pastel patterns of red, yellow, pale and bright blue, ochre and umber against the tropically lush greenery that weaves its way through the city. Further south lies the Yucatán Peninsula and its capital Mérida, a Mayan-descended colonial town with recent Lebanese influence added to the cultural stew.

A Brief History

One can sit down at a table in Mexico and tuck into a plate of *enchiladas*, or nibble on *antojitos*, or savour a plate of grilled meat rolled into soft tortillas, but the more one learns about Mexico, the more one can taste and appreciate each layer of influence that has gone into creating the cuisine. Aztec, Toltec, Mayan, Zapotec, and other Indians have bequeathed their heritage, as have the Spanish Conquest, brief French occupation and modern North American influence.

The earliest Mexicans were Stone Age people who hunted animals and gathered what food they could find. Sometime after 5200 BC signs of agriculture and domestication appeared: corn, beans, squash and tomatoes were raised; turkeys and dogs were kept for meat. We know that by 3500 BC chillies had been discovered as edible and were being cultivated. This is essentially the beginning of Mexican cuisine.

By 2400 BC pottery was being fashioned, the predecessors of today's rustic *cazuelitas* and *ollas*. By around this time, Mesoamerica (northern Mexico south through Guatemala) was developing a farming culture: terraces, irrigation ducts, religious institutions devoted to Earth's fertility. Indian plant-breeders became skilful, eventually trading seeds and information with other tribes throughout the Americas. (It is estimated that half of the world's present fruits, vegetables and grains is a result of the work of the Indian botanists and farmers.) For the first time, humankind had time to devote to other than scraping a living, and this encouraged the blossoming of artistic and religious culture. By this time *pipiáns*, or stews prepared from ground pumpkin seeds, and chillies had become part of the diet, much as they are today.

From 1200 to 400 BC the Olmecs lived in what is today the region of Tabasco, south of Veracruz. They were the first to use a calendar of 365 days, and one of the most outstanding characteristics of their culture is their sculpture, great deformed creatures and faces cut out of stone that still have not been explained. From 300 to 900 AD was Mexico's Classic Period, when life no longer centred in the villages but in the cities. Artistic, cultural, and religious life prospered, as did economic life: a merchant and artisan class developed, and landlords took control of the fields, essentially enchaining the farmer. The Maya were at the apex of this culture, which also included the Zapotec, Toltec, and Totonac, and were the first to use the concept of zero in mathematics. It could be said that they were obsessed with time: their calendars were calculated for centuries and centuries to come. In general this was a time of great achievement. The cultural level has been compared with that of the Etruscans. They have left reliefs and frescoes, pyramids, hieroglyphics, figurines, all depicting joyfulness and a rich life.

Around 800 to 900 AD some sort of major disruption occurred: the paintings of the time show war and major migration; people evidently wandered from their homes and lost faith in their gods, and the fabric of society unravelled. Then, around the 1300s, the Aztecs settled into the Mexico Valley on Lake Texcoco, with the island of Tenochtitlán their capital. It, along with its surroundings that expanded into states and territories, grew extremely rich. Gold, food, clothing, perfumes, all were in abundance; events of state or religion entailed elaborate ceremony.

Most of the people lived on a diet of corn, prepared in the same way *pozole* is today, often ground into flat cakes, and a variety of beans, augmented with an occasional scrap of meat (especially the little hairless dogs they raised as food) or fowl. Everything was seasoned with any of the wide array of chillies. To forget their troubles, the Indians drank *pulque*, the fermented sap of the maguey, still drunk today in the more rural areas of the republic.

The ruling classes also had such luxury foods as chocolate, in addition to their occasional cannibal feasts of sacrificial victims'

◁◁◁▷▷

arms and legs. Though we have no Aztec recipes and records, some of the early Spanish visitors described the royal feasts: a myriad of dishes, many still eaten in modern Mexico, though in a somewhat changed form. Sweet *tamales*, birds cooked with chillies and seeds, turkey with tomatoes, squash seeds and chillies, *tamales* with beans, birds with dried corn, and a wide variety of tortillas were among the dishes described by Bernadino de Sahagun, the Spanish friar who chronicled the Conquest. He also described the different chocolates, each with its own colour, consistency and fragrance.

The Aztecs were undoubtedly a warlike people, but they developed a culture of great richness and diversity. Tenochtitlán, the island capital, was grander than anything in Europe at the time. A pyramid sat at the centre of the town, and before it was an enormous open-air market where women sold corn tortillas, much as they do today. Canals wove through the city transporting sleek canoes piled high with fruit, vegetables and flowers destined for the market.

In 1519 Hernán Cortés landed in what would later be called Veracruz. When he made his way to Tenochtitlán and surveyed the riches he decided he wanted it all. Montezuma II, the Aztec emperor, tried to tempt the Spaniards away with gold but that only whetted their greedy appetites. The Spaniards' chief resource was sheer bravado, hardly a match for the huge numbers of fierce Aztecs, and history would have been very different if it hadn't been for the legend of Quetzalcoatl. This legend told of a high priest and leader of the Toltecs at Tula, who stopped human sacrifice and transformed the warlike Toltecs into peaceful farmers and artisans. The old priests, who depended upon human sacrifice for their livelihood, drove him away by tricking him into breaking his vows of chastity, and as he sailed away into the Caribbean he promised to return in a future age.

When Montezuma saw Cortés arrive from the sea he thought it was the prophecy fulfilled, and doubtless felt unable to do battle with this godly reincarnation. And so began the Conquest with its horrendous battles and cruel domination which resulted in the Mestizo culture, that of modern Mexico. For an eyewitness account of this period read Bernal Díaz's *Historia Verdadera de la Conquista de la Nueva España*. An abridged version is available in translation – *The Conquest of New Spain* by J. M. Cohen (Penguin Classic).

The Spanish may have intended only to reap the gold and riches of this vast empire but in the end they contributed much to developing the culture of Mexico. The Indians were quick to take to some of the crops and domestic animals that the Spanish introduced – pigs especially, for their fat changed Indian food more than any other ingredient: it gave the Indians the means to fry, thereby increasing their culinary range. Pre-Columbian Indians lacked milk, butter and cheese as well as wheat flour; they had no chickens and the only eggs they had were from wild birds that they managed to steal from a nest. As a mixed-race culture developed, so too did a cuisine based on both Indian and Spanish foods.

I always wondered why olives/olive oil and winemaking never secured a foothold in the combination of Indian and Spanish cultures/cuisines. No doubt the fruits would grow well in much of the region and they are, after all, an important part of Spanish Mediterranean cuisine. In early years, however, the Spanish viewed Mexico as a place to take riches from rather than create any competition in the marketplace, and they punished anyone cultivating olives or wine grapes with fines and imprisonment. (Baja California now produces some quite decent wines, and olives and olive oil do figure, if not very prominently, in Mexican cookery.)

Spain ruled Mexico until 1821, realizing as early as the 1550s that the Indians were more easily subdued by the quietly determined monks than by the erratic and volatile conquistadors. By the time independence came to Mexico, many of the Indians had been converted to Christianity, including those in the region of New Spain, which is today the California coast, north to San Francisco. Political upheaval never abated, and governments rose and fell with alarming rapidity until the French intervention in 1861. While the country was in a state of civil war, Napoleon III of France ordered his troops to advance on Mexico City, with the intention of placing Archduke Maximilian of Habsburg on the throne of Mexico. This succeeded, with the support of Mexican conservatives, but it was a short rule, and despite Maximilian's good intentions he was executed in 1867. The French occupation did, however, leave an imprint on the cuisine, including good crusty rolls and creamy pastries.

By the twentieth century, political stability was still lacking in Mexico, but the Mexican Revolution, with such 'leaders of the people' as Pancho Villa and Emiliano Zapata, eventually paved the way for contemporary democracy. A new culture emerged, in which European ideals were abandoned and pride in the Mexican heritage, including the indigenous cuisine, took their place. Food in modern Mexico remains determinedly regional and close to the land. It incorporates each layer of heritage, culture and influence, sharply reflecting the long and fascinating history of the country.

Meals and Meal Times

From desert to tropical jungle, seaside to mountain, city to countryside, meal times in Mexico vary greatly. Throughout the country there are traditionally five daily meals, though few would eat all of them on any given day, and many people in the larger cities have taken to the American-style three-meals-a-day eating pattern, with the larger meal in the evening.

Breakfast, *desayuno*, is early, as the nation rises with the dawn to get a head start on the heat of the coming day. Mugs of *café de olla*, *café con leche* or hot chocolate, sweet rolls or *churros* are consumed in the city, rustic sweet *tamales* in the country.

A second breakfast, *almuerzo*, is eaten around 11 AM to noon. It consists of robust egg dishes, tortillas, perhaps some meat, and is accompanied by *café con leche*, cooling juices, or fruit and milk drinks.

Lunch, *comida corrida*, the traditional main meal of the day, is served around 2 PM. In the Mediterranean/European tradition it consists of a leisurely procession of courses and a several-hour siesta afterwards. Almost always beginning with soup, it progresses to a *sopa seca*, a main plate of meat or fish, one or two of vegetables, and perhaps a plate of simple beans. Lovely fresh tortillas, loosely wrapped in a clean cloth, appear in an endless parade, and finally there is dessert – a fresh or cooked fruit dish, or perhaps a custard – and then coffee to settle it all in.

◁◁◁◁◁◁◁◁◁◁◁◁◁◁◁◁◁◁◁◁◁◁◁◁◁◁◁◁◁◁◁◁▷▷▷▷▷▷▷▷▷▷▷▷▷▷▷▷▷▷▷▷▷▷▷▷▷

Around 7 or 8 PM is *merienda*, coffee or hot chocolate again, or perhaps a mug of *atole*. *Tamales*, or a sweet or savoury pastry, might accompany the drinks.

Supper (*cena*) might be eaten around 9 or 10 PM. It could be a main course, or a one-pot soup-stew, or leftovers from lunch; it might be *tostadas*, *tacos* or *tortas*. If it is a celebration, it will be a heavy meal, lasting well into the night. Generally, however, it is light, and often it is skipped altogether.

SALSAS Y RECADOS

Salsas, Hot Sauces, Condiments and Spicy Seasonings

Raw chillies, chopped and combined with a few equally fresh and assertive flavours, enliven nearly everything they touch. Sauces such as these, known as salsas, give distinction to the simple foods of the Mexican table. Salsas can also be elaborate, simmered with spices, fruits, and/or herbs. They can be made from pickled chillies whirled into a fiery and tangy sauce, or can be a simple tomato sauce seasoned with a sprinkling of chillies and coriander, or crumbled dried hot chillies combined with vinegar.

Serving a bowl of salsa transforms even the simplest meal into a distinctly Mexican one. Eggs and rice, grilled fish, meat kebabs, simple broth, fried chicken – all of these and many more welcome a splash of these zesty sauces and relishes.

Fresh salsa can be frozen in ice-cube trays. While it may lose some of its punch when defrosted, it is still much better than anything found in shops; you can always add a little more chilli, coriander or onion to freshen it up.

Salsa Cruda
Raw Table Salsa of Chillies and Tomatoes

This is a simple, typical *salsa cruda*, a variation of a food that dates back to antiquity, perhaps one of the oldest dishes eaten today.

Makes 250 to 350 ml/8 to 12 fl oz

1 clove garlic, chopped (optional)
1 small to medium onion, chopped
3 fresh green chillies, chopped
5 ripe tomatoes, peeled, seeded and chopped
Salt to taste
2 tablespoons chopped coriander leaves

1. Combine all the ingredients and serve. (Note: for a smoother consistency, purée in a liquidizer or food processor.)

Salsa de Chiles y Ajo
Garlic and Chilli Salsa

This reeks deliciously of garlic. When I have some of this fragrant salsa on hand I use it rather generously; one little trick I enjoy is heating a spoonful of oil in a pan, then adding a spoonful or two of this salsa and cooking it to a near-paste consistency, then adding simple stock. It makes the basis for soup that tastes much more complex than it actually is.

Makes 200 to 250 ml/7 to 8 fl oz

6 cloves garlic, chopped
4 to 5 medium-hot fresh green chillies, chopped
2 ripe tomatoes, seeded, peeled and chopped
1 teaspoon cumin
Salt to taste
25 g/1 oz coriander leaves (or parsley, or combination of the two), chopped
Dash of vinegar of choice or lemon juice

◁◁◁◁◁◁◁◁◁◁◁◁◁◁◁◁◁◁◁◁◁◁◁◁◁▷▷▷▷▷▷▷▷▷▷▷▷▷▷▷▷▷▷▷▷▷▷▷▷▷

1. In a liquidizer or food processor whirl the garlic and chillies into a paste-like consistency.
2. Add the tomatoes, cumin, salt, coriander or parsley and vinegar or lemon juice. Blend until it is a greenish mixture, and the consistency you desire – either chunky or smooth.

Salsa con Limón y Cilantro
Chilli Salsa with Lime and Coriander

Tart and limey, nearly green from fresh coriander, this zesty condiment can be enjoyed with fresh seafood or roasted meats.

Makes 300 to 350 ml/10 to 12 fl oz

4 cloves garlic, finely chopped
3 medium-hot fresh green chillies, such as jalapeños, finely chopped
2 to 3 ripe tomatoes, diced or chopped
50 g/2 oz coriander leaves, finely chopped
Juice of 1 to 1$^1/_2$ limes
Salt to taste

1. Combine all the ingredients and serve. This salsa is at its best when served within several hours of preparation.

Salsa de Chile Güero
Smooth-Textured Salsa of Cooked Hot Chillies and Tomatoes, Sonora-Style

This is usually prepared with chile güero, hence its name. The güero is not generally available in the UK, but for this salsa a jalapeño, or similar medium-hot chilli such as a Kenyan, works just fine.

The salsa can be quite hot – it all depends upon your chillies. You can use a combination of hot green chillies and milder yellow wax peppers if they are available, or omit the chilli seeds.

I find this salsa at its best, however, when it stings just enough to make things interesting.

Makes 250 ml/8 fl oz

> 3 to 4 medium-sized, medium-hot fresh green chillies such as jalapeño or similar
> 1 to 2 cloves garlic (depending on their size), chopped
> 150g/5 oz tomatoes, diced (tinned are fine; include a little juice)
> Juice of ¹/₂ lemon
> Salt to taste
> ¹/₄ to ¹/₂ teaspoon oregano leaves, crumbled
> 50 ml/2 fl oz water

1. Place the chillies in a saucepan with water to cover. Bring to the boil and simmer, covered, for about 10 minutes. Leave until cool enough to handle.
2. Remove the stems from the chillies and peel away as much of the tough, membrane-like skin as possible, but leave the seeds. Place the chillies in a liquidizer with the garlic and blend until smooth, adding only enough of the tomatoes to produce a saucelike consistency. When it is smooth, gradually add the remaining tomatoes, lemon juice, salt, oregano and water.
3. Taste for seasoning and serve.

Salsa Campeche
Orange and Banana Salsa made from Mild Red Chillies, Yucatán-Style

In the lush region of Yucatán, tropical fruits grow with abandon, and are used in the savoury dishes of the area nearly as often as in the sweet ones. In this salsa, orange juice and diced banana combine with the sweet red pepper flavour of the mild pasilla chilli. Mild chilli powder mixed with paprika makes a reasonable substitute for the pasilla.

◄◄►►

Serve with grilled seafood *tacos*, or with Pollo de Plaza (page 156) or Pollo Pibil (page 150).

Makes 500 ml/16 fl oz

250 ml/8 fl oz orange juice
3 whole pasilla chillies, or 2 smooth-skinned and 1
    wrinkled-skinned dried red chillies (or 2 tablespoons
    each mild chilli powder and paprika)
¹/₂ onion, finely chopped
1 clove garlic, chopped
¹/₂ underripe banana, diced
Salt to taste if needed

1. Heat the orange juice in a pan to just boiling. Place the chillies or chilli powder in a bowl and pour the hot juice over, then cover and let cool to room temperature.
2. If using whole chillies, cut them open lengthwise when cool, then scrape the flesh away from the tough skin. Place the scraped flesh in a bowl with enough of the orange juice to make a thinnish paste. If using chilli powder, simply let cool and pour off excess liquid if it seems too runny.
3. Add the onion, garlic and banana to the chilli-orange juice mixture. Let the flavours meld for at least an hour before serving.
4. Add salt to taste if needed.

Salsa Verde
Green Salsa

Salsa Verde is ubiquitous; a small bowl of this tart and tangy, often quite hot salsa is offered to accompany whatever else is on the menu. Based on the tomatillo verde, or husk tomato (*physalis edulis*), its distinctive flavour adds verve to simmered chicken, fish or egg dishes, corn-based dishes such as *chilaquiles* or *enchiladas*, *tacos* and *tamales*. Salsa Verde is particularly good added to gazpacho, creating an exciting bowl of fire and ice.

◁◁◁◁◁◁◁◁◁◁◁◁◁◁◁◁◁◁◁◁◁◁◁◁◁◁◁◁◁▷▷▷▷▷▷▷▷▷▷▷▷▷▷▷▷▷▷▷▷▷▷▷▷▷▷▷

Salsa Verde makes a contrast both in colour and flavour when it is served in addition to red tomato or chilli-based sauces. Often a combination of red salsa, green salsa and a dollop of soured cream are used to garnish a dish, the colours representing the colours of the national flag.

Makes 500 ml/16 fl oz

450 g/1 lb fresh tomatillos, quartered, or 1 large can
2 to 3 fresh medium-hot green chillies, chopped (seed if
   desired)
1 small onion, chopped
1 clove garlic, chopped
12 g/$^1/_2$ oz coriander leaves, chopped
Salt to taste
Cumin to taste (optional)

1. If using fresh tomatillos, place in a saucepan and just cover with water. Bring to the boil, then reduce the heat and simmer until the tomatillos are soft but not mushy. This should take about 10 minutes. If using tinned tomatillos, simply drain gently from the tin, taking care not to lose the tomatillo flesh.
2. Place the tomatillos in a liquidizer or food processor along with the other ingredients and blend until fairly smooth.
3. Chill, then serve at cool room temperature.

VARIATIONS

Cooked Verde: simmer Salsa Verde for 5 to 10 minutes, or long enough to smooth out the sharp flavours of raw onion and garlic. This is particularly good spooned on to creamy mild cheese such as Mozzarella, then grilled until melting. Eat with soft corn tortillas.

Mole Verde: decrease the amount of chillies by half and thin the salsa with enough stock to make a cooking liquid for simmering pork, chicken, or fish. Delicious as an *enchilada* sauce.

◁◁◁◁◁◁◁◁◁◁◁◁◁◁◁◁◁◁◁◁◁◁◁◁◁◁◁◁▷▷▷▷▷▷▷▷▷▷▷▷▷▷▷▷▷▷▷▷▷▷▷▷▷▷▷▷

Salsa de Chile Pasilla
Pasilla Salsa

Salsa de Chile Pasilla is rich with dark, mild chilli flavours and given a tang from the addition of tomatillos and lime. It makes a delicious spread for warm corn tortillas wrapped around shredded pork, duck or black beans, or a dip for crisp-fried tortilla strips or grilled fish. Try spreading it on crusty bread or naan bread and top with shredded meats, lettuce, beans, etc, for a *torta*-style sandwich.

Makes 350ml/12 fl oz

4 dried pasilla chillies or 2 pasilla and 2 ancho chillies
4 tomatillos, cooked
1 clove garlic, chopped
1 small onion, chopped
$1/4$ medium-hot fresh chilli such as jalapeño, chopped
Juice of $1/4$ lime
Salt to taste

1. Lightly toast the chillies over an open flame, then place in a bowl and cover with hot (just under boiling) water. Place a plate over the bowl and leave for at least 30 minutes, preferably an hour, until the chillies have plumped up and softened completely.
2. Remove the stems from the softened chillies and carefully scrape the flesh from the tough skin using a bluntish knife. Discard the skins and place the flesh in a liquidizer with the tomatillos, garlic, onions and fresh chilli.
3. Whirl until saucelike in consistency, adding a little soaking liquid if necessary. Season with the lime juice and salt.

Salsa de Jalapeños en Escabeche y Jitomate
Pickled Chilli, Tomato and Onion Salsa

A nose-tingling, invigorating salsa. Feel free to vary the number of jalapeños: seven results in an intense salsa, four is a bit calmer, two still gives enough heat for interest but leaves your mouth relatively unmolested. Of course, it also depends on the heat of your chillies.

Since this salsa is so tangy and sharp, I like it with a richly spiced but mild dish such as *tacos* made of chicken or turkey, and Mole Poblano (page 159).

Makes about 100 ml/4 fl oz

2 to 7 pickled jalapeños, according to taste
½ onion, chopped
1 clove garlic, chopped
1 medium ripe tomato, diced
Salt to taste
Several generous pinches of dried oregano, crumbled
   between your hands

1. Slice the jalapeños and blend in a liquidizer to a chunky purée.
2. Add the onion, garlic and tomato and blend until fairly smooth.
3. Season with salt and oregano.

Salsa de Chiles al Carbón
Flame-Roasted Chilli Salsa

Roasted chilli gives a new dimension to salsa. This one is based on mild green peppers as well as chillies.

Makes about 250 ml/8 fl oz

2 green peppers
5 medium-hot fresh green chillies, or to taste
3 cloves garlic, chopped
Juice of ½ lime, or to taste
1 teaspoon salt
2 teaspoons olive oil

1. Roast the peppers and chillies over an open flame or under a very hot grill until scorched and charred. Put them in a paper

◁◁◁◁◁◁◁◁◁◁◁◁◁◁◁◁◁◁◁◁◁◁◁◁◁◁◁◁◁◁▷▷▷▷▷▷▷▷▷▷▷▷▷▷▷▷▷▷▷▷▷▷▷▷▷▷▷▷

or plastic bag, or a tightly covered bowl, to 'sweat'; then, when cool enough to handle, peel off the skin and dice the flesh.

2. Purée or liquidize the garlic, then add the peppers, chillies, lime juice and salt. Blend until it forms a saucelike consistency, then stir in the olive oil. Taste for seasoning, and if needed, add more chillies.

Salsa a la Yucateca
Very Hot Roasted Chilli Salsa, Yucatán-Style

This is either very hot or tinged with fire, depending on the chilli you use. I've heard it referred to as '*salsa de los machos*', that is, 'salsa for he-men', in honour of its potency. The habanero, or Scots bonnet, is most authentic, but it is volatile. You could also use a large mild green pepper for bulk and body, and add one Scots bonnet for heat and flavour. Alternatively, make the sauce with mild to medium fresh green chillies.

Whether you make this with a torrid heat level or tone it down to near gentility, it is a lovely salsa, with the delicious flavours of roasted peppers/chillies and the tart accent of lime.

Makes 100 to 150 ml/4 to 5 fl oz

1 green pepper plus 1 Scots bonnet, or 6 medium-sized
   mild to medium fresh chillies
50 ml/2 fl oz lime juice
Salt to taste

1. Roast the pepper and chilli or chillies in an ungreased frying pan to char evenly. Remove and leave in a covered dish or sealed bag until cool enough to handle.
2. Remove the hard papery skin, scraping with a sharp paring knife, and take out the seeds, membranes and stem. Chop the flesh coarsely.
3. Combine the chopped chillies with the lime juice and salt.

ⵕⵕⵕⵕⵕⵕⵕⵕⵕⵕⵕⵕⵕⵕⵕⵕⵕⵕⵕⵕⵕⵕⵕⵕⵕⵕⵖⵗⵗⵗⵗⵗⵗⵗⵗⵗⵗⵗⵗⵗⵗⵗⵗⵗⵗⵗⵗ

Salsa Picante
Vinegar-Based Hot Salsa

This is pure fire, its incendiary pleasure best shaken out in tiny drops. And it is *muy delicioso*, transforming even the simplest, blandest dish with an electric shock of chilli infused in sour vinegar. This only makes a tiny amount, since it is powerful stuff, but by all means make a larger amount if desired: it lasts nearly for ever.

Makes about 100 ml/4 fl oz

    6 to 10 small hot dried chillies, crumbled
    100 ml/4 fl oz vinegar
    ¹/₂ teaspoon salt

1. Whirl chillies in a blender with the vinegar and salt until it forms a thin sauce.

VARIATION

To the above hot sauce add 1 medium-sized diced tomato and a generous pinch of oregano. Whirl until fairly smooth. Unlike the above sauce, this one must be kept in the refrigerator and lasts only several days.

SALSAS PARA COCIDAR
Sauces for Cooking With

The Mexican kitchen is rich with unpretentious yet flavoursome sauces for marinating, simmering, baking or saucing whatever is on the menu. There are other sauces throughout the book, such as the one for Mole Poblano (page 159) or Pollo de Plaza (page 156), which can also be served with other dishes.

⫷⫷⫷

Salsa Ranchera
Tomato and Mild Chilli Sauce with Green Peppers

Salsa Ranchera is a peasant-style mixture of onions, peppers and tomatoes; it may be chunky or smooth and can be used to blanket a sautéed chicken or simmer a handful of prawns, served alongside a thin grilled steak, or ladled over fried eggs for the classic Huevos Rancheros (page 128).

It is an informal sauce, one that I usually prepare according to the dictates of my store-cupboard: as long as there are tomatoes and a few fresh chillies, there is the making for Salsa Ranchera. Onions, garlic, coriander, peppers, or a dash of cinnamon or cumin might add their savour. It is always delicious.

Makes about 750 ml/1¼ pints

- 2 small to medium onions, coarsely chopped or sliced lengthwise
- 2 to 4 cloves garlic, coarsely chopped
- 1 green pepper, cut into strips
- 2 to 3 medium-hot chillies, chopped (for more heat, use the seeds as well; for less heat, roast and peel first, discarding skin and seeds)
- 25 ml/1 fl oz bland vegetable oil
- 1 teaspoon cumin
- ½ teaspoon mild chilli powder, or to taste
- 10 ripe tomatoes, roasted, seeded and peeled (see Appendix 1: Cooking Techniques), then diced (or 450 g/1 lb tinned tomatoes, diced, with only enough of the juice to make a good sauce)
- Generous pinch of oregano, crumbled between the hands
- Salt to taste
- 2 tablespoons coarsely chopped coriander leaves (optional)

1. Lightly sauté the onions, garlic, green pepper and chillies in the oil until the onions are softened; sprinkle with the cumin and chilli powder and cook a few minutes longer.
2. Add the tomatoes, oregano and salt and simmer until saucelike in consistency.
3. Serve as desired, sprinkled with coriander, if using.

◁◁

Southwestern Green Chilli Salsa

Unlike its Mexican counterpart which is green from the tart husk tomato, or tomatillo, the *salsa verde* served in New Mexico, Arizona and Sonora is green from a large quantity of mild chillies. There, the chilli is doted on not only for its heat but for its fine vegetable flavour, the heat a welcome incidental.

This sauce is relatively mild, and based on stock and tomatoes as well as chillies. It is used in cooking to simmer meat, layer tortillas, or to roll up in *burritos* or *tacos*.

Since the sort of chillies used in New Mexico, Arizona and Sonora are not usually available in the UK, I have experimented with combinations of roasted green sweet peppers combined with medium chillies.

Makes about 750 ml/1¹/₄ pints

4 green peppers (or 8 to 10 large, very mild fresh green chillies)
3 to 4 medium chillies (omit if using chillies, above)
350 ml/12 fl oz chicken or other stock
1 medium onion, chopped
3 cloves garlic, chopped
25 ml/1 fl oz vegetable oil
1 tablespoon flour
325 g/12 oz tomatoes, chopped (tinned, with their juice, is fine)
¹/₂ teaspoon ground cumin (optional)
Salt and pepper to taste

1. Roast the peppers and chillies over an open flame or under a hot grill.
2. Place in a sealed plastic or paper bag, or a pot with a tight-fitting lid, and leave for about 30 minutes to loosen the skins, then scrape off the skin with a paring knife. Remove the stems and seeds and dice the flesh.
3. Place the peppers and chillies in a liquidizer and add about 100 ml/4 fl oz stock. Whirl until a chunky mixture has formed, then set aside.
4. Sauté the onion and garlic in the oil until softened, then

sprinkle in the flour and cook for a few minutes longer. Add the reserved pepper purée, stir around well to incorporate the flour, and continue to cook for a few minutes.
5. Add the remaining stock and the tomatoes and simmer for about 10 to 15 minutes. Season with salt, pepper, and cumin if using.

Mild Red Chilli Sauce

This absolutely simple purée of mild red chillies is thick and brick red, with the flavour of pure sweet chilli. It is popular in northern Mexico as well as America's Southwest. Clear meat broths, bowls of simmering hominy, chunks of rugged meats, are all enlivened by spoonfuls of this sauce.

Makes about 250 ml/8 fl oz

  5 large dried New Mexican chilli pods (or pasilla, or any
     smooth-skinned large mild red chillies)
  250 ml/8 fl oz water, heated to just under boiling
  1 to 2 cloves garlic, chopped
  Large pinch of salt

1. Remove the stems from the chillies, then cut open and shake out the seeds.
2. Lightly toast the chillies either over a medium heat in an ungreased frying pan or over an open flame until fragrant. Do not let them darken too much or burn.
3. Crumble or tear the chillies up, then place in a bowl and pour the hot water over them. Cover the bowl with a plate and leave for about an hour or until the chillies are softened.
4. Whirl the chillies and their soaking liquid in a liquidizer or food processor with the garlic and salt, blending until smooth.
5. Press through a strainer or sieve to remove the coarse skin.

◁◁◁◁◁◁◁◁◁◁◁◁◁◁◁◁◁◁◁◁◁◁◁◁◁◁◁◁◁◁▷▷▷▷▷▷▷▷▷▷▷▷▷▷▷▷▷▷▷▷▷▷▷▷▷▷▷▷

VARIATION

Southwestern Enchilada Sauce: cook 2 tablespoons flour in an equal amount of oil, and when cooked through add the above chilli paste, stirring to mix well. Simmer to thicken, then thin down with enough stock to reach the desired consistency. Add a squeeze of fresh lime juice. Use as desired, especially for simple, Southwestern-style *enchiladas*: that is, pour the sauce over oil-warmed tortillas that have been wrapped around shredded or minced browned meat, chicken or cheese, then top with grated cheese and pop into a hot oven to melt the cheese and meld the flavours. Serve garnished with soured cream, diced black olives, shredded lettuce, spring onions, etc.

Pipián
Pumpkin Seed Sauce

Pipián sauces are an ancient food based on ground seeds. They are eaten all over Mexico but are especially enjoyed in the Yucatán. When Cortés's men were fêted by Montezuma, *pipián* was on the menu. Use it in a variety of dishes throughout the book; it freezes particularly well.

Makes about 500 ml/16 fl oz

   325 g/12 oz hulled pumpkin seeds
   1 teaspoon vegetable oil
   1 teaspoon cumin
   1 teaspoon salt
   2 jalapeño or other medium-hot chillies, roasted and peeled
      (see Glossary)
   2 cloves garlic, chopped
   2 tablespoons chopped fresh coriander leaves
   Juice of ¹/₂ lime
   Stock as needed

1. Lightly fry the pumpkin seeds in the oil until golden. Add the cumin and salt and continue frying a few minutes more, until fragrant and slightly browned.

◁◁◁◁◁◁◁◁◁◁◁◁◁◁◁◁◁◁◁◁◁◁◁◁◁◁◁◁◁▷▷▷▷▷▷▷▷▷▷▷▷▷▷▷▷▷▷▷▷▷▷▷▷▷▷▷▷▷▷

2. Purée or grind the seeds with the chillies, garlic, coriander, lime juice, and enough stock to form the desired consistency.

SALSAS PICANTES
Relishes and Condiments

Chunky mixtures of raw chillies and/or pickled vegetables (*en escabeche*) are often served instead of or in addition to a smooth salsa.

Pico de Gallo
Diced Raw Chilli Relish, Texas- and Sonora-Style

Pico de Gallo usually refers to a relish-like mixture of diced crisp ingredients. In Central Mexico the mixture is usually jicama and orange, more a snack than a relish. In Texas, however, Pico de Gallo usually refers to a salsa-like condiment eaten with *fajitas* and other mammoth barbecued meat dishes; the strips of grilled meat are rolled up into soft flour tortillas with a spoonful of the relish.

Makes about 500 ml/16 fl oz

    4 to 5 ripe tomatoes, diced
    5 to 6 spring onions, thinly sliced
    5 radishes or 50 to 75 g/2 to 3 oz jicama, coarsely chopped
    Coarsely chopped coriander leaves to taste
    2 to 3 medium-hot green chillies, diced (for greater heat
        include seeds, for less heat, remove and discard)
    Juice of 1/2 lime
    Salt to taste

1. Combine all the ingredients and serve immediately.

◁◁◁◁◁◁◁◁◁◁◁◁◁◁◁◁◁◁◁◁◁◁◁◁◁◁◁▷▷▷▷▷▷▷▷▷▷▷▷▷▷▷▷▷▷▷▷▷▷▷▷

Salsa Mexicana
Chunky Chilli Table Relish

The consistency of this relish should be decidedly chunky – bits of tomato and onion dotted with flecks of coriander and breathtakingly hot green chilli. It is an invigorating relish, perhaps the most basic dish of the Mexican kitchen, and can accordingly be varied endlessly: a squeeze of lime and/or orange, a few mashed tomatillos, spring onions instead of white onion, and so on.

Makes about 250 to 350 ml/8 to 12 fl oz

4 small to medium ripe tomatoes, diced
1 small to medium onion, diced
12 g/¹/₂ oz coriander leaves, chopped
6 fresh green hot chillies such as serrano, jalapeño, etc
Generous shaking of salt

1. Combine all the ingredients.

Cebollas con Jalapeños en Escabeche
Chopped Onions with Pickled Chillies

This is a simple relish, and a good way of making use of the brine from pickled jalapeños. Tart lemon adds a piquant accent to the pungent onions and hot pickled chillies.

Makes about 100 ml/4 fl oz

1 to 2 onions, finely chopped
Several pickled jalapeño chillies, chopped, plus a few
    spoonfuls of the brine
Pinch of oregano
Juice of ¹/₂ lemon

1. Combine all the ingredients and serve as an accompaniment to hearty foods, especially grilled ones, rice dishes and beans.

◁◁◁◁◁◁◁◁◁◁◁◁◁◁◁◁◁◁◁◁◁◁◁◁◁◁◁◁◁◁◁◁◁▷▷▷▷▷▷▷▷▷▷▷▷▷▷▷▷▷▷▷▷▷▷▷▷▷▷▷▷▷▷

Sometimes I spoon it on to hot jacket potatoes or grilled marinated potato slices.

Cebollas en Escabeche a la Yucateca
Pickled Red Onion Slices, Yucatán-Style

This simple tangy relish is served in *panuchos* or *tacos*, with various roasted and simmered chicken dishes, with seafood, Pollo Pibil (page 150) and indeed nearly anything you might eat in this region.

Makes about 500 ml/16 fl oz

3 large red onions, thinly sliced
White wine vinegar or cider vinegar, either mild or diluted
    with a little water and a dash of lime or lemon juice
Large pinch of dried oregano leaves, crumbled
Salt and pepper to taste

1. Place the onions in a bowl. Pour boiling water over them, then immediately drain in a colander.
2. Return the drained and wilted onions to the bowl. Add the remaining ingredients, using just enough vinegar to cover, and chill for at least 30 minutes.

Legumbres en Escabeche
Marinated Mixed Vegetables

In Mexico and the US one can buy jars of mixed vegetables, much like the Italian *giardiniera* pickles, only fiery from a generous amount of hot chillies. In fact, the *giardiniera* vegetables could easily be given a South of the Border flavour by adding some quickly sautéed hot chillies and a big pinch of oregano.

Makes about 500 ml/16 fl oz

◁◁◁◁◁◁◁◁◁◁◁◁◁◁◁◁◁◁◁◁◁◁◁◁◁◁◁◁◁◁▷▷▷▷▷▷▷▷▷▷▷▷▷▷▷▷▷▷▷▷▷▷▷▷▷▷

4 carrots, thickly and diagonally sliced (or use a crinkly-cut
   knife)
1 or 2 onions, thinly sliced
25 ml/1 fl oz vegetable oil, or more if needed
$1/_2$ cauliflower, cut into florets
1 stalk celery
4 or 5 medium-hot green chillies
100 ml/4 fl oz white wine vinegar
1 teaspoon salt
1 teaspoon oregano leaves, crumbled

1. Quickly sauté the carrots and onions in half the oil, then set
   aside in a bowl. Sauté the cauliflower and celery and set aside
   when crunchy-tender.
2. Sauté the chillies in the remaining oil, add the vinegar and
   heat, then pour it all over the mixed vegetables. Season with
   salt and oregano.
3. Let cool and store in the refrigerator, where it will keep for
   about a week, covered. Enjoy with all sorts of dishes,
   especially crisp *tacos*.

VARIATION

Escabeche de Col: a Mayan version of Legumbres en Escabeche.
Use $1/_2$ thinly sliced cabbage in place of the cauliflower and celery, and decrease the amount of carrots by half. Serve with
grilled meats, chillied black beans, and tortillas.

Camarones en Escabeche
Prawns with Pickled Chillies

Nuggets of cooked prawns tossed with pickled jalapeños make a
sensational relish, especially for potato *tostadas* or cheese melted
on to a flour tortilla. Try to find excellent *jalapeños en escabeche*,
chock full of seasonings and flavour. If your chillies are a little
pale, add a pinch of oregano and other seasonings to taste.

‹‹‹

Makes about 500 ml/16 fl oz

1 part pickled jalapeños, including about 100 ml/4 fl oz of
   the flavourful brine
2 parts cooked prawns, or as desired

1. Combine and serve. Because of the prawns this will not last as
   long as other pickled foods. Keep it refrigerated, and only for
   a few days.

RECADOS
Spice Pastes

In Spanish, *recaudo* is the term for seasonings. In Mexican
Spanish, however, it has evolved into *recado*, a term for spice
pastes. Throughout Mexico spice pastes are used as the basis for
countless sauces, *moles*, *pipiáns* and marinades. They are available
in foil- or paper-wrapped tablet-like chunks, or in jars, but they
are at their best when sold loose, as they are in the Yucatán
where these spice pastes form the subtle and distinctive flavours
of the cuisine. The array of *recados* in the Mérida marketplace
looks like an artist's palette, with large piles of pure colour: yellow, red, black, green, and so on. The Mayan vendor, with her
strong, proud, inscrutable face, will scrape off a little for you and
wrap it in a cone of paper.

Recado
Paste of Spices and Roasted Garlic

Unlike many of the *recados*, there are no chillies at all in this mixture. This paste is especially good in Pollo de Valladolid (page
152) or try adding a spoonful or two to sautéed swordfish and top
with Cebollas en Escabeche (page 38). The paste can be diluted
with a little grapefruit or Seville orange juice, if preferred.

Makes about 75 ml/3 fl oz

> 12 large cloves garlic, unpeeled
> $1/_2$ teaspoon cumin seeds
> 1 teaspoon coarsely ground black pepper
> $1/_2$ teaspoon cloves (about 25 cloves, the little head of the
>   nails only), crushed
> 2 teaspoons oregano leaves
> $1/_2$ teaspoon salt
> 1 tablespoon sherry vinegar or cider vinegar
> 1 level tablespoon flour

1. In an ungreased heavy frying pan cook the whole unpeeled garlic cloves until they are charred in places and softened through. Remove from the heat and let cool.
2. Lightly toast the cumin seeds over a low to medium heat until they grow fragrant and darken slightly. Remove from the heat and let cool.
3. In a liquidizer or spice grinder combine the black pepper, cloves, oregano leaves, salt and cumin seeds, grinding into a well-combined mixture.
4. Squeeze the soft flesh of the garlic cloves into the spice mixture and blend to a paste, then add the vinegar and flour, mixing well. Place in the refrigerator and leave for at least 2 hours; overnight is even better.

Recado Negro
'Black' Seasoning Paste

Not really black, rather a deep, dark colour that comes from taking dark ancho chillies and charring them over an open flame. To ensure that they really blacken, the chillies are first sprinkled with vodka or tequila; as they hit the stove they burst into flame.

A spoonful of Recado Negro is good added to strips of sautéed *nopales*, along with a few leaves of epazote, or make a soft *taco* of corn tortillas warmed in a lightly oiled pan and spread with a small amount of Recado Negro, with a generous spoonful of

◁◁◁◁◁◁◁◁◁◁◁◁◁◁◁◁◁◁◁◁◁◁◁◁◁◁▷▷▷▷▷▷▷▷▷▷▷▷▷▷▷▷▷▷▷▷▷▷▷▷▷▷

soured cream, and a sprinkling of coriander. Recado Negro also makes an excellent seasoning paste for *frijoles negros refritos* (refried black beans). Add a spoonful or two to the sautéing onions before you add the mashed beans.

Makes about 200 ml/6 fl oz

> 6 large ancho chillies
> Tequila or vodka for sprinkling
> 2 tablespoons annatto seeds, soaked overnight in 100 ml/4
>   fl oz mixed orange and grapefruit juice (or substitute
>   paprika for the annatto and mix with the juices without
>   leaving to soak)
> 6 cloves or allspice berries, crushed (or pinch of ground
>   cloves)
> $1/2$ teaspoon ground cumin
> $1^1/2$ teaspoons black pepper
> 1 head garlic, roasted and peeled (see Appendix 1: Cooking
>   Techniques)
> $1^1/2$ teaspoons oregano leaves, crumbled
> 1 teaspoon salt

1. Sprinkle the chillies generously with tequila or vodka.
2. Char over an open flame, but take care as the liquid is flammable and will ignite. I find the safest way to do it is to place the chillies on top of an UNLIT gas ring, then turn it on and light it quickly. The chillies will catch fire immediately, and only need cooking for a minute or so. Turn off the gas and let the flames burn themselves out. You'll probably have to do this in several batches. Alternatively, you could line the sprinkled chillies on a baking sheet and grill, letting them catch fire and burn themselves out in the same way.
3. Take the charred, blackened chillies and remove the stems and seeds. Cut or tear the chillies into small pieces and place in a liquidizer or food processor. Whirl until they form a powder or meal, then add the remaining ingredients, puréeing until the mixture attains the consistency of a paste.
4. Store well covered in the refrigerator, where it should last up to about 5 days.

◄◄◄◄◄◄◄◄◄◄◄◄◄◄◄◄◄◄◄◄◄◄◄◄◄►►►►►►►►►►►►►►►►►►►►►►►►►

Yucatecan Achiote Paste

Since this is most often used to prepare Pollo Pibil, directions appear in that recipe (page 150). Like the other *recados*, it may be added to a variety of dishes: smear it on to meats for grilling, use to season rice dishes, or thin it with a little Seville orange juice (or orange juice and grapefruit juice mixed half and half), then mix with chopped onions, roasted red peppers, green olives and chopped coriander or parsley. Serve over fish.

For a variation on Achiote Paste, add some turmeric, or a spoonful of chopped fresh mint.

Recado Rojo Enchilado
Red Chilli and Citrus Spice Paste

Use this paste for any marinade or wherever a citrus and chilli paste is called for. It adds an extraordinary savour.

Makes about 250 ml/8 fl oz

3 cloves garlic, finely chopped
1 to 3 small or medium medium-hot chillies, either red or
   green, chopped
35g/1¹/₂ oz New Mexico chilli powder
35g/1¹/₂ oz ancho chilli powder (note: if neither is available,
   use a combination of mild chilli powder and paprika)
1 teaspoon cumin seed
¹/₂ teaspoon oregano
¹/₂ teaspoon salt
35ml/1¹/₂ fl oz olive oil
Juice of 1 orange, plus ¹/₂ the grated rind
Juice and grated rind of ¹/₂ lime
1 tablespoon tequila (optional)
25 g/1 oz coriander leaves, chopped (optional)

1. Combine all the ingredients and mix well.
2. Use to coat meat, fish, or poultry, letting it marinate for 30
   minutes to overnight, depending upon the meat or fish

chosen. This paste lasts up to a week, well covered, in the refrigerator, and nearly indefinitely if frozen.

VARIATION

For a subtle fragrance and unique presentation, serve the chilli paste wrapped up in softened corn husks, *tamal*-style. Spice pastes have been served in the Veracruz region like this since pre-Hispanic times.

APERITIVOS, BOCADOS Y ANTOJITOS

Appetizers and Snacks

Mexican cuisine, with its distinctive flavours, its tradition of street food and strong drink, offers a wide variety of savoury snacks. They can be almost crudely simple – potato crisps with salsa, prawns marinated with chillies, fruit sprinkled with cayenne pepper – but they are always filled with the zest that characterizes life South of the Border.

Many of the foods served as main courses in Mexican restaurants outside Mexico are dishes that Mexicans eat as snacks, party appetizers, or street food. *Enchiladas*, *tacos* and *tostadas* (see Tortillas, Tortilla Dishes and Tamales) may all be prepared in diminutive portions small enough to snack on or to start a meal with. Since many of Mexico's best starters are based on fish and seafood, refer to that chapter too for ideas.

◁◁◁◁◁◁◁◁◁◁◁◁◁◁◁◁◁◁◁◁◁◁◁◁◁◁◁◁◁◁◁▷▷▷▷▷▷▷▷▷▷▷▷▷▷▷▷▷▷▷▷▷▷▷▷▷▷▷▷

Legumbres Mixtas
Cooked Vegetable Salad in Mustard Sauce

This mixture of steamed and sautéed vegetables, awash in a deliciously gaudy sauce, is often found in *cantinas* and bars, served with toothpicks for spearing.

1 medium onion, sliced
2 cloves garlic, peeled and halved
75 ml/3 fl oz olive or vegetable oil
1 small or ¹/₂ medium yellow pepper, cut into strips
1 tablespoon French mustard
3 tablespoons white wine vinegar or sherry vinegar
3 or 4 medium potatoes, boiled, cooled and diced
3 or 4 medium carrots, boiled, cooled and sliced
175 g/6 oz green beans, cooked *al dente*, or use frozen (no
    need to defrost – they will once you toss them with the
    marinade and vegetables and let them sit for a while)
1 pickled jalapeño chilli, thinly sliced
Salt and pepper

1. Sauté the onion and garlic in about 1 tablespoon oil until softened and lightly browned in places. Remove and place in a bowl, then quickly sauté the yellow pepper until crisp-tender and add to the onion.
2. Mix the mustard with the vinegar then whisk in the remaining oil and add to the onion, garlic and pepper.
3. Add the remaining vegetables, the sliced jalapeño, and seasoning, and toss together well. Serve immediately or leave to marinate (the green beans are loveliest when freshly dressed; they turn slightly grey if left, say, overnight).

Semillas Tostadas de Calabaza
Toasted Chillied Pumpkin Seeds

Pale, drab green in colour with an earthy flavour, pumpkin seeds are widely used in Mexican food – in sauces, *tamales*, stews, and eaten simply spiced and toasted for a crunchy snack.

◁◁

Soaking the seeds before roasting them gives a particularly brittle crispness. They shatter deliciously between the teeth.

350 ml/12 fl oz water
225g/8 oz raw pumpkin seeds, hulled
1 teaspoon mild chilli powder
1 teaspoon salt
1 teaspoon garlic powder or several cloves garlic, finely
  chopped (optional)

1. Bring the water to the boil then pour it over the seeds. Soak overnight at room temperature.
2. Drain the seeds and spread them evenly over a 25 to 37.5 cm/10 to 15 in baking dish.
3. Bake in the oven at 180°C/350°F/gas mark 4 for 25 to 35 minutes or until the seeds are dry and puffed up. They will pop and sputter in the oven as they roast. After about 20 minutes add the seasonings.
4. Remove from the oven and leave to cool, stirring occasionally. Other seasonings such as cumin seeds, hot pepper, or soy sauce are good in place of the chilli and garlic; alternatively, they are good without any seasoning whatsoever, except a little salt.

Queso Fundito
Melted Cheese

As with many other simple dishes, this one tastes too good to be true. It is eaten throughout Mexico's Republic as well as in Texas, in one guise or another. In the state of Jalisco it is called *queso fundito*, or *queso al horno*, and is served simply garnished with a few fresh or pickled chillies. In Sonora in the North, where meat rules supreme, the melted cheese is called *queso flameado* and is topped with sautéed chorizo sausage and eaten as a prelude to Carne Asada (page 183), a sort of mixed grill. In the Yucatán a similar dish is served with a cinnamon-scented tomato sauce and either minced meat or tiny shrimp.

Melted cheese can be prepared on a barbecue, under the grill,

ᗽᗽᗽᗽᗽᗽᗽᗽᗽᗽᗽᗽᗽᗽᗽᗽᗽᗽᗽᗽᗽᗽᗽᗽᗺᗺᗺᗺᗺᗺᗺᗺᗺᗺᗺᗺᗺᗺᗺᗺᗺᗺᗺᗺᗺ

or in a hot oven. Choose a softish, meltable cheese and cut into slices. Place in a baking dish and either bake or grill. If desired top the cheese with any of the following before cooking: 1. a splash of Salsa Ranchera seasoned with a dash of cinnamon and a handful of crab or cooked prawns. 2. 1 or 2 fairly mild chopped chillies. 3. About 225g/8 oz browned crumbled chorizo sausage. 4. Roasted and peeled red, yellow and green peppers plus several chillies.

Serve when hot and bubbly, accompanied by either warm soft tortillas or crisp *tostada* wedges.

Queso al Horno
Baked Cheese with Fresh Salsa

Melted cheese with fresh chilli salsa is one of those simple pairings that can be varied endlessly. It is a great dish to make when you have a selection of cheeses languishing in the refrigerator.

To prepare, take a combination of grated cheeses of choice and place a handful each in individual ramekins. Top with a spoonful of good homemade salsa. Bake in a hot oven and serve sizzling, with a stack of warm flour or corn tortillas alongside to roll around bits of melted cheese.

A delicious variation is to top thick slices of fresh white cheese such as Pecorino or Mozzarella with green salsa, then bake until bubbling.

Nachos
Tortilla Chips Topped with Melted Cheese and Beans

Nachos are basically crisp corn tortilla chips served with spicy melted cheese. *Nachos* can be simple, prepared with just cheese and salsa, or elaborate, with refried beans, spicy meat sauce, soured cream, guacamole and so on. Sometimes the corn chips are heated through with the cheese and other toppings.

Nachos have trekked from Sonora, Mexico, into mainstream American food. You can buy them at baseball games, but I don't recommend it – the tortillas come topped with a disgusting

◁◁▷▷▷▷▷▷▷▷▷▷▷▷▷▷▷▷▷▷▷▷▷▷▷▷▷▷▷▷▷▷▷▷

gloppy orange sauce. Restaurant *nachos*, on the other hand, run the gamut of quality, from awful to addictively good.

> 200 to 225 g/7 to 8 oz *frijoles refritos* (page 196, or use tinned)
> 175 g/6 oz cheese, grated – a combination of Cheddar and a crumbly, white cheese is good
> Pinch of cumin seeds or ground cumin
> Tortilla chips

Toppings

> 50 ml/2 fl oz soured cream
> Thinly sliced fresh chillies or pickled chillies, or good hot salsa, to taste
> 1 tablespoon coarsely chopped coriander leaves
> 2 tomatoes, diced
> Handful of shredded lettuce

1. Spread the beans in a shallow baking dish, then top with the cheese and sprinkle with the cumin.
2. Bake in the oven at 190°C/375°F/gas mark 5 for about 10 minutes or until the cheese is bubbly and browned.
3. Remove from the oven and stick tortilla chips all around the edges, then place some more in a basket to serve alongside. Top the hot bean mixture with everything else, preferably arranged attractively.
4. Serve immediately, surrounded by corn or tortilla chips and fresh salsa.

VARIATIONS

Southwest Blue Corn Tortilla Chip Nachos: use blue corn chips. Add a handful of thinly sliced spring onions to the cheese, and use an orange or combination of white and orange cheeses.

The beans may be omitted, or black beans may be used in place of the usual pinto beans.

Black Bean Nachos: use refried black beans in place of refried pinto beans. Add slices of avocado to the toppings.

◁◁◁◁◁◁◁◁◁◁◁◁◁◁◁◁◁◁◁◁◁◁◁◁◁◁◁▷▷▷▷▷▷▷▷▷▷▷▷▷▷▷▷▷▷▷▷▷▷▷▷▷▷

Guacamole con Jitomates
Guacamole with Tomatoes

Guacamole, that unctuous green purée of avocado, is nearly synonymous with Mexican food. Since the delicate avocado pear is so mild and creamy on its own, I always feel that lots of lemon or lime and enough chilli are the key to a good guacamole. The consistency can vary tremendously. Many mash it into a purée while others retain a chunky texture. I lean towards the latter category, though if the guacamole is to be used as a sauce, a smoother texture is better.

Guacamole may be served as a dip surrounded with raw vegetables and/or tortilla chips, or it may be used as a sauce for *tacos*, rich roasted meat dishes or chillied stews, soups, grilled fish, robust sandwiches on crusty rolls, *enchiladas* and so on.

The standard method of preventing guacamole becoming discoloured is to save the stone from the avocado pear, place it in the bowl of guacamole, then cover the whole thing tightly and store it in the refrigerator. I'm not so sure it works all that well, however. If I have to keep guacamole for any length of time I sprinkle the top with lemon juice and press a thin film of plastic directly on to the surface. If, finally, the top still discolours, I stir it into the fresh mixture underneath until it all looks green once again.

The recipe below is for a classic guacamole, and since I usually serve it as an appetizer for a largish group the quantity should be enough for 6 to 8 at least.

4 ripe black-skinned avocados
2 cloves garlic, chopped
1 small onion, chopped
4 small ripe tomatoes, chopped
Juice of 2 limes or lemons
2 tablespoons chopped coriander leaves
1/4 teaspoon cumin
Pinch of mild chilli powder
1/2 to 1 fresh green chilli, seeded and chopped
Salt and Tabasco sauce to taste

<<<<<<<<<<<<<<<<<<<<<<<<<<<<<>>>>>>>>>>>>>>>>>>>>>>>>>>

1. Cut the avocado pears in half. Remove the stones and scoop out the flesh.
2. Combine the avocado flesh with the garlic, onion, tomatoes, lime or lemon juice, coriander, cumin, chilli powder and green chilli, and mash together.
3. Season with salt and Tabasco to taste, and add extra chilli if needed. Serve shortly after preparation.

Tortas
Hot Crusty Sandwiches

Walking down the streets of any bustling Mexican town you will see signs on the food stalls that line each street advertising *tortas* for sale. Variations of these hearty sandwiches are to be found throughout the country, filled with *carnitas* – shredded beef, fish or poultry, even shredded shark. It is a satisfying combination: hot crisp roll, soft buttery beans, crisp and refreshing lettuce shreds wilting from the heat of the filling, all set off with a hint of hot chilli. This robust and lusty snack is so messy to eat that it is impossible to retain any vestiges of one's dignity: beans and soured cream soon smudge the face and shreds of lettuce hang errantly from the corners of one's mouth.

◁◁◁◁◁◁◁◁◁◁◁◁◁◁◁◁◁◁◁◁◁◁◁◁◁◁▷▷▷▷▷▷▷▷▷▷▷▷▷▷▷▷▷▷▷▷▷▷▷▷▷▷

Tortas del Mercado
Marketplace Tortas

4 crusty rolls
Hot lard, butter or olive oil for brushing on to the rolls
Good homemade salsa
About 100 g/4 oz hot *frijoles refritos* (page 196, or use tinned)
225 to 275 g/8 to 10 oz shredded meat or poultry
Generous handful of thinly sliced lettuce
1 tomato, diced
1 small to medium onion, chopped
2 tablespoons chopped coriander leaves
1 avocado, sliced and tossed with lemon or lime juice to
    prevent discolouring
Soured cream as desired
Several slices of pickled jalapeño chilli or chipotle chilli
    (optional)

1. Split the rolls open and brush the insides with the hot lard,
   butter or olive oil. Brown under a grill or on a hot heavy
   frying pan.
2. Spread the bottom half of each roll with salsa, then beans,
   then top with the meat or poultry. Place some lettuce,
   tomato, onion, coriander, avocado, soured cream, and a small
   amount of pickled jalapeños or chipotle, if using, on top of
   the meat.
3. Close the sandwiches up. Sit back and enjoy with glasses of
   chilled lager.

ALTERNATIVE FILLINGS

Ropa Vieja (page 178)
Mole Poblano de Guajalote (page 159)
Grated cheese
Crumbled browned chorizo mixed into the refried beans
Chillied-roasted chicken from Pollo de Plaza (page 156)
Leftover Pato con Naranja y Yerba Buena (page 163)
Thin and tender, rare grilled steak (such as Fajitas, page 186)
with onions and peppers

Melted cheese and *nopales*

Shredded meat browned with a little garlic, then simmered with tomatoes and *nopales* and seasoned with chipotle chilli, if available

Tortas de Jaiba y Aguacate
Crab and Avocado Tortas

4 chewy crusty rolls, cut lengthwise but left attached
Butter, softened for spreading
225–275 g/8 to 10 oz cooked crabmeat
Several spoonfuls of mayonnaise and soured cream
$1/_2$ teaspoon mild chilli powder
$1/_2$ onion, finely chopped
Juice of $1/_4$ lime or lemon
$1/_4$ head iceberg lettuce, thinly sliced or shredded
1 to 2 small, ripe tomatoes, diced
1 avocado, peeled and sliced
Salt and pepper to taste
Salsa of choice

1. Pull out some of the soft insides from the rolls, then butter the rolls.
2. Brown on both sides in a hot heavy frying pan, or bake in the oven at 200°C/400°F/gas mark 6 for about 10 minutes or until crisped.
3. Meanwhile, mix the crabmeat with enough mayonnaise and soured cream to bind it together, then season with the chilli powder, onion, and lime or lemon juice.
4. When the rolls are hot and crisped, remove from the oven and stuff with the crab salad, shredded lettuce, diced tomato and avocado. Sprinkle with salt and pepper and serve immediately with salsa.

◁◁◁◁◁◁◁◁◁◁◁◁◁◁◁◁◁◁◁◁◁◁◁◁◁◁◁▷▷▷▷▷▷▷▷▷▷▷▷▷▷▷▷▷▷▷▷▷▷▷▷▷

Rellenitos de Plátano Macho
Patties of Mashed Plantains Filled with Meat and/or Black Beans

2 ripe plantains
100 g/4 oz cooked pork, shredded
1½ tablespoons vegetable oil
½ teaspoon mild chilli powder
1 clove garlic, chopped
Salt and pepper to taste
275 g/10 oz very tender cooked black beans
75 g/3 oz tomatoes, chopped (tinned is fine)
2 eggs
35 g/1½ oz flour, plus extra for flouring hands and forming patties
Oil for frying
75 ml/3 fl oz soured cream
About 6 lettuce leaves, thinly shredded

Tomato-Chilli Relish

75 g/3 oz tomatoes, diced (tinned is fine)
2 spring onions, thinly sliced
1 clove garlic, chopped
1 small hot fresh chilli, chopped, or to taste
Salt to taste

1. Peel the plantains and cut into pieces. Place in a saucepan with water to cover and bring to the boil. Cook for about 5 to 8 minutes or until tender, then drain and mash.
2. Meanwhile, brown the pork in about 1 teaspoon of the vegetable oil, seasoning it with the chilli powder, garlic and salt. Set aside.
3. Purée the beans with the tomatoes. Heat the remaining vegetable oil in a heavy pan and add the bean purée, cooking until it forms a thick paste. Add salt and pepper to taste then set aside.
4. Mix the mashed plantains with the eggs and flour, mixing well to form a batter. It will be quite sticky.

5. Form patties by taking a tablespoon or two of the plantain mixture into your well-floured hand, placing a little of both the meat and beans on top, then topping it with more plantain mixture. Work on a plate that is liberally coated with flour – this is a rather messy business but not too difficult. If a bit of the filling seeps out, do not worry in the least.
6. Heat oil for frying in a heavy pan, then add the patties and let brown. Turn over and pat down so that they are fairly flat rather than plump. Brown on the second side, then remove from the pan.
7. Mix the relish by combining the tomatoes, spring onions, garlic, chilli and salt to taste.
8. Serve the patties spread with some relish, then a layer of the soured cream, then topped with a flurry of shredded lettuce.

Gusanos de Maguey
Maguey Worms, Hidalgo-Style

When you purchase a bottle of the potent alcoholic mexcal, you'll find a maguey worm curled up at the bottom. It may alarm the squeamish, but that little worm gives the drink its distinctive flavour.

The maguey worm, a grub which burrows into the maguey plant, has been a celebrated delicacy since before the Conquest. Tender, delicate and vaguely saline, they are served wrapped in tortillas and fried into crisp *tacos*, chopped and used as an omelette filling, or dipped into chilli salsa. In the state of Hidalgo they are fried until crisp and served in a pile, accompanied by wedges of lime and green salsa.

I include this recipe for its curiosity value; if you ever have the opportunity to prepare and eat maguey worms, you should take advantage of it. Serve as a first course, accompanied by crusty bread or with either soft or crisp-fried tortillas with which to make *tacos*.

ᐊᐊᐊᐊᐊᐊᐊᐊᐊᐊᐊᐊᐊᐊᐊᐊᐊᐊᐊᐊᐊᐊᐊᐊᐊᐊᐊᐊᐊᐊᐊᐊ◇▷▷▷▷▷▷▷▷▷▷▷▷▷▷▷▷▷▷▷▷▷▷▷▷▷▷▷▷▷▷▷▷

500 ml/16 fl oz vegetable oil
450 g/1 lb maguey worms, cleaned
Salsa Verde (page 26)
Avocado and tomato slices
Wedges of lime

1. Heat the oil in a heavy deep pan until very hot, then fry the worms until crisp. You will probably need to do this in several batches. Remove from the hot oil with a slotted spoon and dry on absorbent paper.
2. Serve immediately with Salsa Verde, garnished with avocado, tomatoes and lime wedges.

A FEW SIMPLE MEXICAN NIBBLES

Garbanzos con Chiles: sold in little stalls, these are chickpeas doused with hot sauce such as Tabasco, then sprinkled with salt and piled into little waxed paper cones for nibbling.

Bocadillo de Papas Cocidas: boiled waxy potatoes, at room temperature, cut into bite-sized dice then splashed with a vinegar-based chilli sauce (bottled is fine) make a popular street snack.

Papitas con Chiles y Limón: in Guadalajara I've eaten these freshly made potato crisps, served with a splash of green salsa or a good vinegar-based hot sauce and wedges of lime. Sweet potato crisps are good this way too, seasoned with a dusting of mild chilli and paprika.

Cold cooked prawns dressed in olive oil and lemon: seasoned with pickled jalapeños, chopped onion, tomato, pimiento-stuffed green olives, parsley and crumbled oregano makes a refreshing appetizer.

ANTOJITOS

Antojitos is a term that encompasses *tacos*, *tostadas* (see Tortillas, Tortilla Dishes and Tamales), and all of the snacklike *masa*-based goodies that we have come to associate with Mexican food. *Antojitos* means 'little whims': an appropriate expression, since the corn-based dishes can be varied endlessly depending upon the whims of the cook and the vagaries of the marketplace.

In addition to the tortilla-based *antojitos*, *masa* is also prepared in a wide variety of little cups, boats, patties and other shapes that can either be fried first and stuffed later or vice versa. They often have amusing names, such as *gorditas* ('little fat ones'), *cazuelitas* ('little pots'), *chalupitas* ('tiny boats from the floating gardens of Xochimilco'), and *huaraches* ('sandals'), among others. They may be filled and piled with whatever one fancies; aim for a pleasing variety of flavours and textures.

Cazuelitas
Small Fried Masa Pots

These two-bite *antojitos* are made from *masa* lightened with self-raising flour then formed into little pots and fried until crisp. They can be stuffed with refried beans, shredded meats, or mashed vegetables, and, most importantly, with a dab of strongly flavoured salsa or a strip of chilli and shreds of cabbage, lettuce and/or onion. It should all crackle with the excitement of contrasting flavours and textures.

    6 heaped tablespoons *masa harina*
    2 heaped tablespoons self-raising flour
    250 ml/8 fl oz warm water (more if needed)
    Vegetable oil for deep frying

1. Mix the *masa* with the self-raising flour then add enough water to make a firm yet moist dough. You might need more water, but do not let the dough get too soupy. If it does, leave it to dry for a while then proceed (or add a little more *masa* or flour).

ᐊᐊᐊᐊᐊᐊᐊᐊᐊᐊᐊᐊᐊᐊᐊᐊᐊᐊᐊᐊᐊᐊᐊᐊᐊᐊᐊᐊᐊᐊᐊᐊ◇ᐅᐅᐅᐅᐅᐅᐅᐅᐅᐅᐅᐅᐅᐅᐅᐅᐅᐅᐅᐅᐅᐅᐅᐅᐅᐅᐅᐅᐅᐅᐅᐅ

2. Heat the oil until hot enough for frying.

3. Pull off walnut-sized pieces of the dough then, working with your hands, shape them into pots, making the sides and base as thin as possible without tearing. (The dough may also be pressed into tiny tartlet shells then put into the hot oil, tin shell and all, to fry. The shell should be easy to remove afterwards.)

4. Fry the little pots in the hot oil, ladling the hot oil into the centre of each pot and letting it sizzle away as the bottoms brown in the pan.

5. Drain on absorbent paper. To keep warm for a short period of time, transfer to a baking sheet and place in a moderate oven.

6. Stuff as desired (see below) and serve immediately.

SUGGESTED FILLINGS (OR ANY *TACO* OR *TOSTADA*
FILLING, SEE PAGES 86–99)

Refried beans, Carnitas en Otro Estilo (page 169), a shred of chipotle chilli, if available, and a sprinkling of shredded cabbage.

Guacamole, chopped spring onions, crumbled Feta-type cheese.

Potato-courgette filling: coarsely mash 1 to 2 boiled potatoes and mix with 2 boiled, coarsely chopped courgettes and about 75 g/3 oz grated Cheddar or similar cheese. Stuff *cazuelitas* with this mixture, then heat in a hot oven until the cheese melts. Serve topped with chopped spring onions and a dab of soured cream – a sprinkling of chopped fresh chillies is optional.

Shredded chicken or pork, julienned carrots, pickled jalapeños, and shredded cabbage.

Shredded chicken, avocado slices, strip of pickled jalapeños, thinly sliced or diced radishes, dab of soured cream, thinly sliced onion.

Garnachas Veracruzana
Small Cups with Assorted fillings

Garnachas Veracruzana are small, two-bite affairs: the sort of nibbles that chilled lager and warm nights under the stars were made for.

   1 onion, finely chopped
   2 cloves garlic, finely chopped
   1 tablespoon brine from pickled jalapeños
   Masa mixture (see Cazuelitas, page 57), pressed into tiny
      tartlet shapes and fried until golden
   175 to 225 g/6 to 8 oz shredded pork or *carnitas* (pages 167
      to 170), hot
   2 cold waxy boiled potatoes, diced
   Soured cream (optional)

1. Blend the onion, garlic and chilli brine in a liquidizer or food processor until it forms a salsa-like mixture (alternatively, use a ready-prepared salsa).
2. Spoon a little of this into the bottoms of the tartlet shells, then top with some pork and diced potatoes. A garnish of soured cream is optional, but nice with the onion-meat-potato filling.

Sopitas
Masa 'Cups' with Meat and Fresh Cheese

These *masa* snacks filled with finely chopped or puréed meat or poultry are topped with a fresh salsa then garnished with a sprightly blend of Feta or other slightly salty cheese and shredded cabbage. Refried beans could be substituted for meat in a vegetarian version.

‹‹‹‹‹‹‹‹‹‹‹‹‹‹‹‹‹‹‹‹‹‹‹‹‹‹‹‹‹‹‹‹‹‹›››››››››››››››››››››››››››

Masa cups, fried until golden (see Cazuelitas, page 57)
100 g/4 oz cooked meat or combination of meat and
   poultry
A little stock (optional)
Salsa Cruda (page 23) or Salsa Mexicana (page 37)
50 to 75 g/2 to 3 oz Feta cheese, crumbled
¹/₂ onion, chopped
About ¹/₈ cabbage, thinly sliced

1. Prepare the *masa* cups and keep warm.
2. Chop the meat (or meat and poultry) finely, or purée with
   enough stock to form a rich meaty paste. Heat through in a
   frying pan.
3. Spread a little of the warmed meat into each *masa* cup, then
   top with a spoonful of salsa, and a scattering of crumbled Feta
   cheese, chopped onion and shredded cabbage.

SOPAS Y CALDOS
Soups and Broths

Mexican soups are one of the sparkling pleasures of the Mexican table. The main meal, or *comida corrida*, always begins with a bowlful; tradition now deems it unthinkable otherwise. Yet the Aztecs and Mayans had no tradition of soup – they preferred stewy dishes, and ate the courses all at once. It was the Spanish who brought the European tradition of the multi-coursed meal, beginning with soup.

Such a soup is usually simple, based on the rich broth that always seems to be bubbling on a back burner, since many Mexican specialities are based on simmered meal and fowl. The flavourful broth, made with whatever vegetables are left over from other dishes, is ladled into bowls steaming hot, infused with a hint of hot chilli, sprinkled with fresh coriander, and served with a wedge of lime floating on top to squeeze in. There are few dishes so satisfying as this simple robust *caldo Mexicana*. Garnishes and variations abound: crisp tortilla strips, a little soft rice, very thin pasta that has been fried golden before being simmered, crumbled cheese, earthy beans, and so forth.

Some Mexican soups are surprisingly elegant, all suave and smooth, wrapped in creaminess rather than spice. There are bean soups with a wide and sophisticated range of flavours: chickpea purée with mint and lemon, and spicy black bean purée enlivened with citrus fruit are two delicious examples.

With over 6,000 miles of beaches, Mexico offers an inspiring array of fish and shellfish soups, many of which are seldom seen outside their regions. A Mexican fish soup can be as simple as a great cauldron of hot briny broth, bubbling away as each small piece of fish and seafood is added. With a wedge of lime and a scattering of coriander and chillies, it is a fragrant joy.

These are all the *sopas aguadas*, or 'wet soups'. There is also the

◄◄◄◄◄◄◄◄◄◄◄◄◄◄◄◄◄◄◄◄◄◄◄◄◄◄◄◄►►►►►►►►►►►►►►►►►►►►►►►►►►►►

unusual category of *sopa seca*, or 'dry soup', a grouping that refers to pasta, rice or tortillas cooked in robust broths. These are served as a separate course; during fiestas and other celebration meals both a *sopa aguada* and a *sopa seca* will generally be served. Refer to Rice, Beans and Pasta Casseroles for dishes of this nature.

The Mexican kitchen also offers several one-pot meal soup-stews. Mole de Olla, from central Mexico, is a deep red chilli broth with chunks of turkey; Caldo de Res, a beef stew. Tripe-based Menudo and pork-based Pozole are classics: both hearty peasant dishes filled with meat and spicy chilli flavours, as traditional a welcome in the morning after a *parranda* – a night of drinking and carousing – as they are for a comforting and warming supper on a cool evening in a mountain village. They are traditionally simmered in a large earthenware pot which subtly flavours the broth as much as does the selection of meats.

Since few of us eat hearty three- to five-course meals that begin with a bowl of sustaining soup, serve Mexican soup instead as a meal in itself, accompanied by a salad or a selection of *tostadas* or *tacos*, or perhaps followed by a simple roasted fish or chicken dish. Whenever you feel in the mood for a bowl of warming – or cooling – soup, try preparing a soup *à la Mexicana*.

Manera de Hacer un Buen Caldo
On Making Good Soup

Good stock is the basis for Mexico's wealth of soups. Seasoned with mashed tomatoes, ground mild chillies, puréed garlic and onion, a handful of epazote, thyme, or bay leaves it provides the beginning of an endless variety of soups.

Rather than giving specific recipes here for basic stocks, I suggest that you simply simmer a meat of choice along with whatever flavours the pot: a nice plump chicken (including its feet) with carrots, celery, onion, and parsley will give a good, grandmother-style chicken soup. Add a parsnip, several slices of leek, or several cloves of garlic all for a slightly differing flavour. Beef – chunks of whichever cuts you like (chuck, shortribs, neck, etc) – may be seasoned with the same ingredients, including

◁◁▷▷▷▷▷▷▷▷▷▷▷▷▷▷▷▷▷▷▷▷▷▷▷▷▷▷▷▷▷▷▷▷▷▷▷▷

perhaps a few bay leaves. For a brown stock, oven-roast or pan-sear the beef and vegetables before adding water and simmering. If your stocks don't have a good strong flavour add several stock cubes to the pan, and omit or decrease the salt.

Once you have your stock prepared you must skim off its fat. The easiest way to do this is to refrigerate it so the fat solidifies and can be lifted off. Next, for sparkling clear broth, you should clarify the stock. For each 1 litre/1³/₄ pints stock use 2 egg whites. Beat until slightly fluffy and add to the cold stock, then place over a low heat, beating constantly with a wire whisk until it comes to a simmer. Remove from the heat and leave for 15 minutes or until it begins to cool. Strain through a cheesecloth placed inside a colander.

Caldo Tlapeño
Broth with Chickpeas, Chicken Breasts and Avocado

Tlapan is a small town to the south of Mexico City, where city folk flock on Sundays for brunches and picnics. Streets are lined with food stalls and restaurants, and a holiday atmosphere prevails with mariachi bands working café to café, table to table. This soup evolved in those food stalls with their simmering soup cauldrons; as one anonymous enthusiastic chef hit on a winning combination, soon the other stalls followed suit.

By the way, in 1983 when the Queen visited the Reagans at their ranch she was served a similar version of this soup.

◁◁◁◁◁◁◁◁◁◁◁◁◁◁◁◁◁◁◁◁◁◁◁◁◁◁◁◁◁◁◁▷▷▷▷▷▷▷▷▷▷▷▷▷▷▷▷▷▷▷▷▷▷▷▷▷▷▷

1 litre/1³/₄ pints rich stock – a nice mixture of chicken and
   pork, simmered with whole garlic cloves, makes a good
   fragrant stock
200 g/7 oz cooked chickpeas (whole cooked hominy could
   be used in its place)
1 to 2 chipotle chillies, cut into thin strips (or substitute a
   pinch of mild red chilli powder and a little smoky bacon,
   diced)
3 spring onions, thinly sliced
450 g/1 lb chicken breasts, cooked, skinned, and torn into
   large shreds
1 avocado, preferably hass, peeled and thinly sliced or diced
2 tablespoons chopped coriander leaves
1 lime, cut into wedges
Tortilla chips (optional)

1. Heat the stock with the chickpeas, then add the chipotle chilli
   (or chilli powder and bacon).
2. Serve in bowls, spooning spring onions, chicken breast,
   avocado and coriander into each one and accompanying each
   portion with a wedge of lime.
3. Crisp tortilla chips make a good accompaniment, either as a
   crunchy contrast or to break and use as croûtons in the soup.

VARIATION

Caldo Xochitle: from Guadalajara, this simple broth is enriched
with a little mild chilli (1 should be enough) soaked in the hot
stock then scraped from its tough skin, or a whiff of mild chilli
powder instead of the chipotle. Omit the chick peas and proceed
as above. A little chopped garlic, too, never hurts.

Caldo de Papas
Potato and Tomato Soup, Yucatán-Style

A heady mixture of sautéed tomatoes and onions, good homemade stock, and diced potatoes, given a good shot of lemon,
chilli and coriander just before serving.

◄◄◄►►►

As with all simple soups, homemade stock is the best. Sometimes, though, I 'stretch' it with an equal amount of water and a stock cube and it is quite adequate.

Invigorating for a first course on a sultry evening, followed by Pescado Yucateca (page 146) and steamed rice topped with chopped chilli, lime, and coriander leaves.

1 to 2 onions, thinly sliced
1 tablespoon olive oil
3 cloves garlic, coarsely chopped
10 ripe tomatoes, peeled, seeded and diced (or 225 g/8 oz tinned)
2 medium to large potatoes, boiled, cooled, then cut into small cubes
1 litre/1³/₄ pints rich homemade stock (or half stock, half water and stock cube)
Salt and pepper to taste
¹/₂ teaspoon oregano, crumbled
1 medium-hot fresh green chilli, chopped
2 tablespoons chopped coriander leaves
Wedges of lemon

1. Sauté the onions in the olive oil, then when they are softened add the garlic. Cook for a few minutes, then add the tomatoes and cook down to a thick sauce.
2. Add the potatoes, stock, salt and pepper, bring to the boil and cook for a few minutes, long enough to combine the flavours.
3. Add the oregano and chilli, then serve each portion sprinkled with chopped coriander and garnished with lemon wedges to squeeze in.

VARIATIONS

Caldo Miche: prepare a fish stew-soup substituting fish for the potatoes and using fish stock. Traditionally Caldo Miche is prepared with catfish, but any firm, white fish fillet, cut into bite-sized pieces, is delicious.

Caldo de Cangrejo: add chunks of crab to the potato soup, and use a seafood or fish stock.

◁◁◁◁◁◁◁◁◁◁◁◁◁◁◁◁◁◁◁◁◁◁◁◁◁◁◁◁◁◁◁◁◁▷▷▷▷▷▷▷▷▷▷▷▷▷▷▷▷▷▷▷▷▷▷▷▷▷▷▷▷▷

Pozole
Hominy Soup-Stew with a Selection of Fresh Toppings

Pozole, a one-bowl meal, is hearty, hefty fare, consisting of a rich broth with meat, served ladled over nuggets of chewy corn, or hominy. A selection of condiments of contrasting textures and flavours is tossed in, or offered separately for each diner to add individually.

Traditionally a whole pig's head is used for Pozole, but other cuts of stewing pork give equally good flavour – a combination of trotters and spareribs, for instance, or stewing pork cut from a leg. A luxury version, like the one below, will include chicken, and this robust potful will supply you not only with pork and chicken for the Pozole, but with lots left over to shred for *tacos* or *tinga* or to serve with *moles*.

Regional variations of Pozole abound, and it seems to be enjoyed in every region of Mexico except the Yucatán. I've included an elegant version below, based on duck. To me duck stock is at once refined and suave, yet gutsy and full of flavour. Removing the skin first makes a nearly fat-free stock and gives you enough skin and fat to fry up as crackling – a delicious addition to your Pozole, or to reserve and nibble or toss into a salad or *taco*.

'White Pozole'

1 kg/2¼ lb hominy (see Glossary)
About 2 teaspoons salt
450 g/1 lb lean pork, cut into cubes
450 g/1 lb spareribs or fattier pork, or several trotters
3 beef stock cubes
2 whole heads garlic
2 onions
2 bay leaves
½ chicken
3 chicken stock cubes

Condiments:

Shredded cabbage
Chopped onion
Wedges of lime
Red chilli flakes
Strips of crisp fried tortilla or *chicharrones* (optional)

1. You will need three big pots. In the first, place the hominy with water to cover. Leave overnight to swell, then bring to the boil, reduce the heat and simmer for about 45 minutes or until tender, adding more water as needed (you will need to add water several times as the kernels swell). The hominy can be cooked without prior soaking but will take about twice as long. When tender, add 2 teaspoons of salt, or less if the stock cubes are very salty. Set aside.
2. In the second pot place the pork, the beef stock cubes, about 3 litres/5$^{1}/_{4}$ pints water, 1 head garlic, 1 onion and 1 bay leaf. Bring to the boil, reduce the heat, and simmer until tender, about 4 hours.
3. In the third pot place the chicken, the chicken stock cubes, 2 litres/3$^{1}/_{2}$ pints water, and the remaining garlic, onion and bay leaf. Bring to the boil, reduce the heat, and simmer until fragrant and rich, about 3 to 4 hours.
4. When ready to serve remove the meat and chicken from the stock. Shred the meat and keep it separate. Skim the stock of fat. Arrange the garnishes on a platter.
5. Spoon a generous amount of cooked Pozole into each bowl, then ladle in the hot broth, shredded pork and chicken, and various garnishes. Offer an extra hot sauce if desired.

VARIATIONS

Pato en Pozole: Duck Pozole is a delightful combination of elegant and rustic. Prepare as above, but in half quantity. Before placing the duck in the pot, remove all the skin, cut it into small pieces and make crackling out of them: place in a heavy pan with about 100 ml/4 fl oz water and some salt. Bring to the boil, cook away the water, then let the crackling brown in its own fat until crisp

⊲⊲⊲⊲⊲⊲⊲⊲⊲⊲⊲⊲⊲⊲⊲⊲⊲⊲⊲⊲⊲⊲⊲⊲⊲⊲⊲⊲⊲⊲⊲⊳⊳⊳⊳⊳⊳⊳⊳⊳⊳⊳⊳⊳⊳⊳⊳⊳⊳⊳⊳⊳⊳⊳⊳⊳⊳⊳⊳⊳⊳

and crunchy. It will be substantially reduced in quantity.

Serve the Pozole as above. For a first course, serve with only a few shreds of duck and a small portion of hominy. Reserve any of the leftover duck for elegant *tacos*.

In Michoacán dried oregano is offered in a small bowl for diners to crumble into their Pozole.

In Guerrero the addition of about 325 g/12 oz cooked tomatillos puréed with 275 g/10 oz toasted ground pumpkin seeds and a little chopped fresh green chilli gives a distinctive flavour and colour to Pozole. Let the mixture simmer in the stock for about 30 minutes, stirring often so that it does not stick on the bottom of the pan.

In Sonora, Mexico, and north into New Mexico Pozole is served with a drizzle of mild chilli sauce based on mild chilli powder such as ancho, New Mexico, guajillo or California. Mild chilli powder mixed with paprika works well: lightly sauté in a little oil, then combine with a little hot stock until it reaches the desired consistency.

Pozole Rojo: a red Pozole favoured in Michoacán gets its colour from the mild red chillies added to the stew: ancho, guajillo, New Mexico, etc. Lightly toast and rehydrate the mild chillies and scrape away the skin or purée and strain as desired (see Glossary). Add this chilli purée to the soup. About 4 to 6 chillies should be good. Mild chilli powder may be used, though the result is not as sweetly fresh as the whole chillies are.

Sopa de Garbanzo
Mint-Scented Purée of Chickpeas, Oaxaca-Style

Like many Mexican dishes, this smooth and elegant purée contains not a whiff of chilli. Such dishes – usually based on vegetables or beans – often come as a surprise to those who have preconceived ideas of Mexican food as anything smothered in chillies and wrapped in a tortilla.

◁◁◁◁◁◁◁◁◁◁◁◁◁◁◁◁◁◁◁◁◁◁◁◁◁◁◁◁◁◁◁◁◁◇▷▷▷▷▷▷▷▷▷▷▷▷▷▷▷▷▷▷▷▷▷▷▷▷▷▷▷▷▷

Sopa de Garbanzo, with its aroma of olive oil and fragrance of mint, has the distinct Arabian overtones that appear mysteriously throughout the foods of this great nation. It's really no mystery, however, since at the time of the Spanish Conquest Moorish influence was still strong in Spain.

More usual garnishes for this soup include crisp browned croûtons or eggs fried in olive oil, but I prefer wedges of lemon squeezed in: they give it a tart and fresh lift.

    1 onion, coarsely chopped
    2 cloves garlic, chopped
    2 tablespoons olive oil (or vegetable oil)
    400 g/14 oz cooked chickpeas
    750 ml/1¼ pints chicken stock
    1 to 1½ teaspoons dried mint, crumbled, or 2 tablespoons
        fresh mint, chopped
    Salt (omit if using stock made from a cube) and black
        pepper to taste
    Lemon wedges
    Fresh mint for garnish (optional)

1. Lightly sauté the onion and garlic in the oil until softened and lightly browned. Add the chickpeas and stir through the onion mixture, cooking for a minute or two.
2. Add the stock, bring to the boil and cook for a moment.
3. Place the chickpeas in a liquidizer (this makes a smoother purée than a food processor) or food processor and blend until smooth, then with the machine still running slowly pour in the stock.
4. Season with the mint, salt if needed, and pepper, and serve each portion of soup with a lemon wedge either squeezed in or served on the side for each guest to squeeze. Garnish with fresh mint leaves if liked.

◁◁◁▷▷▷▷▷▷▷▷▷▷▷▷▷▷▷▷▷▷▷▷▷▷▷▷▷▷▷

Sopa de Frijole Negro y Tortillas
Black Bean Soup with Three Citrus Fruits and Fresh Tortillas

Black bean soups are ubiquitous in many regions of Mexico, especially Oaxaca and Yucatán. The rich, almost smoky flavour and hearty quality of the beans lend themselves to a wide variety of seasonings. While meaty stocks and chunks of sausage are classic, I like this vegetarian version best. Its strong Yucatecan citrus flavours, the smooth texture of soured cream, and the chunks of soft earthy tortillas broken into the bowl combine to make a strikingly delicious soup.

2 teaspoons vegetable oil
2 cloves garlic, chopped
$1/2$ teaspoon cumin seeds
275 g/10 oz cooked black beans, puréed
Pinch of mild chilli powder (optional)
500 ml/16 fl oz stock of choice (stock cubes are fine)
1 tablespoon finely chopped fresh coriander leaves
1 fresh medium-hot green chilli, such as jalapeño, seeded
    and finely chopped
$1/2$ orange
$1/2$ lemon
$1/2$ lime, cut into 4 wedges
About 50 ml/2 fl oz soured cream
2 spring onions, thinly sliced
4 freshly made, fairly thick corn tortillas, broken into bite-
    sized pieces

1. Heat the oil in a saucepan and warm the garlic and cumin seeds in it; when fragrant but not browned, stir in the black beans (and chilli powder, if using) and cook for a minute.
2. Pour in the stock, add the coriander, cover and simmer for 5 to 8 minutes.
3. Ladle out into 4 bowls; sprinkle with chilli and squeeze in the juice from the orange and lemon halves, then squeeze in the lime juice and place a lime wedge in each bowl (the essential oils from the lime peel add their flavour and perfume, plus the diner can squeeze the lime wedge with his or her spoon to extract more of the tangy juice).

◁◁◁◁◁◁◁◁◁◁◁◁◁◁◁◁◁◁◁◁◁◁◁◁◁◁◁◁◁◁◁▷▷▷▷▷▷▷▷▷▷▷▷▷▷▷▷▷▷▷▷▷▷▷▷▷▷▷▷▷

4. Stir well, then top each bowlful with a dollop of soured cream, sprinkle with spring onions, and garnish with tortilla pieces.

Sopa de Tortilla
Vegetable Soup with Crisp Tortilla Strips, Cheese, Lime and Chillies

Sopa de Tortilla could almost be called *sopa Mexicana*, for variations are to be found on nearly every table in the Republic. The formula is flexible: simmering stock filled with vegetables, the whole thing served with crisp tortilla strips, wedges of lime, and chillies – all ingredients close at hand in the Mexican kitchen.

The richly flavoured stock makes a perfect foil for the contrasting flavours and textures. If you have no big pot of simmering broth, *à la Mexicana*, you can improvise by simmering a few bits and pieces of vegetables along with several pieces of various meats – the neck of a duck, for instance, the odd chicken wing, a few pieces of meat or bones. Throw them into the stock pot along with an onion, several garlic cloves, a chopped carrot, and several stock cubes (this will shortcut your soup preparation). By combining several different types of meat in the stock, you develop layers of flavour and complexity that would not occur with only one type. For a vegetarian broth use vegetable stock cubes, a head of garlic or two, a few strips of red pepper and so on.

Once you have a lovely stock made, the rest of the soup is easy. It is brilliantly simple and tastes essentially of the Mexican table.

◁◁◁◁◁◁◁◁◁◁◁◁◁◁◁◁◁◁◁◁◁◁◁◁◁◁◁◁◁◁◁◁◁◁◁◁◇▷▷▷▷▷▷▷▷▷▷▷▷▷▷▷▷▷▷▷▷▷▷▷▷▷▷▷▷▷▷▷▷▷▷▷

Stock
use 1 or 2 of the following:

> 1 duck neck/2 chicken feet /3 chicken or duck wings/
> A chunk of beef with bone/A pig's trotter, or similar
> piece of meat
> 3 tomatoes, chopped
> 1 clove garlic, coarsely chopped
> $1/_4$ green pepper, cut into strips
> 1 teaspoon pure red New Mexico or ancho chilli powder
> (or mild chilli powder)
> 750 ml/$1 1/_4$ pints water
> 2 stock cubes
>
> 1 or 2 small to medium carrots, julienned or diced
> 1 courgette, diced
> $1/_2$ red pepper, cut into strips
> 50 ml/2 fl oz tomato sauce or juice
> $1/_4$ to $1/_2$ medium-hot fresh chilli, such as jalapeño, chopped
> 6 corn tortillas, cut into strips
> About 175 ml/6 fl oz vegetable oil for frying tortilla strips
> 225 g/8 oz Cheddar cheese, coarsely grated or diced
> 1 lime, cut into wedges
> 2 tablespoons chopped coriander leaves
> Salsa to taste, or chopped fresh chillies

1. Place all the ingredients for the stock in a pot and bring to the
   boil. Simmer for an hour or until it has a good flavour.
2. Remove the duck neck, wings, or whatever meat you are using
   from the stock. Add the carrots, courgette, red pepper,
   tomato sauce or juice and green chilli. Bring to the boil and
   simmer for an additional 30 minutes or so, until the
   vegetables are tender.
3. Fry the tortilla strips in the hot oil until lightly golden
   browned. Drain on paper towel and set aside.
4. Place some cheese in the bottom of each serving bowl, then
   ladle in the stock and vegetables, filling the bowls nearly all
   the way. Top each portion with a handful of crisp golden
   tortilla strips, a wedge of lime and a sprinkling of coriander.
   Offer salsa or chillies for those who want more heat.

◁◁◁◁◁◁◁◁◁◁◁◁◁◁◁◁◁◁◁◁◁◁◁◁◁◁◁▷▷▷▷▷▷▷▷▷▷▷▷▷▷▷▷▷▷▷▷▷▷▷▷▷▷▷

Sopa Roja de Elote
Sweetcorn, Red Pepper and Tomato Soup

Soups made from sweetcorn abound throughout the regions, often enriched with cream, cheese, onions, and either red or green chillies. Sometimes the soups are mild and smooth, other times fiery. This one is only judiciously spicy, with a smoothness that comes from swirling in a little cream cheese. The tomatoes and red pepper give the soup a pleasing texture and character.

Serve as a first course, followed by Chuletas a la Parilla (page 184) and a fresh and sassy salad.

   4 small or 3 medium onions, coarsely chopped
   25 g/1 oz butter
   1 tablespoon mild chilli powder
   1 to 1$^1/_2$ teaspoons cumin powder
   225 g/8 oz sweetcorn kernels (frozen is fine)
   1 red pepper, roasted, peeled, and diced
   1 litre/ 1$^3/_4$ pints chicken or vegetable stock
   325 g/12 oz canned, diced, tomatoes in juice
   1 small can diced, peeled, green chillies
   225 g/8 oz cream cheese
   2 tablespoons chopped coriander leaves or spring onions

1. Lightly sauté the onions in the butter. When softened, add the chilli powder, cumin, sweetcorn, and red pepper, stirring to combine the flavours of the spices and vegetables.
2. Add the stock, tomatoes and green chillies. Bring to the boil, then remove from the heat. Stir the cream cheese until smooth, then slowly add a little of the hot soup to the cream cheese, stirring as it is absorbed. Repeat until the cream cheese is a sauce consistency.
3. Add this cream cheese mixture to the hot soup, stir well to combine and heat until tiny bubbles form around the edge of the pot.
4. Serve immediately, each portion topped with coriander or spring onions.

◄◄

Sopa de Pechuga de Pollo y Almendras
Chicken and Almond Purée

This deliciously unusual soup is thickened with puréed chicken
breast and almonds. It has a nutty, meaty quality yet is smooth.
Though it is traditionally prepared warm, I like it best at cool
room temperature. Serve as a first course, followed by Chuletas a
la Parilla (page 184) and Arroz con Elote (page 192), or Arroz con
Mariscos (page 189) and a plate of green beans with red peppers.

 85 g/3$^1/_2$ oz blanched almonds
 1 medium onion or 2 small onions, diced
 6 cloves garlic, peeled but left whole
 4 spring onions, thinly sliced
 2 tablespoons olive oil
 2 small cooked chicken breasts (about 175 g/6 oz total)
 About 900 ml/1$^1/_2$ pints rich chicken stock
 25 to 35 g/1 to 1$^1/_2$ oz coriander leaves, coarsely chopped
 Salt and pepper to taste

1. Sauté the almonds, onion, garlic and spring onions in the
   olive oil until golden brown.
2. Dice the chicken breasts. Place half the chicken in a liquidizer
   with the almond and onion mixture. Purée, adding enough
   stock to make a fairly smooth mixture.
3. Add the coriander and blend until the mixture turns into a
   green-flecked purée.
4. Remove from the liquidizer and add the remaining diced
   chicken. Taste for salt and pepper, and serve cool.

Sopa de Frijole
Tarascan Pinto Bean Soup with Crisp Tortillas and Mild Red Chilli Strips

Bean soups of all types are eaten throughout Mexico. They are an ideal way of stretching a small amount of meat to feed many people.

This soup is in the style of the Tarascan Indians, from the region of Pátzcuaro. It begins as a simple, rather bland bean broth, but is enlivened by chunks of cheese, tart lemon juice, quickly fried shreds of mild red chillies, and crisp tortillas. Then the bland flavour of the beans works as a juggler, artlessly tossing the various flavours and textures to form an exciting and delicious bowlful.

  2 small to medium onions, chopped
  2 tablespoons olive oil
  Large pinch of cumin seeds
  2 tomatoes, seeded and diced (tinned is fine)
  Large pinch of oregano leaves
  275 g/10 oz cooked pinto beans
  750 ml/1^1/$_4$ pints stock of choice – vegetable, beef or
    chicken
  1 large, mild, smooth-skinned dried red chilli
  3 corn tortillas, slightly stale
  100 to 175 g/4 to 6 oz white melting cheese such as
    Cheddar, cut into dice
  ^{1}/$_2$ lemon, cut into wedges
  Hot salsa or chilli sauce

1. Lightly brown the onions in half the olive oil, then sprinkle in the cumin seeds and toast them for a minute or two with the onions.
2. Add the tomatoes, oregano and beans. Coarsely mash about half the beans with a fork, then add the stock. Bring to the boil, then reduce the heat and simmer together for a few minutes to combine the flavours.
3. Meanwhile, cut the chilli with scissors into very thin strips,

almost shreds. Cut the tortillas into thin strips too.

4. Heat the remaining oil and fry the chilli and tortillas together until the tortilla strips are golden and the chillies darken in colour. Do not let them burn.

5. Place the diced cheese into 4 bowls. Ladle over it the bean soup, squeeze in some lemon juice, then top with fried chilli and tortilla strips.

6. Serve immediately, accompanied by a hot salsa or hot chilli sauce to taste.

SIMPLE MEXICAN SOUPS TO MAKE WITH GOOD HOMEMADE STOCK

Sopa de Aguacate: a dollop of guacamole floating in a bowl of rich chicken stock.

Caldo de Res: simmer puréed tomatoes with diced carrots, onions, potatoes, courgettes, cabbage, chunks of corn on the cob, and a handful of chopped coriander leaves in a beef stock with chunks of tender simmered beef. Serve with a salsa, a bowl of crushed hot dried chillies, or hot sauce.

Sopa de flor de Calabaza: remove the stems from a handful of squash blossoms, then cut them in julienne strips. Sauté an onion in a little butter, then when soft, add the blossoms. Add chicken stock and simmer for about 5 minutes. Serve immediately. Sometimes a little cream is added to this, or the broth is flavoured with a sprig of epazote.

Rich Spicy Broth: whirl an onion, several cloves of garlic, a chopped medium-hot green chilli and several tomatoes in a liquidizer, along with a handful of coriander leaves. When the mixture is the consistency of a paste, heat a spoonful of oil in a heavy soup pan and fry the paste in this oil until it has reduced and intensified. Add a good rich stock and simmer for 15 minutes or so.

Caldo Chile Rojo: simmer several dried mild red chillies in some rich stock. When the stock is ready and the chillies tender,

remove and either purée and strain the chillies or scrape the flesh
from the tough skin. Return the chilli flesh to the stock and serve
as the basis for a variety of simple soups: add a spoonful of leftover Arroz Mexicana (page 188) and a slice or two of avocado;
garnish with a few strips of crisp golden-fried tortilla chips,
wedges of lime, and a sprinkling of coriander; serve with thin
strips of cooked chicken or meatballs.

Mole de Olla: prepare a rich turkey broth with chunks of turkey
and vegetables such as carrots, potatoes, red and/or green peppers, onions, garlic, fresh coriander. Season either with dried
mild red chilli, as in the above Caldo Chile Rojo, or with small
spoonfuls of Recado Rojo Enchilado (page 43) to taste.

Caldo de Albóndigas: simmer meatballs in beef stock flavoured
with garlic, coriander, cumin (and chipotle chilli if you have it).
Add diced courgettes and a cinnamon stick, and serve with
wedges of lime and a salsa of choice. Caldo de Albóndigas is
often served as a first course for a meal in which meat will not
otherwise appear, or for a main course accompanied by *tacos* or
tostadas.

Vermicelli Soup: sauté broken vermicelli in butter or olive oil with
several cloves of sliced garlic then add to rich stock. When the
pasta is nearly tender, add diced chicken breast and cook until
just done. Serve garnished with a little chopped fresh green
chilli, diced tomato and/or avocado, and a wedge of lemon or
lime.

Tex-Mex Sopa de Pollo: add several spoonfuls of leftover Arroz
Mexicana (page 188) or other rice dish to the stock. Simmer to
heat through, then serve with diced avocado, salsa, and wedges of
lime.

Caldo de Huevo: poach 1 egg per person in rich stock. Serve the
egg floating in a bowl of the soup, garnished with strips of crisp
fried tortillas and a sprinkling of coriander. Add hot salsa to taste.

Sopa de Calabaza: simmer a head of garlic in stock, then add

‹‹

several diced courgettes, a handful of raw rice, several chopped tomatoes and some oregano. When all is tender, serve sprinkled with crumbled Caerphilly cheese. Meatballs, seasoned with mild red chilli or chipotle chilli, turn this soup into a hearty meal.

TORTILLAS, PLATOS DE TORTILLAS Y TAMALES

*Tortillas, Tortilla Dishes
and Tamales*

TORTILLAS

The distinctive scent of bland earthy *masa* (corn, or maize), the
basis of tortillas, being ground or cooked on the *comal* lets you
know you are in Mexico. It is a fragrance like no other, ancient
and ageless. Indeed, tortillas are an ancient food, the bread of the
Aztec, Maya and other Mexican-Indian nations.

Early in the development of the civilization, the native tribes
of Mexico developed the process of soaking and boiling grains of
corn to yield a dough. Eventually the stone *metate*, a primitive
though effective grinder like a mortar and pestle, was used for
grinding the corn into a dough, which was then patted into nourishing flat breads.

The original names for these pancake-like breads were many,
depending on what type of corn was used: *iztactlaolli* referred to
white corn, *yauhtlaolli* to black corn, etc. When the Spanish
arrived they were confused: one could starve to death before
spluttering out such long phrases as *tatonqui tlaxcalli tlacuelpacholli*
(large white tortilla). To simplify things, the Spanish called them
tortillas, or 'little cakes', the same name that refers to the flat
omelettes of Spain.

Fresh off the grill, sweetly fragrant, the ever-present stack of
tortillas, covered in a clean cloth, appears at every meal table in
Mexico. Indeed, a stack of soft, fresh and tender tortillas served
with a bowl of spicy salsa turns even the simplest foods into a
Mexican meal.

Tortillas provide the basis for *tacos, tostados, enchiladas, tostaditas*
and so on. As an edible container, they may be wrapped around
nearly any filling: shredded meats, soupy beans, chunks of

roasted chicken or fish, a wedge of piquant cheese, scrambled eggs and vegetables, or simply a slice of avocado and a smear of hot chilli salsa. Before the Conquest, tortillas were the eating utensils as well as the food; in many parts of Mexico it is still so.

Tortillas provide an endless variety of sustaining and delicious dishes that form the diet of rich and poor alike. In Mexico and most of America's Southwest, tortillas are cheap and plentiful. You can count on their availability to throw together an impromptu meal, even if other ingredients are limited.

In the UK, without a large Mexican population, this is obviously not the case. However, good tortillas are available frozen (see Sources) and you can store them in your freezer for months at a time, retrieving a handful at will. And you can make your own. Homemade tortillas have such an earthy, basic flavour that it is worth acquiring the skill. In my own kitchen I have found that homemade tortillas are rather thicker than purchased ones: therefore I make them myself when they are to be eaten on their own, served as *tostadas*, or stuffed with cheese for *quesadillas*, etc. If I want thin tortillas, such as for *enchiladas*, crisp *tacos*, *nachos*, etc, I use the purchased ones. Keeping a supply of *masa* and tortillas on hand enables you to prepare simple, authentic Mexican food quickly and easily.

Tortillas de Maiz
Corn Tortillas

Flat, round, fairly small tortillas are eaten daily throughout much of Mexico (though larger wheat tortillas dominate in the Northern Sonora region). They are made from the age-old preparation of soaking field corn in a lime solution to loosen the hull and swell the grain into a mixture known as *nixtaml*.

For the past several millennia the background music of the entire country has been the pat-pat-pat sound of tortillas being patted out between the sturdy, brown hands of ageless women. For all its effortless appearance it is the sort of difficult skill that one possibly needs to grow up practising. Try it one day when you have enough time to scrape the sticky *masa* from your fingers.

TORTILLA PRESS

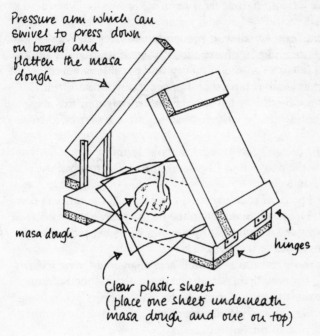

Pressure arm which can swivel to press down on board and flatten the masa dough →

masa dough

hinges

Clear plastic sheets
(place one sheet underneath masa dough and one on top)

However, most fresh tortillas in shops and restaurants are prepared on machines or on homemade presses. It is a simple and effective way of getting an even, fairly thin, tortilla. You can purchase a metal one imported from Mexico at Mexicolore in London (see Sources) or make your own wooden one using the following plan. An endearing quality of this tortilla press is that it doesn't tax your woodworking skills: the rougher its appearance, the more authentic and charming it looks.

Fresh *masa* is used in Mexico, either prepared at home or purchased from the neighbourhood tortilla factory or market. In the absence of fresh *masa*, use dried *masa* flour, moistened with water to make a pliable dough.

◁◁◁◁◁◁◁◁◁◁◁◁◁◁◁◁◁◁◁◁◁◁◁◁◁◁◁◁◁◁◁◁◇▷▷▷▷▷▷▷▷▷▷▷▷▷▷▷▷▷▷▷▷▷▷▷▷▷▷▷▷▷▷

Makes 12 tortillas, approximately 15 cm/6 in in diameter

225 g/8 oz *masa harina* (see Glossary and Sources)
300 to 350 ml/10 to 12 fl oz warm water

1. Mix the *masa harina* with enough warm water to make a
   dough that holds together and is moist. If it is too dry the
   tortillas will be crumbly and dry, and possibly not hold
   together at all. If the dough is too wet it will be difficult to
   handle and possibly fall apart. Experience is your friend in
   this endeavour – if your first batches are not perfect, keep
   at it.
2. Let the dough sit, covered, for about 15 minutes.
3. Divide the dough into 12 pieces. Roll each into a ball with
   your hands.
4. Place a piece of plastic sheet on each side of the tortilla press
   then place a ball of dough in the middle. Close the press,
   encasing the dough ball and flattening it between the plastic-
   sheeted sides of the press.
5. Place the tortilla on a medium-hot, ungreased, heavy frying
   pan (I tip a cast-iron pan upside down and use the bottom).
   It is easiest to peel one side of the plastic off first, then using
   the other sheet of plastic ease it into the pan and peel it off
   directly on to the hot surface.
6. Cook for 1 to 2 minutes, turning frequently. It should be
   speckled lightly brown and appear dry and undoughy, yet still
   soft. It may puff up briefly.
7. Remove from the pan and place in a clean, napkin-lined
   basket or plate, covering the warm tortillas while you
   continue preparing them.
8. Serve immediately, warm and fragrant. Store any leftovers
   well wrapped in the refrigerator. To reheat sprinkle with a
   few drops of water and heat on a hot ungreased pan, turning
   quickly to cook both sides. If they seem to be sticking,
   moisten the pan with a tiny bit of oil.

◁◁◁▷▷▷▷▷▷▷▷▷▷▷▷▷▷▷▷▷▷▷▷▷▷▷▷▷▷▷▷▷▷▷▷▷▷▷

VARIATIONS

Oaxacan Black Tortillas: use the black cooking liquid from cooking black beans, along with a little of the mashed beans, in place of the more usual water.

Oaxacan Thin Tortillas and New Mexico Piki Bread: these paper-thin discs are both prepared in a similar manner: the dough dabbed in a huge circle on to a hot heavy pan, the excess scraped off. When the dough is cooked through it is exquisitely thin, like tissue paper, and is eaten rolled up into a scroll either stuffed or simply rubbed with a little chilli paste. In New Mexico, Piki bread may be tinted with somewhat garish colours of red, yellow or blue, while in Oaxaca the dough may be grey from ashes used in place of lime for soaking the corn.

Tortillas Rojo: add about 1¹/₂ teaspoons mild chilli powder and paprika to the *masa* dough.

Blue Corn Tortillas

The native blue corn of Mexico has a rustic flavour that conjures up the ruggedly austere landscape it grows in. On the stalk its ears grow blue-black-purple but they dry to a greyish blue and are usually treated as hominy: cooked in lime then ground into flour for tortillas, *tamales*, etc. At this stage it looks somewhat like powdered concrete; moistened and patted into tortillas etc, it can cover a range of blue hues. A dash of baking soda turns it a darker blue-to-greenish colour; add a dash of acidic liquid and it becomes more purple.

Blue corn chips have become extremely popular throughout much of the US in recent years. They are crunchier and more brittle than regular corn chips and particularly pleasing dipped into salsa as an appetizer or served with hot, cheese-topped beans, *nacho*-style. I often see them in the UK in healthfood shops and occasionally in restaurants.

As cornmeal, blue corn has found its way into the traditional American kitchen in the form of waffles, muffins, cornbread and the like. Blue cornmeal has also begun appearing in healthfood shops in the UK.

To prepare tortillas using blue *masa* instead of regular white *masa* proceed as for regular tortillas but keep in mind that the blue ones will be sturdier and less flexible. You will probably need more water than for regular ones (2 parts blue *masa* to 1 part water). Some prepare blue corn tortillas more like crêpes, adding milk, salt and egg to the dough. This produces a lighter, more delicate and pliable tortilla, suitable for making *enchiladas*. Blue corn tortillas are especially good used in the New Mexican speciality of stacked *enchiladas* layered with cheese and mild chilli sauce and crowned with a fried egg or two.

Tortillas de Harina
Flour Tortillas, in the Style of Sonora and the US Southwest

Hot off the griddle, warm flour tortillas are chewy, fragrant and eminently satisfying. Homemade ones are thicker and sturdier than shop-bought ones, best for eating immediately rather than for use in any delicate dishes.

Though they are traditionally prepared with lard or vegetable shortening, I often use oil and find the results fine. Sometimes I use olive oil for a flatbread that is more like the Italian *piadine*, and good with cheeses, cold meats, or jam for breakfast. Bean *burritos*, beef *chimichangas*, or fruit *chimichangas* are all made with flour tortillas.

Makes 10 tortillas

> 225 g/8 oz flour
> 1¹/₂ teaspoons baking powder
> 1¹/₂ teaspoons salt
> 60 g/2¹/₂ oz lard or solid vegetable shortening, or 60 ml/2¹/₂ fl oz oil
> 175 ml/6 fl oz hot water

1. Combine the flour, baking powder and salt. .
2. Cut in the fat until the mixture resembles coarse meal, or stir

≪≪≪≪≪≪≪≪≪≪≪≪≪≪≪≪≪≪≪≪≪≪≪◇≫≫≫≫≫≫≫≫≫≫≫≫≫≫≫≫≫≫≫≫≫≫≫

in the oil, if using. Add the water and mix with a fork until the liquid is absorbed. Gently knead with the hands for 10 to 15 seconds: if the dough is too sticky and wet, add a spoonful or two of flour. Cover the bowl and leave for at least 15 minutes.

3. Divide the dough into 10 pieces. Roll each round in flour then leave for 15 to 20 minutes.

4. Pat each dough portion into a flattish round, then roll, using strong pressure on the dough, until it is 0.3 cm/⅛ in thick.

5. Heat an ungreased well-seasoned or lightly oiled heavy frying pan or griddle until very hot, then cook each tortilla on the hot pan until bubbles appear all over the surface. Turn and lightly brown the other side (do not overcook or it will be dry and cracked). Place in a cloth-lined basket and serve as soon as possible.

Tostadas and Tostaditas (known in Michoacán as Totopos)
Crisp Fried Tortillas and Tortilla Chips

Tostadas are crisp fried tortillas, layered with savoury fillings then piled high with fresh greens and vegetables.

Tostaditas – warm, brittle, crisp wedges of fried tortilla – served in napkin-lined baskets along with a bowl of fresh salsa are one of life's great temptations. The tortillas may be cut either into strips or wedges. They are delicious in soups, as a garnish to sauced dishes, or to dip in salsa. Wedges may be arranged in an oven-proof dish, topped with cheese and/or beans, baked, then served as an appetizer with salsa.

This is the basic recipe for either *tostadas* or *tostaditas*.

12 corn tortillas
About 450 g/1 lb lard or shortening, or 500 ml/16 fl oz
    vegetable oil

1. Cut the tortillas into 6 wedges each for *tostaditas*, or leave whole for *tostadas*. They are easier to cut with strong scissors than with a knife.

2. Heat the fat in a heavy frying pan until a cube of bread dropped into it turns golden immediately.
3. Fry 6 tortilla wedges or 1 whole tortilla at a time until just crisp.
4. Drain on absorbent paper and serve (see pages 95 to 99 for *tostada* recipes and suggested toppings).

Fried Flour Tortillas

Savoury: flour tortillas, cut into fairly large wedges, are delicious fried golden and topped with a spoonful of *mole* sauce and a sprinkling of chopped spring onions for an unusual appetizer.

Sweet: crisp golden fried tortillas can be dusted with cinnamon and sugar and served as an accompaniment to a simple fruit dessert or ice-cream. For a particularly attractive presentation they can be cut into shapes such as stars, arrows, abstracts, flowers, leaves and so on before frying. Flour tortillas may also be stuffed with fruit and fried, or the hot golden tortillas may be sprinkled with chocolate and left to melt. See Desserts and Baked Goods for complete recipes.

CORN TORTILLA DISHES

Tacos

Tacos are probably the first introduction anyone has to Mexican food. They are eaten in one form or another throughout the Republic. Over the border into the Southwest, *tacos* have become as American as the hamburger or hot dog.

Tacos consist of savoury ingredients wrapped up in tortillas, which are then served either soft, fresh and warm or fried until crisp. Crisp *tacos* may also be made from fried tortilla shells, then stuffed afterwards.

Throughout Mexico, *tacos* reflect the regional cuisine. The marketplace is the best place to sample them, especially when the tortillas are soft and warm, pulled off the griddle and wrapped around some sort of savoury morsel. Almost any stewed, grilled, fried or dressed mixture can be used to fill a *taco*. *Tacos de carbón* are shreds of charcoal-grilled meats, unforgettably delicious. In the Yucatán *tacos* are filled with exquisitely refreshing *fiambres*, cool, vinaigrette-dressed mixtures of seafood, poultry or meat.

Tacos de Pollo
Chicken Tacos with Guacamole

An excellent way to use leftover chicken that has been simmered in a soup pot. Salsa Verde (page 26), that tangy green, tomatillo-based hot sauce, is especially delicious with this simple *taco*.

Serves 2 as a main course, 4 as an appetizer

225g/8 oz boiled chicken, cut or shredded into bite-sized
  pieces
Oil for frying
$1/2$ to 1 teaspoon cumin seeds
2 cloves garlic, chopped
$1/2$ teaspoon mild chilli powder, or to taste
Salt and pepper to taste
4 corn tortillas
2 tablespoons chopped coriander leaves
2 tablespoons finely chopped onion
Handful of shredded lettuce
Soured cream (optional)
Salsa or a little finely chopped raw chilli
1 quantity guacamole (see page 50 – or make a simple one
  by mashing 2 avocados with lots of lemon or lime juice,
  then adding a chopped tomato and hot salsa)

1. Quickly brown the chicken in a little oil with the cumin seeds and garlic, then sprinkle in the chilli powder. Season with salt and pepper.
2. Heat the tortillas, one at a time, in an oiled pan until pliable, then place on a plate. Place several spoonfuls of the chicken

mixture inside each tortilla and roll up.

3. Either serve straight away, topped with the coriander, onion, lettuce, soured cream, if using, salsa or chilli, and guacamole, or fry until crispy. To fry, heat a pan until quite hot, add enough oil for deep frying, then quickly fry the *tacos* until golden brown. You may need to close the *tacos* with toothpicks to secure the edges and prevent the filling leaking out.

Tacos de Tinga Poblana
Smoky-Flavoured Shredded Pork Tacos with Avocado, Puebla-Style

This dish tastes of Mexico – its fragrant simplicity, the earthy corn flavours playing against the richness of the meat and smoky heat of the sauce. Like so many of Mexico's robust savoury dishes, this one begins with a pot of simmering meat. The broth is used for soup, the meat for this dish the next day. The meat must be cooked enough to enable you to shred it with two forks. Pork is the usual choice.

By the way, *tinga* translates roughly as 'vulgar', only enhancing my affection for this full-flavoured *taco*.

450 g/1 lb cold simmered pork
2 shallots, chopped, or 1 onion, chopped
25 to 50 ml/1 to 2 fl oz vegetable oil
1 rasher bacon, diced (optional)
2 tomatoes, seeded, peeled and diced (tinned are fine)
About 175 ml/6 fl oz stock from cooking the meat
1 to 2 chipotle chillies, mashed, plus a bit of the marinade
    (or use mild chilli powder to taste)
8 fresh warm corn tortillas
2 avocados, sliced, or guacamole made from mashing 2
    avocados with lemon juice and a little hot pepper
    seasoning or salsa
Soured cream
Chopped coriander leaves, chopped radishes, shredded
    lettuce, to garnish as desired

1. Shred the meat into small pieces using two forks.
2. Sauté the shallots or onion in the vegetable oil until softened (with the bacon and mild chilli powder, if using).
3. Add the meat and sauté for a few minutes with the onion, then add the tomatoes and stock and cook until it reduces to a sauce, mashing the meat a little as it cooks. Add the chipotle chillies (or mild chilli powder) and continue to cook and mash until the sauce and meat are nearly one.
4. Serve warm tortillas topped with or rolled around several spoonfuls of the meat mixture, adding a slice of avocado or a spoonful of guacamole, and a drizzle of soured cream. Eat immediately, garnished with a sprinkling of coriander leaves and/or chopped radishes or shredded lettuce.

VARIATION

Often Mexican chorizo is added to the mixture. Spicy Spanish chorizo, while the texture is not the same, can be diced and added for additional flavour, especially if chipotle chilli cannot be found.

Tacos de Huachinango con Salsa Verde
Red Snapper Tacos with Green Salsa

Red snapper is extremely popular in Mexico as well as California. It is a light-flavoured yet firm-textured fish, especially good when combined with the strong, bright flavours of chillies, garlic, tomatoes, etc. Chunks of red snapper are especially good splashed with a tangy salsa, especially a green one, then rolled up into *tacos*. If Salsa Verde is not available, use any homemade salsa such as Salsa de Chiles y Ajo (page 23), or Salsa Cruda (page 23).

◁◁◁◁◁◁◁◁◁◁◁◁◁◁◁◁◁◁◁◁◁◁◁◁◁◁◁◁◁◁◇▷▷▷▷▷▷▷▷▷▷▷▷▷▷▷▷▷▷▷▷▷▷▷▷▷▷

2 fillets of red snapper or bass, 275 to 325 g/10 to 12 oz in
   total
Salt and pepper to taste
1 teaspoon cumin
1 teaspoon chilli powder
1/2 teaspoon oregano leaves, crumbled
2 cloves garlic, chopped
1 to 2 tablespoons olive oil
Juice of 1/2 lime or lemon
8 corn tortillas
Oil for heating tortillas
Salsa Verde, either homemade (page 26) or bottled
2 tablespoons chopped coriander leaves
2 tablespoons chopped onion

1. Place the fish in a baking dish, then sprinkle with the salt,
   pepper, cumin, chilli powder, oregano, garlic, oil and lime or
   lemon juice. Cover tightly and bake in the oven at
   230°C/450°F/gas mark 8 for 15 minutes or until just cooked
   through. Remove from the oven and keep warm.
2. Heat the tortillas by warming them gently, one at a time, in a
   lightly oiled heavy frying pan over a low-to-medium heat.
   Stack them on a heavy plate, keeping them covered as you go
   to keep them warm and pliable.
3. Assemble the *tacos*: break the fish into bite-sized pieces, divide
   between the tortillas, sprinkle with salsa, coriander and onion,
   then roll up.
4. Serve immediately with extra salsa for dipping.

Flautas de Camarones con Guacamole
Crisp Tacos of Prawns with Guacamole

Flautas are thin, flute-like *tacos* that have been filled then rolled
up and fried until a golden crisp. Often two tortillas are used,
overlapping slightly to form a much longer surface and more
flute-like shape.

Flautas may be filled with chicken, crab, or anything else instead of the prawns. Since they are fried, however, choose a filling that is not too moist or rich.

Cooling and fresh guacamole makes a lively counterpoint to the crisp fried *tacos*, as does a bowl of a mild salsa or Pico de Gallo (page 36).

325 g/12 oz prawns, cooked and diced
1 teaspoon pure mild chilli powder such as ancho, pasilla,
 etc, or combination of mild chilli powder and paprika
¹/₂ onion, finely chopped
1 tablespoon chopped coriander leaves (optional)
Salt to taste
8 corn tortillas
Oil for frying

Toppings

Guacamole (page 50)
Salsa or Pico de Gallo (page 36)
Chopped onion
Chopped coriander leaves
Chopped tomatoes

1. Combine the prawns with the chilli powder, onion, coriander, if using, and salt.
2. Prepare either 8 small *flautas*, or 4 long ones by using either 1 corn tortilla per *flauta* or 2. If using 2, line them up so that they are slightly overlapping, then fill with the prawn mixture and roll. For small *flautas* simply place some filling on a tortilla and roll it. Do not stuff too full and do not fold over at the edges to seal – just roll them very tight and seal with a toothpick if necessary.
3. Fry in hot oil until crisp and golden, then drain each *flauta* on absorbent paper as it is cooked.
4. Serve immediately, garnished with guacamole and salsa or Pico de Gallo, chopped onions, tomatoes and coriander.

◁◁

Tacos en Estilo San Luis
Tacos Filled with Beans, Meat and Nopales

These *tacos* are a memorable mélange of flavours and textures, wrapped into a chewy, toasty corn tortilla. They are not as complicated to make as the long list of ingredients implies.

Meat Filling

> 450 g/1 lb minced beef or tender cooked and shredded beef
> 6 spring onions, thinly sliced
> 6 to 8 cloves garlic, coarsely chopped
> 1 to 3 small to medium boiled potatoes, cooled and diced
> 175 g/6 oz tomatoes, chopped (either tinned or very ripe fresh ones)
> 2 pickled jalapeños, chopped or thinly sliced
> Salt to taste

Nopales Filling

> 2 small to medium onions, thinly sliced
> 2 cloves garlic, coarsely chopped
> 1 tablespoon vegetable oil
> 225 g/8 oz precooked *nopales* (see Glossary)
> Salt and pepper to taste
> 2 teaspoons coarsely chopped fresh coriander leaves

Refried beans

> 225 g/8 oz tin *frijoles refritos*, or use homemade (page 196)

> 8 corn tortillas
> A little oil

1. Prepare the meat filling by browning the meat in a frying pan. Pour off the fat, add the spring onions and garlic and continue cooking a few minutes, then add the potatoes and cook a minute or two longer, taking care not to break up the potatoes too much. Add the tomatoes and pickled chillies; taste for salt. Set aside and keep warm.

2. Prepare the *nopale* filling: sauté the onions and garlic in the vegetable oil until softened, then add the *nopales* (drained if tinned). Season with salt, pepper and coriander. Set aside.
3. Heat the refried beans and keep warm.
4. Heat the tortillas one at a time in a medium-hot lightly oiled pan. As soon as each one is hot and pliable, spread with *frijoles refritos*, then top with a few spoonfuls of the meat mixture and the *nopale* mixture. Roll up or fold over.
5. Either eat immediately, or place in a dish to keep warm in the oven while you prepare the rest.

VEGETARIAN VARIATION

Since this dish has such a wide range of flavours and textures, I think that a good soya-based minced beef substitute would work extremely well.

Tacos de Camarones
Prawn Tacos Splashed with a Tangy Sauce

Sloshing a bit of mild sauce on these *tacos* stretches the definition of *tacos*. They are both crisp and sauced, somewhat like *enchiladas*. The filling, too, is rather different from other *taco* presentations: using raw shrimp instead of cooked gives an almost Asian result.

The sauce is more reminiscent of a French reduction than a Mexican salsa, and while simple to prepare it is a very sophisticated dish.

Stuffing

> 3 cloves garlic, chopped
> 1 onion, chopped
> 1 to 3 roasted medium to hot green chillies, peeled and seeded, then chopped (according to taste)
> 3 ripe tomatoes, chopped (tinned is fine)
> 1 tablespoon chopped coriander leaves
> 450 g/1 lb fresh raw prawns, chopped or diced
> Salt to taste

Sauce

3 cloves garlic, chopped
1 onion, chopped
4 tomatoes, quartered or chopped (tinned is fine)
1 tablespoon vegetable oil
500 ml/16 fl oz fish stock
1 tablespoon vinegar or lemon or lime juice

8 corn tortillas
Vegetable oil for frying

Toppings

$1/_4$ cabbage, shredded
Pickled carrots, courgettes or jalapeños
$1/_2$ onion, thinly sliced or chopped

1. Mix all the ingredients for the stuffing and set aside.
2. In a liquidizer or food processor whirl the garlic, onion and
   tomatoes to a paste.
3. Heat the oil in a frying pan, then add the garlic-onion-tomato
   mixture and fry for a few minutes to concentrate the flavour,
   then add the stock and cook for a few minutes longer.
   Remove from the heat and add the vinegar or lemon or lime
   juice.
4. One at a time heat the corn tortillas in a lightly greased frying
   pan over a medium heat and when pliable fill with the prawn
   filling and fold over, *taco*-style.
5. When all the tortillas are filled, fry them several at a time,
   until they are golden and crisp. Drain on absorbent paper.
6. Serve each portion of 2 *tacos* splashed with the warmed
   reserved sauce and topped with the shredded cabbage, the
   pickled carrots, courgettes or jalapeños, and chopped or sliced
   onions.

◁◁◁▷▷▷

SIMPLE TOPPINGS AND FILLINGS FOR *TACOS*

Browned chorizo and potatoes.

Browned minced meat with red chilli and avocado slices.

Chunks of cooked fish with a fresh, invigorating salsa.

Grated cheese and chopped spring onions: grill until bubbly then serve with salsa, avocado, and soured cream.

Shredded cooked meat of choice, chopped spring onions, soured cream, radishes.

Diced lobster (or crab) and avocado with chopped onion and salsa.

Sautéed red, yellow and green peppers with tomatoes, cumin, chilli, melted cheese and soured cream.

Tostadas

Tostadas at their most basic refer to fried tortillas, but the word is generally used to describe those crisp fried tortillas used as a base on which to pile a variety of savoury fillings and fresh salady ingredients. At their garish extreme, in California and the Southwest, huge tortillas are deep fried into gargantuan edible plates and piled high with robust meat and salad ingredients, far too much for one person but too enticing to leave unfinished.

Tostada shells are sold in most supermarkets. They do not taste as good and authentic as those you fry yourself, but they are convenient, and make *tostadas* something you can throw together with little advance preparation. Do remember, however, that with shop-bought crisp *tostada* shells the ingredients need to be rather more flavourful. When preparing your own homemade

ⵀⵀ

fried tortillas you can rely more on their corn flavour and use more subtle toppings such as guacamole, grated cheese, herbs, seafood, and so on.

Nearly anything can top *tostadas*: creamy refried pinto or black beans can act as a delicious base for toppings that range from diced vegetables to seafood, to shredded or sauced meats. Piles of fresh shredded cabbage or lettuce, diced radishes and thinly sliced onion, a sprinkling of coriander and/or diced tomatoes, strips of pickled chillies or chipotle chilli, slices of avocado, soft, cooling soured cream – all of these things, and more, might be found on a *tostada*.

Tostadas Compuestas
Tostadas Topped with a Selection of Ingredients

Great fun for informal entertaining, these hot bean- and sauce-topped *tostadas* can be offered on a platter with a selection of toppings for guests to help themselves to.

325 g/12 oz Mexican chorizo (or use minced meat plus $1/_2$ teaspoon mild chilli powder, $1/_2$ teaspoon paprika, $1/_2$ teaspoon oregano, and salt and pepper)
1 onion, chopped
2 cloves garlic, chopped
4 corn tortillas fried to a crisp, or *tostada* shells
175 g/6 oz *frijoles refritos*, tinned or homemade (page 196)
100 g/4 oz fairly sharp cheese, grated
Shredded lettuce

Toppings

Chopped onion
Diced tomatoes
Roasted mild green chillies
Salsa of choice
Sliced avocados
Chipotle chillies in strips and/or pickled chillies
Any pickled vegetable such as cabbage, carrots, etc
Soured cream
Chopped coriander, spring onions, radishes

1. Brown the chorizo (or meat and spices) in a pan with the onion and garlic.
2. Spread the refried beans on the *tostada* shells then top with the meat mixture, grated cheese and shredded lettuce. Either divide the toppings between them or offer them separately in bowls.

VARIATION

Tostadas Tapatia: in Guadalajara, *tostadas* of pickled pig's trotters are quite popular. Omit the chorizo topping, chipotle chillies and soured cream. Over the layer of hot beans and cheese place pieces of boneless pig's trotters, and top with shredded lettuce tossed with a little oil, vinegar and a dash of salt. Hot chilli salsa to taste.

ⰔⰔⰔⰔⰔⰔⰔⰔⰔⰔⰔⰔⰔⰔⰔⰔⰔⰔⰔⰔⰔⰔⰔⰔⰔⰔⰔⰔⰔⰔⰔⰕⰕⰕⰕⰕⰕⰕⰕⰕⰕⰕⰕⰕⰕⰕⰕⰕⰕⰕⰕⰕⰕⰕⰕⰕⰕⰕⰕⰕⰕⰕ

Tostadas de Papas
Potato Tostadas with Salsa Verde and Soured Cream

The tangy flavour of tomatillo salsa pairs particularly well with the earthy, spicy chillied potatoes. A smoky whiff of chipotle chilli is a delicious counterpoint to this delightfully tart salsa, but if it is unavailable, thin rings of pickled jalapeños are good, too. Soured cream cools it all off, and the crunch of shredded cabbage gives additional textural interest.

> 3 medium potatoes, peeled and diced
> 1 tablespoon vegetable oil
> 1 small onion, diced
> 2 cloves garlic, chopped
> 1 teaspoon mild chilli powder
> 1 teaspoon paprika
> 4 *tostada* shells, homemade (page 95) or shop-bought
> *Frijoles refritos*, homemade (page 196) or from a tin (optional)
> Salsa Verde (page 26), or several cooked tomatillos mashed
>   with a chopped chilli and a little chopped onion or garlic,
>   and salt to taste
> 50 to 75 ml/2 to 3 fl oz soured cream, or as desired
> 1 tablespoon chopped fresh coriander leaves
> 1 chipotle chilli or 2 pickled jalapeños, sliced
> Handful of shredded cabbage

1. Lightly brown the potatoes in the vegetable oil with the onion. When the potatoes are nearly tender, add the garlic, chilli powder and paprika. Set aside and keep warm.
2. Heat the *tostada* shells under the grill or in a hot oven for just long enough to heat through, then spread with *frijoles refritos*, if using. Pile with the cooked potatoes, then garnish with Salsa Verde, soured cream, coriander, chipotle or pickled jalapeño, and shredded cabbage. Serve immediately.

VARIATION

Tostadas de Papas y Camarones (Potato and Prawn Tostadas): add a handful of warm prawns to the *tostadas*, scattered on after the potatoes.

◁◁◁◁◁◁◁◁◁◁◁◁◁◁◁◁◁◁◁◁◁◁◁◁◁◁◁◁▷▷▷▷▷▷▷▷▷▷▷▷▷▷▷▷▷▷▷▷▷▷▷▷▷▷▷

SUGGESTED *TOSTADA* TOPPINGS

Picadas, Puebla-Style: spread soured cream on *tostadas* then top with any tender shredded or chopped meat (such as *carnitas*). Garnish with Salsa Verde (page 26) and strips of chipotle chilli, if available, and serve with a sprinkling of finely chopped onion.

Tostadas de Frijoles y Huevos: spread hot crisp *tostadas* with mashed seasoned black beans; top with eggs scrambled with garlic, chilli, tomato and fresh coriander.

Tostadas de Guacamole: spread hot *tostadas* with a layer of guacamole and a layer of soured cream, then sprinkle with chopped onion.

Tostadas de Queso: make a layer of cheese and chopped spring onion on top of a soft corn tortilla. Grill until bubbly and lightly browned. Serve with salsa and avocado.

Tostadas de Frijoles y Jocaqui: spread *tostadas* with refried beans, then sprinkle with grated cheese. Grill until melting. Mix soured cream with chopped mild green chillies, then spread this over the hot cheese-topped *tostadas*.

Spread *tostadas* with puréed black beans; top with shreds of roasted duck, chopped onion, coriander, salsa, soured cream, and a little chipotle chilli, if available.

Panuchos: in the Yucatán, tortillas are slit open to form a pocket, then stuffed, fried crisp, and topped with a variety of savoury ingredients. A simpler version of this is the following *tostada*: spread a crisply fried *tostada* with mashed black beans. Top with torn or shredded simmered chicken or several slices of hard-boiled egg, Cebollas en Escabeche a la Yucateca (see page 38, or marinate thinly sliced onion in lemon juice), a little thinly sliced lettuce and sliced pickled jalapeños.

Any *antojito* filling (pages 57 to 59) is suitable for topping *tostadas*.

◁◁◁◁◁◁◁◁◁◁◁◁◁◁◁◁◁◁◁◁◁◁◁◁◁◁◁◁◁◁▷▷▷▷▷▷▷▷▷▷▷▷▷▷▷▷▷▷▷▷▷▷▷▷▷▷▷

Quesadillas
Savoury Turnovers

Quesadillas are uncooked tortillas that are stuffed and folded then either fried in oil or cooked on an ungreased heavy pan. A dough of straight *masa* gives a good flavour but the consistency is a bit sticky; using *cazuelita* dough gives a more manageable pastry.

Traditional fillings include meat, vegetables, *mole* or *adobo* mixtures, chorizo, potatoes, beans and cheese. But simple cheese and chillies are possibly the best, to my taste, the rich turnover topped with a fresh relish of diced tomato, chilli, onion and coriander.

Stuffed with cheese and topped with avocado or guacamole, *quesadillas* are delicious for breakfast. Smaller versions make an excellent first course or appetizer.

For each *quesadilla* take either a freshly made uncooked tortilla (i.e. round of *masa* dough, pages 80–82) or 1 corn tortilla lightly warmed in a little oil to make it pliable. Place a few spoonfuls of the filling of choice in the centre, fold over, then fry on both sides either in oil or in an ungreased heavy pan. Serve immediately, garnished with strips of fresh or pickled chilli or a good-quality salsa, chopped onions, guacamole or diced avocado.

SUGGESTED FILLINGS (OR ANY *TACO*, *TOSTADA* OR *CAZUELITA* FILLINGS)

Grated cheese and roasted green chillies, cut into strips. Cook the *quesadillas* until the cheese melts and oozes out of the edges. Topped with Pico de Gallo (page 36) or Salsa Verde (page 26).

Machaca de Camarones: sauté chopped onion, then add some chopped green chilli and tomatoes. Cook until it is a thick sauce, then add lots of diced raw prawns. Cook over a very low heat until it is a relatively dry dish. Season with salt and pepper.

◁◁◁◁◁◁◁◁◁◁◁◁◁◁◁◁◁◁◁◁◁◁◁◁◁◁◁◁▷▷▷▷▷▷▷▷▷▷▷▷▷▷▷▷▷▷▷▷▷▷▷▷

Sesos: soak one pair of lamb or beef brains in cold water to cover for 1 hour, then remove the covering membrane and the veins. Place in boiling water with several cloves of garlic, 1 bay leaf, a spoonful of vinegar and some salt. Reduce the heat and simmer for 30 minutes. Cool in its liquid, then drain and cut into large dice. Make a simple salsa by sautéing 1 chopped onion and 2 tomatoes in a little butter or oil; season with mild chilli powder and paprika, chopped coriander, and a little seeded, chopped fresh green chilli. Add the brains to the salsa and heat through. Stuff into *quesadillas* or *tacos* and serve garnished with shredded lettuce and salsa of choice.

Enchiladas

Enchiladas are corn tortillas dipped first in a savoury sauce then into hot oil and rolled up. The word *enchilada* translates to 'chillied up', referring to the chillied sauce in which the tortillas are dipped. Usually, but not always, they are wrapped around a filling of some sort: meat, fish, cheese, poultry, vegetables, or simply chopped onion, chillies and herbs. Most commonly rolled, *enchiladas* may also be stacked, as in New Mexico, or folded, as in Oaxaca. They may be served plain, or covered with sauce and cheese then baked.

Good authentic *enchiladas* should be prepared with slightly stale corn tortillas. Since corn tortillas can be hard to find, I've experimented using shop-bought *taco* shells. It simplifies things immeasurably and in many of the dishes works well.

◁◁◁

Enchiladas de Papas
Potato and Cheese Enchiladas

Filling corn tortillas with a mild, cheesy potato mixture then baking them in an unusual coriander sauce makes a surprisingly deli-
cate-flavoured, though hearty and filling, dish. Since it is not
dipped into a chilli sauce, this is authentically not considered an
enchilada, more a baked *taco*.

Serve a small portion as a first course, Mexican-style, followed
by a mild chilli-grilled fish, or accompany with a large salad for a
cosy supper.

   6 to 8 medium, slightly mealy potatoes, boiled until tender
      then mashed
   225 to 275 g/8 to 10 oz cheese such as Caerphilly or
      Cheshire, crumbled
   300 ml/10 fl oz soured cream
   8 spring onions, thinly sliced
   3 or 4 medium-hot chillies such as jalapeño, roasted (see
      Glossary), peeled, seeded and chopped
   Generous pinch of mild chilli powder (optional)
   Salt and pepper to taste
   8 corn tortillas (or 8 shop-bought *taco* shells)
   Oil for frying, if using corn tortillas
   100 g/4 oz Cheddar cheese, coarsely grated

Sauce

   2 cloves garlic, chopped
   6 ripe tomatoes, roasted (see Glossary), seeded and peeled,
      or use tinned
   1 green pepper, roasted, peeled and diced
   1 to 2 fresh medium-hot green chillies
   250 ml/8 fl oz chicken or vegetable stock
   25 g/1 oz coriander leaves, coarsely chopped
   Juice of 1 lime
   1 tablespoon vegetable oil

◁◁◁◁◁◁◁◁◁◁◁◁◁◁◁◁◁◁◁◁◁◁◁◁◁◁◁◁◁◁▷▷▷▷▷▷▷▷▷▷▷▷▷▷▷▷▷▷▷▷▷▷▷▷▷▷▷▷

Toppings

Shredded lettuce
Salsa of choice

1. Mix the mashed potatoes with the cheese, soured cream, spring onions, chopped chillies, and mild chilli powder, if using. Season with salt and pepper and set aside.
2. Warm the tortillas in hot oil one at a time, place several spoonfuls of filling in the centre of each tortilla and roll up. Place in a baking dish. If using shop-bought *taco* shells, do not bother heating them, just fill with the mashed potato mixture.
3. Make the sauce: in a liquidizer or food processor purée the garlic, then add the tomatoes, green pepper, chilli, stock, coriander and lime juice. Process until it makes a sauce consistency.
4. Heat the vegetable oil in a heavy frying pan, then add the sauce, several spoonfuls at a time at first, then the rest, letting it fry and reduce in volume until it darkens in colour and intensifies in flavour. This should take only a minute or two.
5. Pour the sauce over the potato-stuffed tortillas and sprinkle with the cheese.
6. Bake in the oven at 200°C/400°F/gas mark 6 for about 10 minutes, or just long enough for the cheese topping to melt and the ingredients to heat through.
7. Serve sprinkled with shredded lettuce and offer salsa of choice.

Enfrijoladas
Bean-Topped Enchiladas

This hearty casserole consists of *enchiladas* topped with a layer of refried beans and a layer of cheese, then baked until the cheese melts. It is the sort of ribsticking dish that warms the depths of any winter's evening. Though the filling in the recipe is a simple one of minced beef or pork, any browned meat makes a good filling.

◁◁◁◁◁◁◁◁◁◁◁◁◁◁◁◁◁◁◁◁◁◁◁◁◁◁◁◁◁◁◁◁◁◁◁◁◁◇▷▷▷▷▷▷▷▷▷▷▷▷▷▷▷▷▷▷▷▷▷▷▷▷▷▷▷▷▷▷▷▷▷

550 g/1¼ lb minced beef or pork
2 small to medium onions, chopped
2 tablespoons chopped coriander leaves
2 chillies, roasted (see Glossary), peeled and chopped if hot,
   left raw and chopped if mild
Salt and pepper to taste
8 corn tortillas (or 8 shop-bought *taco* shells)
Oil for frying, if using corn tortillas
325–450 g/12–16 oz *frijoles refritos*, tinned or homemade
   (page 196)
350 g/12 oz Cheddar cheese, coarsely grated

Toppings

150 ml/5 fl oz soured cream
1 small to medium onion, chopped
About 6 lettuce leaves, shredded
Hot salsa of choice

1. Brown the meat and onions in a pan, crumbling the meat as it
   cooks. Pour off excess fat, then add the coriander, chillies, salt
   and pepper. Set aside.
2. If using corn tortillas, heat in a little oil until softened. If
   using *taco* shells, no preparation is necessary. Stuff either the
   corn tortillas or *taco* shells with the meat mixture, laying each
   stuffed tortilla parcel into a casserole dish.
3. Top the layer of tortillas with an even layer of *frijoles refritos*.
   Then top with a layer of grated cheese.
4. Bake in the oven at 200°C/400°F/gas mark 6 until the cheese
   is melted and all the ingredients are heated through.
5. Serve topped with soured cream, chopped onion, shredded
   lettuce, and hot salsa of choice.

VEGETARIAN VARIATION

Simply omit the meat and dip the tortillas in mild chilli sauce
before rolling them round a little chopped onion, coriander and
chilli. Top with *frijoles refritos* and cheese and bake as above.

New Mexico Enchiladas Verdes
Green Enchiladas, New Mexico-Style

These *enchiladas* are stacked rather than rolled, which inexplicably seems to make a difference to the flavour.

    12 corn tortillas, slightly stale if possible
    Oil for heating the tortillas
    1 quantity Salsa Verde (page 26)
    325 g/12 oz stewing pork or beef, cut into bite-sized pieces,
        simmered in water/stock until tender (save the cooking
        liquid for soup)
    325 g/12 oz sharp cheese such as Cheddar, grated
    ¹/₂ teaspoon cumin seeds (optional)
    250 ml/8 fl oz stock of choice (water mixed with a stock
        cube is fine, though do not add extra salt)

Toppings

    2 eggs per person, lightly fried *or*
    Soured cream
    Chopped onions
    Coriander
    Shredded lettuce

1. Heat the tortillas one at a time in a small amount of hot oil. Dip immediately into a little of the Salsa Verde (have some on a plate or shallow bowl), then place the first 2 tortillas next to each other on a baking sheet.
2. Top these 2 tortillas with a layer of the meat, a little more sauce, and some cheese, then repeat with a layer of tortillas, meat, sauce and a layer of cheese. Keep repeating, ending with sauce and a lavish sprinkling of cheese.
3. Sprinkle with cumin seeds if desired, then pour the stock gently over and around the two stacks.
4. Bake in the oven at 190°C/375°F/gas mark 5 for 20 minutes, or until the cheese is melted and bubbling, perhaps lightly browned in parts.
5. Serve immediately, topped either with fried eggs or with the soured cream, onions, coriander and lettuce.

◄◄◄►►

Papa-dzules

Papa-dzules are Yucatecan *enchiladas*, flavoured with pumpkin seeds and spicy tomato sauce. Often the tortillas are dipped in a *pipián* sauce, then garnished with a rich green oil pressed from pumpkin seeds. This recipe is a simplified version, hard-boiled egg filling seasoned with chopped pumpkin seeds rather than a *pipián* sauce. It is an ancient dish, once prepared by the Aztecs to impress Cortés and his Spanish entourage.

    8 hard-boiled eggs, shelled and coarsely chopped
    1 to 2 spring onions, thinly sliced
    Salt, cumin, oregano and black pepper to taste
    Several tablespoons pumpkin seeds
    8 corn tortillas
    Oil for frying
    Salsa Ranchera (page 32)
    Cebollas en Escabeche a la Yucateca (page 38)
    2 hot chillies, seeded and sliced

1. Mix the eggs with the spring onions, salt, cumin, oregano and pepper. Set aside.
2. Lightly toast the pumpkin seeds in a heavy frying pan, adding a tiny bit of oil if needed to toast them to a golden colour. Remove from the pan and chop or grind. Add to the egg mixture.
3. Warm the tortillas in a little oil. Spoon the egg mixture down the centre of each, then roll up and place in a dish.
4. Heat the Salsa Ranchera, and pour over the rolled tortillas. Serve immediately, garnished with the pickled onions and sliced chillies.

VARIATION

Stuff the tortillas with browned minced pork and scrambled eggs as well as ground pumpkin seeds or Pipián (page 35), then top with Salsa Ranchera.

SOME SIMPLE *ENCHILADA* DISHES

Chard or Spinach Enchiladas: warm flour tortillas (or white chapattis – not authentic, but very acceptable) in a little oil; stuff with sautéed and chopped chard or spinach seasoned with a little onion, garlic and chilli. Roll up and sauce with a mild (New Mexico) chilli sauce, top with lots of grated cheese, and bake briefly until melted and bubbling. Serve with soured cream, diced black olives and chopped onion.

Enchiladas Verdes: dip corn tortillas into either a little hot oil or heated mild Salsa Verde (page 26) to make them pliable. Fill with shredded cooked chicken or grated cheese and roll up. Top with lots of mild Salsa Verde and more cheese and bake briefly in a hot oven until the cheese melts. Serve topped with soured cream, shredded lettuce, and coriander.

Enchiladas Bandiera Mexicana: warm tortillas in a little oil, then stuff with any filling: browned, shredded or minced meat, cooked chicken, cheese, cooked seafood. Top with a stripe of each of Salsa Verde (page 26) and Salsa Ranchera (page 32), bake briefly, and serve with a stripe of soured cream. The three stripes signify the colours of the Mexican flag.

Enchiladas de Jocaqui: mix grated cheese with enough soured cream to moisten. Season with chopped spring onions and cumin, then use to stuff warmed corn tortillas. Sauce with a mild (New Mexico) red chilli sauce, top with more grated cheese and bake in a hot oven just long enough to melt the cheese. Serve topped with more soured cream, spring onions and shredded lettuce.

◁◁◁◁◁◁◁◁◁◁◁◁◁◁◁◁◁◁◁◁◁◁◁◁◁◁◁◁◁◁◁▷▷▷▷▷▷▷▷▷▷▷▷▷▷▷▷▷▷▷▷▷▷▷▷▷▷▷▷

Chilaquiles

Translated literally, *chilaquiles* means 'broken old sombreros'. In culinary terms, however, it refers to a casserole of torn stale tortillas, fried until crisp and layered with chilli sauce or stock, cream, cheese, and meat or chicken, etc. Authentically, if the dish contains chilli it is called *chilaquiles*, if it does not, it is called a *sopa seca*. To further confuse things, a *sopa seca* may be made with chorizo or ingredients already spiced with chillies so the name is almost irrelevant. Whatever it is called, this casserole is versatile, economical and completely delicious in an earthy, hearty way. It is quintessentially Mexican in taste, texture and appearance.

In the absence of stale tortillas I have used shop-bought *tostada* or *taco* shells, broken into several pieces and layered. They are acceptable, bordering on very good, in such casseroles.

Once the sauce is made and the tortillas prepared the casserole is quick and easy to make. It doesn't, however, keep its texture long. In *mercado* cafés throughout Mexico, *cazuelas* of *chilaquiles* might be prepared freshly for the lunch crowds; by the end of the afternoon, they have become the consistency of polenta, or porridge.

Leftover *chilaquiles* are often served for breakfast, accompanied by one or two fried eggs and hot chilli salsa. Try nearly any sort of *chilaquiles* for brunch, especially made in individual ramekins, topped with an egg each as they bake in the oven.

Accompany with beans, either black or pinto/pink ones, crusty bread, a platter of lush fruits, and lots of strong, cinnamon-scented coffee with milk. A pitcher of tequila and tropical fruit juice enhances the spirit of the morning.

Chilaquiles de Legumbres
Vegetable Chilaquiles

This consists of broken fried tortillas and cooked courgettes and mashed potatoes, baked for a short while in an *enchilada*-type sauce of cinnamon-scented tomato and pasilla chilli. It is served topped with vegetables tossed in vinegar, hot salsa, shredded lettuce and coriander.

◁◁◁◁◁◁◁◁◁◁◁◁◁◁◁◁◁◁◁◁◁◁◁◁◁◁◁◁◁◁◁▷▷▷▷▷▷▷▷▷▷▷▷▷▷▷▷▷▷▷▷▷▷▷▷▷

Sauce

6 pasilla chillies
500 ml/16 fl oz hot vegetable stock (water plus a vegetable
    stock cube is fine)
1 small to medium onion, chopped
2 cloves garlic, chopped
1/2 teaspoon oregano
325 g/12 oz tomatoes, chopped (or use tinned)
1 to 2 chipotle chillies (or pinch of mild chilli powder or
    dash of smoky barbecue sauce)
Generous pinch of cinnamon
25 to 50 ml/1 to 2 fl oz oil of choice
Juice of 1/4 lime

Toppings

2 or 3 small to medium potatoes, cooked, peeled and diced
4 carrots, cooked but still firm, sliced or diced
75 g/3 oz fresh peas, cooked, or frozen ones, defrosted
2 teaspoons white wine or sherry vinegar, or to taste
Hot salsa of choice
6 to 10 lettuce leaves, shredded
12 g/1/2 oz coriander leaves, coarsely chopped

Filling

4 to 5 small to medium potatoes, cooked and coarsely
    mashed
2 courgettes, steamed or boiled and diced
Large pinch of cumin seeds or ground cumin
175 g/6 oz white cheese, crumbled or grated
175 ml/6 fl oz soured cream

To assemble

24 crisp fried tortillas – either homemade (pages 79–81) or
    shop-bought *tostadas* or *taco* shells – broken into several
    pieces each
175 g/6 oz white cheese, grated or crumbled

◁◁◁◁◁◁◁◁◁◁◁◁◁◁◁◁◁◁◁◁◁◁◁◁◁◁◁◁◁◁▷▷▷▷▷▷▷▷▷▷▷▷▷▷▷▷▷▷▷▷▷▷▷▷▷▷▷▷▷▷

1. To make the sauce, place the pasilla chillies in a bowl and pour the hot stock over them. Cover with a plate and leave until soft – at least 30 minutes, preferably an hour.
2. Remove the stems and seeds from the chillies then scrape the softened flesh from the skin with a blunt knife. Reserve the soaking liquid and any juice from the chillies.
3. Put the chilli flesh, onion and garlic into a liquidizer or food processor and whirl together briefly to chop and combine. Add all the remaining ingredients except the oil and lime juice, blend until well mixed, then add the reserved soaking liquid.
4. In a heavy frying pan heat the oil then pour the sauce into it. It might splutter – stand back until it calms down. Cook down over a relatively high heat for 5 minutes or so. Remove from the heat, add the lime juice and set aside.
5. To make the vegetable topping, combine the diced potatoes and carrots and peas, toss with the vinegar and set aside.
6. To assemble, arrange half the broken tortillas in a large baking dish. Cover with a layer of the filling ingredients: mashed potatoes, courgettes, cumin, cheese and soured cream. Top with the remaining tortillas then pour the sauce over.
7. Top with a layer of cheese then bake in the oven at 200°C/400°F/gas mark 6 for about 10 minutes, or just long enough to melt the cheese. If the casserole bakes for too long it sinks into a mushy consistency.
8. Serve immediately, garnished with a little hot salsa, the vinegared vegetables, shredded lettuce and coriander leaves.

<<<<<<<<<<<<<<<<<<<<<<<<<<<<<<<<<<>>>>>>>>>>>>>>>>>>>>>>>>>>>>>>>>

Chilaquiles de Chorizo
Chorizo Chilaquiles

This makes a luscious brunch dish, accompanied by scrambled eggs and tomato-coriander salsa, with refried beans on the side and a pitcher of sangria waiting to be poured.

    2 to 3 chorizo sausages
    175 g/6 oz tomatoes, peeled, diced and seeded (tinned is
        fine)
    2 cloves garlic, chopped
    12 crisp fried tortilla strips or *taco/tostada* shells
    350 ml/12 fl oz stock (homemade if possible), or more if
        needed
    Generous pinch of dried mint, crumbled, or 1 to 2
        teaspoons fresh mint, chopped
    175 g/6 oz Feta or fresh Pecorino cheese, crumbled
    1 small onion, chopped

1. Brown the chorizo sausage in a pan, crumbling it as it cooks. Pour off any excess fat.
2. Add the tomatoes and garlic, cook for a few minutes, then add the tortilla strips or broken-up *taco/tostada* shells. Pour in half of the stock, cover and simmer for a few minutes, then add the rest of the stock. You might need to add more stock if the tortilla pieces remain hard or if the mixture seems unpleasantly dry. Don't, however, stir it all into a mush. Let the pieces of tortilla soften but still retain their shape.
3. When the tortillas have softened and most of the liquid has been absorbed, serve in shallow soup plates, topped with a sprinkling of mint, cheese and onion.

VARIATION

Substitute 325 g/12 oz minced beef for the chorizo sausages and brown it with a generous seasoning of mild chilli powder, cumin, oregano and chopped onion.

FLOUR TORTILLA DISHES

Tortillas made of wheat flour rather than corn are favoured in Mexico's northern regions such as Sonora, as well as in America's Southwest, especially Arizona. Introduced by the Spanish, wheat added a further dimension to the previously corn-dominated Mexican table.

Often in the north of Mexico and in America's Southwest you will find the simplest meals of warm flour tortillas rolled around mixtures of beef or pork, in sauces of brick-red ancho or pasilla chillies or green tomatillos. In such dishes the flour tortillas are the perfect partner to the robust stew and I cannot think of any other dish that is so satisfying to both the body and spirit.

Flour tortillas are used for a variety of *burritos*, *chimichangas*, layered savoury *tortas* and so on. They may also be used for desserts – fry them until golden and dust them with sugar and cinnamon for impromptu *buñuelos* (see Desserts and Baked Goods for other ideas).

California Classic Burritos

These are soft flour tortillas, filled with refried beans, grated cheese and chopped onions, then doused with Salsa Verde or other spicy salsa and rolled up. The tortilla remains chewy, the filling of beans creamy and rich, the onions and salsa a pungent accent. They are really fast-food *burritos*, low-brow food, but one would have to be a terrible snob not to admit that they are delicious.

About 225 g/8 oz refried beans (tinned is fine)
6 to 8 flour tortillas or white flour chapattis
100 to 175 g/4 to 6 oz white cheese, grated
1/2 small onion, chopped
Salsa Verde (page 26) or other spicy salsa

1. Heat the refried beans in a pan and keep warm. Heat the tortillas or chapattis: to keep them flexible and soft, lightly

≪≪≪≪≪≪≪≪≪≪≪≪≪≪≪≪≪≪≪≪≪≪≪≪≪≪≪≪≪≪≪≪≪≪≪≫≫≫≫≫≫≫≫≫≫≫≫≫≫≫≫≫≫≫≫≫≫≫≫≫≫≫≫≫≫≫≫≫

wet them and heat one at a time on an ungreased frying pan
quickly on each side.
2. Spread with several spoonfuls of the hot beans, sprinkle with
the cheese, onions and salsa, and roll up.
3. Serve immediately.

VARIATION

Add diced *nopales* to the refried beans, with or without crumbled,
browned chorizo.

Torta con Queso y Tomatillo
Layered Pie of Cheese and Green Salsa

Butter 6 flour tortillas and toast them under the grill until crisp.
Layer with grated cheese and Salsa Mole Verde (page 27), ending with a layer of cheese. Bake in the oven at 190°C/375°F/gas
mark 5 for about 10 minutes, or until the cheese is melted and
browned. Serve with chopped coriander, soured cream, and
diced tomatoes.

Burritos de Huevos a la Maya
Warm Flour Tortillas Wrapped Around Scrambled Eggs
and Pumpkin Seed Sauce

Eggs are a favourite food in the Yucatán region – you find slices
of hard-boiled egg tucked into *enchiladas*, *tacos*, as a topping for
tostadas, decorating salads and platters of sauced foods, as well as
scrambled and layered into dishes like these *burritos*.

In this dish the eggs are scrambled into soft, creamy curds and
rolled into warm flour tortillas along with a good spoonful of
pipián sauce, or pumpkin seed and vegetable purée. Sprinkle in
a little chopped chilli or hot salsa since the sauce is quite mild.

Enjoy accompanied by platters of black beans, Arroz Mexicana
(page 188), and sautéed chorizo.

◁◁◁◁◁◁◁◁◁◁◁◁◁◁◁◁◁◁◁◁◁◁◁◁◁◁◁◁◁◁◁◁◇▷▷▷▷▷▷▷▷▷▷▷▷▷▷▷▷▷▷▷▷▷▷▷▷▷▷

8 to 10 eggs, lightly beaten
35 g/1$^1/_2$ oz butter
Salt and pepper to taste
8 small to medium flour tortillas or 4 large ones
$^1/_2$ quantity Pipián (page 35)
2 to 3 spring onions, thinly sliced
1 fresh medium-hot green chilli, chopped (and seeded if
    desired), or salsa to taste

1. Scramble the eggs softly in the butter with salt and pepper to
   taste.
2. Heat the flour tortillas in a hot pan one at a time, sprinkling
   each one with a drop or two of water first. If the tortillas
   stick, add a very few drops of oil to the pan.
3. As each tortilla is warmed, spoon in the scrambled eggs, then
   several spoonfuls of *pipián* and a sprinkling of spring onions
   and either chillies or salsa. Serve immediately.

Chimichangas
Crisp Flour Tortilla-Wrapped Parcels, Arizona-
and Sonora-Style

Chimichangas are *burritos* plunged into hot oil and fried to a gold-
en crisp. The most common filling is some type of shredded
meat or poultry rather than the refried beans or cheese that are
often used to fill a tender soft *burrito*. Other fillings for
chimichangas include Picadillo (page 180) made with the traditional
beef, or with the less traditional shredded dark meat of turkey or
chicken; browned shreds of simmered pork; browned and crumbled chorizo (or mild chilli-spiced minced beef) mixed with
refried beans; diced potato and chorizo. They would probably be
quite good filled with spicy fish. Then there is the recipe for
Chimichangas de Papas (page 116). (For a sweet twist on the
genre, try the Chimichangas de Frutas on page 227.)

Chimichangas originated in the region that is now the state of
Sonora, Mexico as well as across the border in Arizona. A good
chimichanga is a contrast of textures: the crisp outside, soft flour

◁◁◁◁◁◁◁◁◁◁◁◁◁◁◁◁◁◁◁◁◁◁◁◁◁◁◁▷▷▷▷▷▷▷▷▷▷▷▷▷▷▷▷▷▷▷▷▷▷▷▷▷▷

tortilla inside, and savoury stuffing, its top slathered with cool soured cream and/or guacamole and spicy-hot salsa.

On a party-giving note, *chimichangas* make excellent cook-ahead fare; the filling may be prepared up to a day ahead and kept refrigerated or the whole parcels may be fried earlier in the day and reheated in the oven at 200°C/400°F/gas mark 6 until warmed through and crisp, about 10 minutes.

Chimichanga de Res
Beef Chimichangas

Hearty Southwestern fare, this is a classic rendition – the shredded meat encased in a golden brittle-crisp tortilla shell, with green chilli salsa and soured cream blanketing the whole thing.

8 large flour tortillas (25 cm/10 in ones are available,
    otherwise use smaller ones)
1 quantity Ropa Vieja (page 178)
Oil for deep frying
Soured cream
Diced avocado or guacamole
Southwestern Green Chilli Salsa (page 33)
4 spring onions, thinly sliced
16 black olives, pitted and halved

1. Heat the tortillas one at a time in a lightly greased heavy frying pan. When softened, place several spoonfuls of Ropa Vieja in a line down the centre of each tortilla, leaving a border at the top and sides.
2. Fold the top and bottom over to encase the filling then roll the sides to form neat parcels.
3. Heat the oil, deep fry the stuffed parcels about 2 at a time, depending on the size of the pan, and cook until golden brown. (Alternatively, they may be sautéed in a frying pan, then baked in a dish in the oven – this method is best for serving a large group.)
4. Serve the *chimichangas* hot, each crisp golden parcel topped

with a dollop of soured cream and diced avocado or
guacamole, a spoonful of salsa, and a sprinkling of spring
onions and black olives.

Chimichangas de Papas
Potato Chimichangas

Flour tortilla parcels filled with cheese, soured cream, and chilli-
spiked mashed potatoes then fried to a golden crisp make an
unexpected treat. Serve with salsa, chillies and more soured
cream.

>   4 flour tortillas
>   Filling from Enchiladas de Papas (page 102), omitting the
>   mild chilli powder
>   Oil for shallow frying

Toppings

>   Soured cream
>   Salsa
>   Chopped spring onions

1. Gently heat the flour tortillas one by one in an ungreased or
   lightly greased pan to soften. Transfer to a plate and fill with
   several spoonfuls of the potato filling, then fold the tops over
   and roll up the sides to form an oblong parcel.
2. Heat the oil and when hot enough to fry add the parcels.
   Cook on a medium-high heat until lightly golden brown then
   drain on absorbent paper.
3. Serve with topping(s) of choice.

Sincronizadas
Crisp Stuffed Flour Tortillas

The name *sincronizadas* refers to the 'synchronization' of the two
flour tortillas, held together with the melted cheese like so much

◁◁◁◁◁◁◁◁◁◁◁◁◁◁◁◁◁◁◁◁◁◁◁◁◁◁◁◁◁▷▷▷▷▷▷▷▷▷▷▷▷▷▷▷▷▷▷▷▷▷▷▷▷▷▷

delicious glue. Other savoury morsels may be added to the cheese filling – see below for suggestions.

Sincronizadas are a speciality of Arizona and Sonora. They make a zesty snack or teatime savoury, or cut into neat wedges they make a good first-course for a dinner party.

For each sincronizada

2 flour tortillas (or white chapattis), as thin and large in diameter as you can find them

Salsa or spice paste of choice – a thick, unrunny one works best; in the absence of a good homemade or shop-bought one, a few drops of Tabasco sauce works, too

75 g/3 oz cheese, sliced

Vegetable oil or bland seed oil for frying

Optional fillings

Sliced ham

Spicy salami

Browned crumbled chorizo

Puréed spiced black beans

1–2 tablespoons cooked, squeezed-dry spinach mixed with creamy Ricotta or goat's cheese

Toppings

Fresh salsa of choice (preferably green tomatillo salsa)

Shredded lettuce

Soured cream or Greek yogurt

Chopped spring onions

Chopped radishes

1. Spread the tortillas lightly with the salsa or spice paste of choice. Arrange the cheese on top of one of the tortillas, then top with optional filling if using.
2. Top with the other tortilla, spread-side downwards, to make a sandwich.
3. Heat the oil in a heavy frying pan and when hot enough to fry place the sandwich (carefully, so that the filling doesn't come

◁◁◁◁◁◁◁◁◁◁◁◁◁◁◁◁◁◁◁◁◁◁◁◁◁◁◁◁◁◁◁◁▷▷▷▷▷▷▷▷▷▷▷▷▷▷▷▷▷▷▷▷▷▷▷▷▷▷▷▷

out) into the hot pan. Over a medium-high heat cook the disc
until it is golden brown and the cheese begins to melt then
turn over and cook the other side. Any cheese that escapes
from the sandwich should fry in the hot oil and become crispy
and luscious, so don't worry about it leaking out as it melts.
4. Drain on absorbent paper, then serve immediately, piled with
salsa, shredded lettuce, soured cream or Greek yogurt,
chopped spring onions and radishes.

TAMALES

The *tamal* is among the most ancient of foods, and its name is
derived from the Aztec *tamalli*, meaning patty, or cake. *Tamales*
were served by the Aztecs, Mayans and other Indian Nations, but
were greatly enhanced by the Spanish introduction of pork and
cooking fat.

This dish of wrapped and steamed corn dough – either *masa
harina* or ground hominy or grits – is popular throughout the
Republic. In city and town streets, village squares and market-
places, street vendors as well as special *tamal* shops sell them, hot
and fragrant in *ollas*, or clay pots, set over charcoal braziers. The
same vendor often sells an accompanying mug of *atole* or black
coffee.

What *tamales* are wrapped in depends upon the area they hail
from: either corn husks in the North and the central mountain
regions, or banana leaves in the South and coastal regions. And
the area influences the type of corn or *masa* used, too, whether it
is a dried mixture or a wetter grind. Occasionally *tamales* are prepared not from dried corn but from fresh sweetcorn, or from
dough made of mashed potatoes or rice flour. One of my
favourites is a dough with lots of sweetcorn kneaded in, sur-
rounding a chunk of cheese and strip of green chilli in the centre.
As the corn *masa* cooks, the cheese melts and it makes a very
delicate *tamal*.

Tamal fillings vary widely: meat, chicken, turkey, duck,
iguana, fish, seafood, pumpkin seeds – indeed, *tamales* are perfect

◁◁◁▷▷▷▷▷▷▷▷▷▷▷▷▷▷▷▷▷▷▷▷▷▷▷▷▷▷▷▷▷▷▷▷▷▷▷▷▷▷▷

vehicles for leftovers in the thrifty Mexican kitchen, with leftover *mole*, *adobo*, *picadillo*, or chilli pasilla or ancho salsa, binding the meat or fish. Diced potatoes and browned chorizo, strips of sautéed chillies and cheese (*rajas*), squash blossoms, mushrooms or corn fungus (*huitlacoche*) might be used as fillings, as well. The flavour combinations are further expanded by the sauces splashed on to the *tamales*: green tomatillo salsa or mild chilli pasilla.

Then there are the 'blind' *tamales*, that have been left unfilled, to be served as an accompaniment for dishes such as *mole* or barbecued lamb, or eaten for breakfast with a glass of hot chocolate, coffee or *atole*.

Tamales may be tiny one-bite nibbles, or they might be gargantuan, almost unreasonably plump parcels that make a full meal. They may also be made sweet, the *masa* kneaded with sugar and fruit juice, the dough filled with fruit.

North of the Border in the Southwestern states *tamales* have been traditionally stuffed with chilli-simmered beef, chicken or poultry, though in recent years, as Southwestern food has become very stylish, *nouvelle*-style *tamales* have flourished. Seafood *tamales* especially have become popular North of the Border, where once only meat- or chicken/turkey-filled *tamales* reigned.

The dough for *tamales* must be beaten to a light fluffy consistency or else the *tamales* will be heavy, perhaps leaden. A food processor does the job well but not as effectively as beating by hand.

Pork, Beef, Chicken or Turkey Tamales

This makes a hearty, rustic *tamal*, in classic peasant style. Though it is a basic chillied-meat stuffed *tamal*, its flavours vary greatly depending on the type of *masa* you use and the type of fat.

It may be made either Mexican-style, in smallish parcels, or Sonora/North-of-the-Border-style, big plump packets of *masa*-spread corn husks layered to form a huge *tamal*. (To eat it, the diner peels off layer after layer of corn husks, scraping the

ᐊᐊᐊᐊᐊᐊᐊᐊᐊᐊᐊᐊᐊᐊᐊᐊᐊᐊᐊᐊᐊᐊᐊᐊᐊ◊ᐅᐅᐅᐅᐅᐅᐅᐅᐅᐅᐅᐅᐅᐅᐅᐅᐅᐅᐅᐅᐅᐅᐅᐅᐅ

cooked *masa* from each layer. Many think that this is the best part of *tamal*-eating.)

Meat

   450 g/1 lb stewing pork or beef, cut into chunks, or
      1 kg/2¹/₄ lb meat with bones, or poultry on bones such as
      thighs, breasts, etc
   1.2 litres/2 pints water, plus several stock cubes
   1 head garlic
   1 onion, cut in half
   5 bay leaves

1. Place the meat in a pot with the other ingredients. Bring to
   the boil and simmer until tender, about 2 hours. Set aside.

Chilli Sauce for Meat Filling

   1 onion, chopped
   2 cloves garlic, chopped
   2 tablespoons mild chilli powder
   2 tablespoons paprika
   300 ml/10 fl oz reserved stock from cooking meat
   1 tablespoon bland vegetable oil
   Generous pinch of cumin seed or ground cumin
   Salt to taste
   Juice of ¹/₂ lime

1. In a liquidizer or food processor blend the onion, garlic, chilli
   powder, paprika and a little stock until it forms a paste, then
   thin it with a little more stock.
2. Heat the oil in a frying pan, then add the onion-chilli paste
   and 'fry' until it becomes concentrated, about 5 minutes, then
   add the remaining stock and the cumin. Cook for a few
   minutes longer.
3. Season with salt and lime juice.

◁◁◁◁◁◁◁◁◁◁◁◁◁◁◁◁◁◁◁◁◁◁◁◁◁◁◁◁◁◁◁◁◁◁◁◁◁▷▷▷▷▷▷▷▷▷▷▷▷▷▷▷▷▷▷▷▷▷▷▷▷▷▷▷▷▷▷▷▷

Masa

75 ml/3 fl oz softened lard or vegetable shortening
1 teaspoon salt
450 g/1 lb *masa harina*, preferably the white Quaker type
350 ml to 500 ml/12 to 16 fl oz stock from cooking the
   meat, more if necessary
1 teaspoon baking powder

1. Whip the lard or shortening until fluffy, then whip in the salt
   and *masa harina*. It will be like tiny crumbs.
2. Add the stock a little at a time, whipping after each addition,
   then let it rest for a few minutes before whipping it again
   until fluffy. Then beat in the baking powder. When it is ready
   it will be the consistency of a light biscuit dough.

Serving sauce (optional) – or use salsa of choice

12 cooked green tomatillos, puréed
250 ml/8 fl oz stock from cooking meat
Salsa to taste (preferably one with good flavour but not
   excessive heat, such as Salsa de Chile Güero, page 24; if
   no salsa is at hand, substitute a little chopped green
   chilli, onion, garlic and coriander)

1. Combine all the ingredients and warm in a pan when ready to
   serve.

To assemble:

About 15 dried corn husks (see Glossary), soaked in warm
water to cover for at least 3 hours or overnight

1. Remove the corn husks from the water and pat dry. Lay 2
   large or 3 smaller husks out on a work surface, spreading *masa*
   down the edges and overlapping slightly so that they stick
   together and form a rectangle. Spread a layer of *masa* over the
   husks.
2. Spoon a little meat on to the *masa*-spread corn husks as well
   as some chilli sauce, leaving a border of about 2.5 cm/1 in.

◁◁◁◁◁◁◁◁◁◁◁◁◁◁◁◁◁◁◁◁◁◁◁◁◁◁◁◁◁◁◁◁◁◁◇▷▷▷▷▷▷▷▷▷▷▷▷▷▷▷▷▷▷▷▷▷▷▷▷▷▷▷▷▷▷▷▷▷▷

Cover with more *masa* and make a parcel by folding over first the long sides to cover the meat and chilli filling and then the top and bottom.

3. Repeat steps 1 and 2 with most of the remaining corn husks and filling. The filling should be completely enclosed.

4. Layer the stuffed *tamales* in a steamer and cover with a layer of corn husks, then with a clean tea towel, which absorbs the excess steam and moisture and keeps the *tamales* from becoming soggy. Fill the pot with enough water to steam but not enough to reach the *tamales*.

5. Steam over a high heat for about an hour, checking every so often to be sure the pot has not boiled dry.

6. When the *tamales* are ready, place each one on a portion of the serving sauce, or salsa of choice, with a drizzle of the chilli sauce (mixed with the remaining meat) over the top. Each diner peels off the corn husk before eating the *tamal*.

Tamal Camarón: prepare the above *masa* mixture, using fish stock in place of meat stock. Fill with any prawn mixture such as Machaca de Camarón (page 100) or make a salsa of sautéed onion and garlic, and add the flesh of 1 or 2 mild soaked chillies, a few tomatoes, and a dash of cumin. Add prawns to this salsa and cook through.

Tamal de Cazuela con Pollo: this is a pie *tamal*, a casserole lined with *masa* dough then filled with chicken, olives and raisins. It can be prepared in a large pudding basin or small individual ones for tiny cup *tamales*.

Follow the above recipe using chicken and omitting the corn husks. Press one-third of the *masa* filling into a pudding basin or casserole dish, lining the bottom and sides, then layer pieces of boned chicken, the mild red chilli sauce, about 15 pimiento-stuffed green olives, and a handful of raisins that have been soaked in hot water until they plump up. One or 2 seeded and diced tomatoes or tomatillos and 1 chipotle chilli, chopped, can be included.

Flatten the remaining *masa* into a shape to fit the top of the dish and place on top of the chicken and sauce. Seal the edges,

cover with foil and bake in the oven at 180°C/350°F/gas mark 4
for about an hour.

VARIATION

Leftover *tamales* may be unwrapped, cut into pieces and layered
in a casserole, then topped with cheese and baked.

Tamales de Dulce
Sweet Tamales

Before the Spanish Conquest, Mexicans had little in the way of
sweet desserts. Without sugar, butter and flour, their sweet tooth
was satisfied by the wide array of luscious tropical fruits and fragrant honey. Often these were combined with ground corn and
wrapped into corn husks for sweet *tamales*.

Sweet *tamales* are still enjoyed throughout Mexico, often for
breakfast or supper, accompanied by cups of hot strong coffee or
chocolate, or sweet, corn-based *atole*. Strangely, though they are
sweet, they are moistened with chicken stock. Somehow it works,
despite the hefty amount of sugar in the *tamales*. The stock
brings out the earthy flavour of the *masa*.

Like their savoury counterparts, sweet *tamales* may be either
unfilled or filled. Simple sweet things are best: a spoonful of apri-
cot or strawberry preserve, Dulce de Coco (page 230), diced candied fruit mixed with pine nuts, candied pineapple, papaya or
other tropical fruit, quince jam. Sometimes tinned or poached
fruit is used: the fruit is diced and used as a filling, the juice is
mixed with the *masa* in place of stock.

◁◁◁◁◁◁◁◁◁◁◁◁◁◁◁◁◁◁◁◁◁◁◁◁◁◁◁◁◁◁◁▷▷▷▷▷▷▷▷▷▷▷▷▷▷▷▷▷▷▷▷▷▷▷▷▷▷▷

200 g/7 oz lard, or mixture of half lard and half unsalted
   butter
450 g/1 lb cooked hominy, drained
100 ml/4 fl oz lightly salted or unsalted chicken stock
1 teaspoon salt
225 g/8 oz sugar
1 teaspoon cinnamon
1 teaspoon baking powder
About 15 dried corn husks, soaked in warm water to cover
   for at least 3 hours or overnight
Filling of choice (see above) or a handful of raisins

1. Beat the lard or lard and butter until it is the consistency of
    whipped cream. Set aside.
2. Grind the hominy in a food processor or liquidizer. Add to
    the whipped lard a little at a time, along with a little of the
    stock, the salt, sugar, cinnamon and baking powder,
    continuing to beat or whip the mixture into extreme
    fluffiness. The classic test is to drop a small amount of the
    mixture into a cup of cold water; if it floats, it is fluffy
    enough.
3. Drain the corn husks and pat dry. Fill the *tamales* as for Pork,
    Beef, Chicken or Turkey Tamales (page 119), either filling
    each with a spoonful of jam, etc, or mixing the raisins into the
    dough.
4. Steam according to the directions given for Pork, Beef,
    Chicken or Turkey Tamales (page 119). Tiny ones (*tamalitos*)
    will take about 30 minutes, larger ones up to an hour or
    longer.

Tamales Veracruzana
Banana Leaf-Wrapped Tamales, Veracruz-Style

Banana leaf-wrapped *tamales* are prepared with a moister filling,
one made from puréed hominy rather than *masa*. Chillied meat
or poultry fillings are best for these *tamales*, especially with
chipotle chilli added for a smoky nuance.

Banana leaves are considerably larger than corn husks, so they can be cut up to make single-portion *tamales* or left whole to make one huge enough for a whole family to share.

Masa filling

325 g/12 oz cooked hominy, drained well
175 g/6 oz lard or vegetable shortening
2 teaspoons pure chilli powder, or combination of mild
    chilli powder and paprika
1 teaspoon salt

Meat filling

675 g/1¹/₂ lb simmered pork, beef, turkey or chicken
    chunks
1 quantity chilli sauce from Pork, Beef, Chicken or Turkey
    Tamales (page 119)
1 chipotle chilli, chopped (optional), or a little smoky
    bacon, diced
10 pimiento-stuffed green olives, sliced
1 green pepper, roasted, peeled and cut into strips
1 ripe tomato, peeled, seeded and diced
1 or 2 banana leaves

Toppings

Mild chilli sauce of choice
Spicy salsa

1. Mix the *masa* by puréeing the hominy in a processor with the lard or shortening, the chilli powder or chilli powder and paprika, and the salt.
2. Dice the meat and mix with the chilli sauce, chipotle chilli, if using, or smoky bacon, green olives, green pepper strips and chopped tomato.
3. Make the banana leaf or leaves pliable by heating over an open flame. Cut into whatever size pieces you want to work with. Spread each piece with the *masa* filling, then top with some of the meat and chilli mixture. Fold up to enclose the

meat mixture and stack in a steamer.

4. Steam for 40 to 50 minutes or until the *masa* is cooked firm. Serve immediately, with any mild chilli sauce and a spicy salsa to set it all off.

HUEVOS
Eggs

Few cuisines offer as dazzling an array of exciting egg dishes as does Mexican cookery. Yet before the Conquest hen's eggs were unknown. The eggs that were available – from turkeys and other wild birds – were strongly flavoured and not easily obtained.

With the introduction of domestic turkeys and chickens, egg dishes rapidly became an important part of the Mexican diet. The traditional Indian sauces of puréed tomatoes and aromatics bring out the best in the gentle egg, as do the strong flavours of the cuisine: chilli, garlic, tomatoes, lime, cheese, sausages, etc.

The variety of egg dishes is endless. Scrambled eggs are served with salsa and warm tortillas to roll up into tender *tacos*; or they are mixed with browned chorizo, strips of *nopale*, diced potatoes, shrimps and peas, tomatoes, and so on. Soft-boiled eggs are eaten with a squeeze of lime and a sprinkling of fiery cayenne pepper. Eggs are softly poached in rich dark *adobo* sauces or red chilli and meat sauces, or baked in *cazuelitas* with hearty chilli stews until the yolks are just set. Fried eggs might be topped with cheese, grilled to let it melt, then served on a bed of spicy browned meat with a blanket of Salsa Ranchera and a scattering of sliced fresh chillies.

One of the most exotic omelette fillings is from the state of Hidalgo, sautéed ant eggs with lots of coriander or epazote. In the Yucatán, you'll find *enchiladas* and *taco*-style preparations stuffed with scrambled or hard-boiled eggs and sauced with *pipián* (puréed pumpkin seeds). *Chilaquiles*, the delicious casserole of leftover tortillas, is traditionally served with an egg or two alongside, scrambled into a creamy mass or showing its sunny face.

In the countryside, egg dishes have traditionally been eaten at *almuerzo*, the hearty mid-morning meal that follows *desayuno*, the

◄◄◄◄◄◄◄◄◄◄◄◄◄◄◄◄◄◄◄◄◄◄◄◄◄◄◄◄◄◄◄◄◄◄◄◄◄►►►►►►►►►►►►►►►►►►►►►►►►►►►►►►►►►►►

early-morning coffee and sweet rolls. As such they make gorgeous brunch and lazy weekend breakfasts, docile enough to start the day, lively enough to jolt you awake.

Huevos Rancheros
Fried or Poached Eggs with Rustic Tomato Sauce

Huevos Rancheros is one of those simple, utterly memorable dishes – spicy tomato sauce blanketing tender eggs, all resting on a bed of soft corn tortillas. Cut into the egg and let the yolk run into the spicy sauce, fork up each blissful bite, adding a dash of extra salsa if the dish is too mild for your taste. The tortilla underneath becomes slightly soggy and sauce-laden – the best part of the whole dish.

While Huevos Rancheros is ubiquitous throughout the Republic and many parts of America's Southwest, the flavour of the dish depends on the chillies of the region you are in: poblanos, jalapeños, even smoky chipotles, fresh serranos, and so forth. It can be mild and only slightly *picante*, or it can be fierce, with thinly sliced fresh hot chillies lying in wait to assault your unsuspecting palate. In some places the tomato sauce is replaced by a green tomatillo sauce.

Serve the delectable dish for Sunday breakfast or summer supper, accompanied by a platter of tropical fruit, potatoes baked with mild chilli powder and lots of garlic, and a pitcher of tequila mixed with icy grapefruit juice.

250 ml/16 fl oz Salsa Ranchera (page 32)
4 corn tortillas
Oil for heating tortillas
8 eggs
1 tablespoon chopped coriander leaves

1. Heat the sauce and keep it warm.
2. Heat the tortillas in a little hot oil in a heavy frying pan and keep warm, covered, in the oven or on the backburner.
3. Poach or fry the eggs.

◄◄

4. Place a tortilla on each plate; top with 2 eggs, then spoon over the tomato sauce. Serve immediately, sprinkled with the coriander.

VARIATIONS

Huevos en Salsa Jitomate con Frijoles Negros: in Oaxaca a few spoonfuls of mashed cooked black beans are added to the tomato sauce. The rich earthiness of the black beans adds a flash of brilliance to the simple tomato sauce.

Huevos Motul: in this traditional Yucatecan version of Huevos Rancheros, the dish is prepared by stacking up several crisp fried tortillas spread with black beans, with fried eggs sandwiched between the layers. It is given a carnival-like atmosphere by sprinkling green peas, diced pink ham, strips of roasted red peppers, coriander leaves, cubes of mild cheese and sometimes slices of fried banana over the top. Though it is delicious, I find it a bit unwieldy, and streamline it into one concise and splendid layer. Fry 4 tortillas until crisp. Spread each with cooked black beans, then top with 1 or 2 poached or lightly fried eggs. Spoon hot Salsa Ranchera over it all. Sprinkle with tender green peas (briefly cooked, or frozen and defrosted), diced ham, cubes of mild cheese, and coriander leaves. Offer salsa of choice on the side.

Huevos en Salsa Verde: prepare as for Huevos Rancheros, but top with a mild Salsa Verde (page 26) instead of the Salsa Ranchera.

Huevos con Chorizo
Scrambled Eggs with Chorizo

Deliciously simple, crumbled chorizo with eggs is one of the humble glories of the Mexican table. It is very much a comfort dish – ridiculously easy to prepare and full of spicy flavour. The chorizo is so assertively flavoured that no other spicing is needed.

250 g/9 oz chorizo (if unavailable, use any soft-textured,
    very spicy and meaty sausage; I've even found the North
    African *merguez* a delicious addition)
8 eggs, lightly beaten
Chopped coriander leaves or spring onions

1. Remove the casing from the chorizo and brown it in a frying
    pan, crumbling it as it cooks.
2. Pour off excess fat, leaving a little to cook the eggs in.
3. Pour in the eggs and scramble them over a medium heat.
    Serve immediately, sprinkled with coriander or spring onions.

VARIATION

Huevos con Papas y Chorizos: fry 4 large potatoes, peeled and
diced, and 2 to 3 medium onions, coarsely chopped, with 450 g/
1 lb chorizo until browned and tender. Pour off excess fat.
Instead of scrambling the eggs, make indentations in the sausage
mixture and break them in. Cover and simmer until the egg
whites are firm. Season to taste and garnish with coriander. Serve
with a rambunctious salsa and lots of chilled *cerveza* or mugs of
strong hot coffee.

Migas
Spicy Scrambled Eggs with Tortilla Strips, Texas-Style

In Spanish, *migas* refers to broken-up fried bread. In Northern
Mexico and parts of Texas it refers to crisp, fried broken-up tortillas added to spicy scrambled eggs. Often in restaurants you will
be able to choose various additions: spicy fried chorizo sausage,
diced avocado pear, strips of sautéed chillies, grated cheese,
chopped onion, tomatoes, and so on. *Migas* is occasionally found
in Mexico proper, where it is called not *migas* but *huevos con
tostaditas*.

Whatever one calls it, it is a delicious blend of contrasting
flavours and textures. It makes a robust brunch dish accompanied
by black beans, avocado pears with salsa, and a platter of tropical
fruits.

◁◁◁◁◁◁◁◁◁◁◁◁◁◁◁◁◁◁◁◁◁◁◁◁◁◁◁◁◁▷▷▷▷▷▷▷▷▷▷▷▷▷▷▷▷▷▷▷▷▷▷▷▷▷▷▷▷

10 to 12 corn tortillas, cut into 1.25 cm/½ in strips (or use
   tortilla chips)
100 ml/4 fl oz vegetable oil for frying, if using whole
   tortillas
6 cloves garlic, chopped
2 green peppers, roasted, peeled, then cut into strips and
   tossed with a good shake of cayenne pepper
35 g/1½ oz unsalted butter
1½ teaspoons cumin
6 ripe, small to medium tomatoes, coarsely chopped
8 eggs, lightly beaten
25 g/1 oz coriander leaves, chopped
3 to 4 spring onions, thinly sliced
Hot salsa of choice

1. Fry the tortilla strips in the vegetable oil until golden brown
   but not dark brown, then drain on absorbent paper. Tortilla
   chips do not need frying.
2. Sauté the garlic and green pepper strips in a third of the
   butter for just a minute. Do not let the garlic brown. Sprinkle
   in the cumin, then add the tomatoes and cook over a medium
   heat for 3 to 4 minutes, until the tomatoes are no longer
   runny. Remove from the pan and set aside.
3. Over a low heat, melt the remaining butter in the pan. Pour
   in the beaten eggs. Cook over a low heat and stir until eggs
   begin to set. Add the reserved chilli-tomato mixture and
   tortilla strips, and continue cooking, stirring until the eggs
   are the consistency you desire. The tortilla strips should be
   neither crisp nor soggy but pliable and chewy. Top with the
   coriander leaves and spring onions.
4. Serve immediately, accompanied by a fresh hot salsa or other
   spicy condiment.

VARIATION

Tacos de Huevos Revueltos: instead of serving the spicy scrambled
eggs tossed with the fried tortillas, roll them into soft corn tortillas and serve as *tacos*.

◁◁◁◁◁◁◁◁◁◁◁◁◁◁◁◁◁◁◁◁◁◁◁◁◁◁◁▷▷▷▷▷▷▷▷▷▷▷▷▷▷▷▷▷▷▷▷▷▷▷▷▷▷▷▷▷

Huevos Oaxacaena
Omelette Strips in a Sauce of Tomatoes and Puréed, Roasted Onions, Oaxaca-Style

This egg dish is strikingly unusual: the sauce is made by blending roasted onions, garlic and chilli with tomatoes then cooking it down in hot oil to a concentrated flavour. Serve with warm corn tortillas for an unusual brunch dish or first course, or with crusty bread for supper.

The recipe uses quite a large number of chillies, though it is not oppressively hot. Removing the seeds and roasting the chillies first helps cut down their sting; if your chillies are very hot, however, reduce the number considerably.

6 small to medium onions, peeled and cut into chunks
9 cloves garlic, whole and unpeeled
5 to 7 fresh green chillies
450 g/1 lb tomatoes, diced (tinned is fine)
75 ml/3 fl oz vegetable oil
A few spoonfuls of tomato purée (optional)
Pinch of sugar (optional)
6 eggs, lightly beaten
Salt and black pepper to taste
3 tablespoons coarsely chopped coriander leaves

1. Roast the onions, garlic and 4 of the chillies on an ungreased heavy frying pan until they char, turning them so that they blacken evenly. Remove from the heat and let cool.
2. When cool enough to handle, chop the onions, squeeze the garlic cloves out of their papery skins, and peel the chillies, remove their seeds and chop. Place in a liquidizer and purée together to form a paste. Add the tomatoes and blend until a saucelike consistency is formed.
3. Heat 50 ml/2 fl oz of the oil in a heavy frying pan, add the puréed mixture and cook until it reduces in volume and the sharpness of the raw onion recedes. Add tomato purée if needed, and season with a pinch of sugar if the tomatoes seem acidic.

4. Remove the seeds from one of the unused green chillies and chop the flesh. Add to the sauce, season, using plenty of salt, and set aside.
5. Cook the eggs in 3 or 4 flat omelettes, removing each to a plate, then rolling up pancake-fashion. Slice each of these rolls into 2 cm/³/₄ in widths.
6. Reheat the sauce in the frying pan, then add the omelette strips, tossing carefully so that they do not fall apart.
7. Serve immediately, sprinkled with the coriander and with the 2 extra chillies, seeded and chopped if desired.

VARIATION

Enchiladas Oaxacaena: omit the omelette strips. Dip corn tortillas in the warm sauce, then sprinkle with crumbled white cheese such as fresh Pecorino or Cheshire and fold them into quarters. Serve with extra sauce and chopped onion.

A FEW SIMPLE MEXICAN EGG DISHES

Soft-boiled eggs with a squeeze of lime juice and a sprinkling of cayenne pepper.

Place Salsa Ranchera (page 32) in individual ramekins or in a large casserole. Arrange 1 or 2 poached eggs per person in the sauce, then top with grated cheese. Grill or bake in a hot oven until the cheese melts.

Eggs with Refried Black Beans and Fried Plantains: heat refried black beans with grated mild white cheese melted atop it. Serve each portion topped with 2 poached or fried eggs, ripe plantain slices that you have browned in a lightly greased, heavy frying pan, and accompanied with a fresh tomato and chilli salsa. Bacon would not be out of place in this robust brunch dish. Serve with warm naan which approximates the Navajo fry bread traditionally served with this meal.

A favourite old-style California dish is beaten eggs combined with lots of roasted mild green chillies and grated Cheddar

◄◄◄◄◄◄◄◄◄◄◄◄◄◄◄◄◄◄◄◄◄◄◄◄◄◄◄◄◄◄◄<>►►►►►►►►►►►►►►►►►►►►►►►►►►►►►►►

cheese, then baked until the eggs have set. Serve either hot or
cold, cut into squares.

Huevos Tapatios, from Jalisco: top warmed corn tortillas with
crumbled browned chorizo or with minced beef seasoned with
mild chilli, cumin and oregano. Top with fried eggs and a sprinkling of grated cheese (it should melt on to the hot eggs) and garnish with guacamole or diced avocado and a tomato and chilli
salsa.

Cheese Omelettes with the Colours of the Mexican flag: prepare a
mild Salsa Verde (page 26) or a simple mixture of chopped roasted and peeled mild green chillies (tinned is fine). Have ready also
a spicy tomato or *ranchera* sauce. Blanket each rolled-up cheese
omelette with a stripe of each, plus one of soured cream, for a
green, red and white garnish.

Tender meats such as leftover pot roast, *carnitas*, etc, are delicious shredded then browned with chillies, garlic and perhaps a
chopped tomato or two. Scramble in as many eggs as you please
and serve the dish garnished with coriander leaves and with chilli
salsa on the side.

PESCADOS Y MARISCOS
Fish and Seafood

To first-time visitors in Mexico, who may be familiar only with *tacos*, *enchiladas*, *nachos*, and the occasional *tamal*, the dazzling array of impeccably fresh, briny-sweet fish and seafood comes as a revelation. With over 6,000 miles of relatively unspoiled coastline there is scarcely an area where fish does not figure prominently in the diet. Spindly-legged crabs, great, tentacled squid and octopus, sweet conch, robust sharkmeat, briny-shelled oysters and clams, the ever-present snapper and hearty swordfish, frog's legs, and beef-like steaks of terrapin – sea creatures abound. Even in mountain regions, myriad lakes offer freshwater fish, most notably the sweet-fleshed, tiny, white *pescado blanco* of Lago Pátzcuaro.

Fish and seafood combine brilliantly with Mexico's dominant seasonings: chillies, garlic, tomatoes. Rarely is the fish blanketed with cream and butter, European-style; rather it is enhanced with zesty spices and clean-tasting seasonings.

In addition to ocean fish and freshwater fish, dried fish are eaten – occasionally salted cod, more commonly tiny dried shrimp. A classic Lenten dish is Tortas de Camarón (page 140) – fried patties of dried shrimp, often served with *nopales* or *romeritos*.

In Mexico City, paella is often eaten for Sunday lunch, but it is a paella that reflects its 400-year residence in the New World: a robust dish that contains Mexican chorizo and a scattering of coriander, and is even better when doused with salsa.

In America's Southwest seafood has not been as important a part of the traditional diet as have meat, corn, and chillies. Yet in recent years, enthusiastic young chefs, combining classic French techniques with full-flavoured local ingredients, have developed seafood dishes of great distinction.

◁◁◁◁◁◁◁◁◁◁◁◁◁◁◁◁◁◁◁◁◁◁◁◁◁◁◁▷▷▷▷▷▷▷▷▷▷▷▷▷▷▷▷▷▷▷▷▷▷▷▷▷

Ostiones con Salsa con Limón y Cilantro
Oysters with Lime-Coriander Salsa

The startlingly tart flavours of lime and chilli are as welcome on raw oysters as the traditional shot of Tabasco or dab of mignonette. Serve on the half-shell, resting on a bed of ice or tendrils of seaweed. Top each oyster with a judicious dollop of Salsa con Limón y Cilantro (page 24).

Ceviche
Raw Fish 'Cooked' in a Citrus Marinade

At its best Ceviche, or Cebiche, consists of pristinely fresh seafood, marinated in lime juice until almost pickled, then dressed in a chunky salsa-like salad or sauce. At its worst, unfortunately, it is mediocre, even inedible, a last-ditch attempt to disguise fish that is no longer fresh.

Many recipes instruct you to combine the fish with the lime juice and sauce ingredients all at once, then let it marinate. I think this is a mistake. A bath in undiluted lime juice – and plenty of it – firms up the fish and readies it for its submersion in the tomatoes and chillies.

In Mexico, Ceviche may be made from any sort of fish or seafood besides white-fleshed fillets: prawns, crab, scallops, or that great sea-snail, the conch.

450 g/1 lb white-fleshed fish fillets
Juice of 7 limes
2 to 3 ripe tomatoes, seeded and diced
3 fresh green chillies or 4 pickled jalapeños, seeded and
    chopped
¹/₂ teaspoon oregano, crumbled
Salt to taste
100 ml/4 fl oz olive oil
1 small onion, chopped
2 tablespoons chopped coriander leaves

◁◁◁◁◁◁◁◁◁◁◁◁◁◁◁◁◁◁◁◁◁◁◁◁◁◁◁◁◁◁◁▷▷▷▷▷▷▷▷▷▷▷▷▷▷▷▷▷▷▷▷▷▷▷▷▷▷▷

1. Cut the fish into bite-sized pieces and place in a glass bowl. Pour on the lime juice and mix well to combine. Refrigerate for at least 5 hours, or until the fish looks opaque. Turn every so often, so that the lime juice permeates the fish evenly.
2. When opaque, add the tomatoes, chillies, oregano, salt and olive oil. Chill for another hour or so.
3. About 15 minutes before serving, remove from the refrigerator so that the olive oil warms slightly if it has become congealed. Serve sprinkled with the onion and coriander.

VARIATION

Drain the fish of the lime juice before adding the other ingredients. This makes a clean-tasting, though less tangy Ceviche.

Camarones a la Parilla
Grilled Chillied Prawns with Papaya

The combination of citrus fruit and chilli powder imparts a distinctive zest to seafood, a flavouring particularly suited to the smoky taste of outdoor grilling. Accompany by sweet and juicy papaya or other tropical fruits and garnish with edible blossoms such as nasturtiums or pansies.

Note that the shells are left on the prawns. This keeps the flesh moist and succulent while grilling but it is admittedly fiddly to eat – be sure to have bowls for the shells. If this is all too messy to contemplate, use shelled prawns with their tails still intact and take care not to overcook.

◁◁◁◁◁◁◁◁◁◁◁◁◁◁◁◁◁◁◁◁◁◁◁◁◁◁◁◁◁◁◇▷▷▷▷▷▷▷▷▷▷▷▷▷▷▷▷▷▷▷▷▷▷▷▷▷▷▷▷

1 orange
2 limes
3 cloves garlic, chopped
1 fresh green chilli, chopped (or to taste)
2 tablespoons mild red chilli powder such as ancho or New
   Mexico
1 teaspoon cumin
$^1/_2$ teaspoon oregano leaves, crumbled between the hands
1 teaspoon salt
2 tablespoons olive oil or vegetable oil
1 kg/2$^1/_4$ lb prawns, with shells left on
1 firm but ripe papaya, peeled and cut into bite-sized pieces
Fresh salsa of choice

1. Grate the rind from the orange and 1 of the limes, then
   squeeze the juice from them both. Cut the other lime into
   wedges and reserve.
2. Combine the juice and the rind, then add the garlic, fresh
   chilli, mild chilli powder, cumin, oregano, salt and oil.
3. Mix with the prawns and marinate for 30 minutes to 1 hour.
4. Arrange on bamboo or metal skewers and grill over a charcoal
   fire if possible, otherwise grill indoors or sauté in a frying
   pan.
5. Serve immediately, each skewer garnished with papaya chunks
   and lime wedges, and accompanied by a salsa of choice.

Camarones 'Cocktel'
Yucatecan Prawn Appetizer

The spicy simplicity of this method of cooking and presentation
captures the essence of sun-drenched Mexican eating.

4 or 5 large raw prawns per person, with shells on
$^1/_2$ lemon
Cruet each of olive oil and vinegar
Small bowls, each filled with a separate ingredient: chopped
   onions, diced tomatoes, chopped coriander, and chopped
   or thinly sliced hot green chillies
Wedges of lime

1. The best way of cooking prawns is by a Chinese method
   known as steeping. Place the unshelled prawns in a saucepan
   with the lemon half and water to cover. Bring to the boil,
   cook for a moment or two, then remove from the heat, cover,
   and let steep until the water is cool. Remove their shells, legs,
   and vein, but leave the tail. The prawns should emerge pink,
   juicy and tender.
2. Arrange the prawns in shallow soup plates in a sunburst or
   flower shape.
3. Pass cruets of olive oil and vinegar, and bowls of raw
   condiments, so diners can help themselves.

Camarones en Frio
Sautéed Prawns Topped with Lime-Marinated Onions

The contrast of tastes and textures comprises the charm of this
dish. The prawns are earthy and rich-tasting, with soft, sautéed
onions and garlic, yet tangy with a splash of vinegar and topped
with crunchy, lime-pickled onions. It is a little dish that could be
enjoyed as part of an appetizer selection or luncheon, as a first
course, or salad.

    2 onions, thinly sliced
    Juice of 1 lime
    2 cloves garlic, coarsely chopped
    2 tablespoons vegetable oil
    450 g/1 lb raw prawns, shells removed
    Pinch each: black pepper, cayenne pepper, paprika,
        oregano
    3 tablespoons white wine vinegar
    Salt if needed

1. Combine one of the sliced onions with the lime juice and chill
   for at least 30 minutes.
2. Sauté the remaining onion with the garlic in the vegetable oil;
   when softened, add the prawns, sprinkle with the black
   pepper, cayenne, paprika, and oregano and stir around. Splash
   the wine vinegar into the pan and let it cook out as the prawns

firm up – it should take only a few minutes. If the prawns are done but the vinegar is still sharp, remove the prawns, and let the vinegar cook a moment longer, becoming a concentrated essence rather than a sauce. Add salt to taste if necessary. Toss the prawns back in the pan then remove to a plate to cool.

3. Serve the cooled prawns and cooked onions topped with the tangy lime-marinated onions.

VARIATION

Other seafood, or firm white-fleshed fish fillets cut into bite-sized pieces, are equally delicious in place of the prawns. I often make it with chicken; turkey would probably be good as well.

Tortas de Camarón
Fried Shrimp and Prawn Patties

Tortas de Camarón are traditional for Lent and Christmas. Certain restaurants are known for their Tortas de Camarón and people come especially during the holidays to sample these seafood fritters.

Tortas de Camarón are usually made with dried shrimp only, but I find that adding fresh prawns lightens them and makes them juicier, more interesting. The patties are usually served in a sauce of either tomatoes or *mole*; sometimes they are simmered with *romeritos*, a rosemary-like green vegetable, or shredded greens. *Nopales*, too, are a traditional accompaniment.

Makes about 10 large fritters or 20 small ones

1 quantity Salsa Ranchera (page 32) or Mole (page 160)
175 g/6 oz sliced cooked *nopales*, rinsed and drained (optional)
50 g/2 oz dried shrimp
100 g/4 oz fresh prawns, cooked and cooled
4 medium eggs, separated
Pinch of salt
25 g /1 oz flour
Oil for frying

◄◄◄◄◄◄◄◄◄◄◄◄◄◄◄◄◄◄◄◄◄◄◄◄◄◄◄◄◄◄►►►►►►►►►►►►►►►►►►►►►►►►►►►►►►

1. Heat whichever sauce you choose; cover and keep warm. If using *nopales*, heat it in the sauce as well.
2. Whirl the dried shrimp in a liquidizer until it is mealy or crumblike in consistency.
3. Chop the cooked prawns, then mix with the ground dried shrimp. Beat the egg yolks until thick and lemon-coloured.
4. Whip the egg whites with a pinch of salt until stiff peaks form, then gently fold the whites into the yolks. Sprinkle the flour over the eggs and gently fold it in, along with the shrimp, to form a batter.
5. In a heavy frying pan, heat enough oil to reach a depth of 2.5 cm/1 in.
6. Spoon 25 ml/1 fl oz batter into the hot oil for small fritters or 50 ml/2 fl oz for larger fritters. Cook until golden brown.
7. Drain on absorbent paper and serve immediately, accompanied by the warm sauce.

Langosta Rosarita
Grilled Lobster with Refried Beans

Not that long ago Rosarita Beach was among the points furthest south one could drive from the US into Baja California. Beyond that lay hazardous terrain, with tales of rough roads frequented by remorseless *banditos*.

Because of its proximity to Los Angeles, its lushly exotic landscape, and the nearby Aqua Caliente racetrack, Rosarita Beach became a favourite get-away spot for old-time Hollywood stars. They came to the Rosarita Beach Hotel, a place that always struck me as a romantic outpost at the edge of the world. There they tucked into the speciality of the area: briny sweet lobster slathered with garlic-herb butter and served with creamy refried beans. The elegant lobster meat combines with the humble, earthy bean in an unexpected and joyous way.

Serve with a stack of fresh warm flour tortillas and a bowl of crisp chunky coriander-flecked chilli and tomato salsa.

This is one of those dishes that is best eaten on a warm beach, as the oppressive heat of the day disappears into a pleasantly mild evening.

◁◁◁◁◁◁◁◁◁◁◁◁◁◁◁◁◁◁◁◁◁◁◁◁◁◁◁◁◁◁◁◁◁◁◁◁◁▷▷▷▷▷▷▷▷▷▷▷▷▷▷▷▷▷▷▷▷▷▷▷▷▷▷▷▷▷

100 g/4 oz unsalted butter, at room temperature
1 teaspoon dried oregano leaves, crumbled between your
   hands
2 or 3 cloves garlic, coarsely chopped
$1/_2$ teaspoon salt, or to taste
Coarsely ground black pepper
2 large cooked lobster tails, split in half, the flesh loosened
   with a knife
275 g/10 oz *frijoles refritos*, tinned or homemade (page 196),
   kept warm
Warm flour tortillas
Salsa Cruda (page 23)

1. Mix the butter with the oregano, garlic, salt and plenty of
   pepper. Spread over the lobster flesh, reserving a little for
   basting and to spread over once the lobster has finished
   cooking.
2. Either grill the lobster over an open flame for about 10
   minutes, or bake in the oven at 180°C/350°F/gas mark 4,
   basting with the reserved butter. Since the lobster is already
   cooked, you just need to heat it with the seasonings. If it is
   overcooked it will be tough and uninteresting.
3. To serve, place each piece of lobster on a plate with a portion
   of the beans, and offer tortillas and salsa as desired.

‹‹‹‹‹‹‹‹‹‹‹‹‹‹‹‹‹‹‹‹‹‹‹‹‹‹‹‹‹‹‹›››››››››››››››››››››››

Mejillones a la Mexicana
Mussels Steamed over Lager with Tomatoes, Chillies and Onions

The slight bitterness of the beer is combined with acidic tomatoes, sweet onions and hot chilli to form a sort of spicy court-bouillon for steaming mussels. It is a rather nice way of using up any leftover lager you might have languishing in the refrigerator. Clams can be used instead of mussels.

500 ml/16 fl oz lager
2 smallish onions, coarsely chopped
1 medium-hot green chilli, seeded and diced
75 g/3 oz tomatoes, chopped (tinned is fine)
1 kg/2¼ lb mussels in their shells, scrubbed and
 de-bearded
Fresh salsa

1. Place the lager, onions, chilli and tomatoes in the bottom of a steamer.
2. Bring to the boil, then add the mussels and steam until their shells pop open. Discard any that have not opened.
3. Serve immediately, accompanied by salsa of choice.

Pescado en Tamal
Corn Husk-Wrapped Chillied fish, Toluca-Style

Fish – in bite-sized chunks or small and whole – have been wrapped in corn husks and steamed, much like a *tamal*, since pre-Hispanic times. The husk-wrapped parcels were stacked into a sort of steamer device based on corn cobs, then water was poured in and the parcels stacked over the cobs, and steamed.

Serve each diner several parcels, so that when he or she unwraps them the flavours steam directly to the diner, tantalizing with their full force. Accompany with warm corn tortillas, avocado slices, and pickled jalapeños or salsa of choice, so diners can make their own soft *tacos* if they wish.

About 16 corn husks (see Glossary), depending on size
(note: this is using Mexican corn husks; when using
African corn husks use the whole husk parcel – they are
still attached at the base)
1 quantity Recado Rojo Enchilado (page 43)
450 g/1 lb white-fleshed firm fish, cut into bite-sized
pieces, or tiny whole sardines, cleaned
2 tablespoons chopped fresh coriander leaves
1 avocado, peeled and sliced
Pickled jalapeños
Warm corn tortillas

1. Soak the corn husks in warm water to cover for 30 minutes.
2. Meanwhile, mix the spice paste with the fish and toss to coat
   well.
3. When the corn husks have become pliable, lay out 2 at a time,
   making a flat oblong surface, then top with a spoonful or so of
   the chilli-seasoned fish.
4. Fold over to enclose the fish well (if using African corn husks,
   place the fish in the centre of the leaves and fold it all over the
   fish filling to enclose).
5. Stack the parcels in a steamer and steam for 10 minutes. Serve
   immediately, accompanied by the coriander, avocado slices,
   jalapeños, and warm corn tortillas.

VARIATION

In place of corn husks, use banana leaves as they do in the
Yucatán. The flavour of the dish will be subtly different according to whether you use corn husks or banana leaves. Cut the
leaves into a workable size, and heat over a low to medium heat
on top of the stove to render them pliable, then place a generous
spoonful of the fish in the middle of each leaf and fold the leaf
over to enclose completely. Steam and serve as with the corn
husks.

Caldo Largo con Limón
Big Soup-Stew of fish, Seafood, Roasted Garlic and Citrus Fruit, Yucatán-Style

This is a seafood rendition of the classic Yucatecan soup, *sopa de lima*, more usually prepared with shredded chicken and tortilla strips. While the original is one of the brilliant soups of the Mexican kitchen, I find the deliciously sharp flavours even better suited to seafood, and with the large proportion of fish this soup makes a full meal.

Serve with crusty bread or soft corn tortillas, and a salad of boiled potatoes, roasted red peppers, tomato wedges, a splash of salsa and a sprinkling of chopped coriander.

Fresh fruit ice-creams, splashed with a little tequila and orange liqueur such as Grand Marnier or triple sec, would be delightful as a sweet course.

Serves 6

2 onions, coarsely chopped
1 medium-hot chilli such as jalapeño, seeded and chopped
15 large garlic cloves
1 tablespoon olive oil
750 ml/1¼ pints chicken stock
500 ml/16 fl oz fish stock or clam juice
6 medium clams, scrubbed
12 medium mussels, scrubbed and trimmed of their 'beards'
8 ripe tomatoes, peeled, seeded and coarsely chopped
¼ teaspoon dried oregano leaves, crumbled between the hands
1 teaspoon finely grated grapefruit zest
1 teaspoon finely grated lime zest
225 g/8 oz medium prawns, raw with their shells
225 g/8 oz firm-fleshed white fish, cut into bite-sized pieces
Salt and black pepper to taste
75 ml/3 fl oz lime juice (juice of approximately 2 limes)

◁◁◁◁◁◁◁◁◁◁◁◁◁◁◁◁◁◁◁◁◁◁◁◁◁◁◁◁◁◁◁◁◁◁◁◁◁◁▷▷▷▷▷▷▷▷▷▷▷▷▷▷▷▷▷▷▷▷▷▷▷▷▷▷▷▷▷▷▷▷▷▷▷

1. Mix a third of the onions with half the chopped chilli; reserve for garnish.
2. Roast the unpeeled garlic cloves on an ungreased heavy frying pan over a medium heat until the skins are charred and the cloves slightly softened, about 4 minutes. Cool slightly, then slip the skins off.
3. Heat the oil in a large saucepan and sauté the remaining onions and chilli until softened, about 5 minutes. Add the roasted garlic, chicken stock, fish stock or clam juice, and 250 ml/8 fl oz water. Simmer to blend the flavours, about 15 minutes.
4. Add the clams, mussels, tomatoes, oregano, and grapefruit and lime zests. Cook over a medium heat until the clam and mussel shells open, 5 to 10 minutes. Discard any unopened ones.
5. Add the prawns, white fish, salt and pepper. Simmer until the prawns and fish turn opaque, just 2 or 3 minutes.
6. Remove from the heat, stir in the reserved onion-chilli mixture and the lime juice, and serve immediately.

Pescado Yucateca
Chillied Bass with Coconut Milk

I first tried this dish on a seemingly endless stretch of beach in the Mexican tropics. It tasted both tropical and exotic, as delicious as the palm tree-fringed scenery.

Almost any of the red chilli pastes makes an excellent coating for this fish; in the Yucatán, achiote seasoning is traditional, but I usually use the Recado Rojo Enchilado (page 43) or the red chilli and tequila paste from Pato con Naranja y Yerba Buena (see page 163). Roasted garlic gives a distinctive Yucatecan flavour to the dish, and slices of orange gently perfume the flesh of the fish. The drizzle of cool coconut milk is rich against the slightly acidic spiced fish.

◁◁◁◁◁◁◁◁◁◁◁◁◁◁◁◁◁◁◁◁◁◁◁◁◁▷▷▷▷▷▷▷▷▷▷▷▷▷▷▷▷▷▷▷▷▷▷▷▷▷

1 whole fish such as red snapper or cod, about
   1.5 kg/3¼ lb, inside cleaned
1 lemon, halved
4 to 5 cloves garlic, unpeeled
Chilli paste (see above)
Several slices of orange, unpeeled
50 ml/2 fl oz coconut milk
Shredded lettuce, chopped chillies and coriander leaves, to
   garnish

1. Place the fish in a baking dish. Rub it inside and out with one lemon half. Slice the other lemon half and reserve.
2. Toast the garlic cloves in an ungreased frying pan for about 5 to 7 minutes or until lightly charred. Remove their skins.
3. Coat the fish inside and out with the chilli paste, then place the charred garlic, orange slices, and several slices of lemon in its cavity.
4. Cover with foil and bake in the oven at 150°C/300°F/gas mark 2 for 1 hour, then remove the foil.
5. Place the fish under the grill and let the top brown and crisp a little.
6. Serve drizzled with coconut milk and garnished with shredded lettuce, chopped chillies and coriander leaves.

A FEW SIMPLE MEXICAN FISH DISHES

Roast a whole fish such as snapper or bass slowly over a low fire, letting the fish develop a smoky flavour. Serve with pickled jalapeños, wedges of lime, and warm corn tortillas, and roll up *tacos* while you knock back glasses of tequila followed by chilled Mexican beer.

Pescado con Ajo: marinate fish fillets in lots of lime juice to firm the flesh. Drain, then top with garlic butter that is exceedingly garlicky and grill until lightly browned. Serve with more garlic butter and a sprinkling of parsley.

Pescado Frito a la Campeche: serve any crisply fried fish fillets with the following sauce: in a pan, combine 2 thinly sliced onions with

❮❮❮❯❯❯❯❯❯❯❯❯❯❯❯❯❯❯❯❯❯❯❯❯❯❯❯❯❯❯❯❯❯❯❯❯

250 ml/8 fl oz cider vinegar, 100 ml/4 fl oz water, a large pinch of oregano and salt. Cook until the onions are transparent and let cool.

Season floured and fried fish fillets with mild chilli powder. Serve sprinkled with coriander and chopped onion and accompanied with wedges of orange, lime, and lemon for each diner to squeeze over as desired.

Serve grilled or poached fish topped with guacamole.

Marinate fish fillets in a mild (New Mexico) chilli sauce seasoned with vinegar and a dash of cumin, oregano, cinnamon and cloves. Bake until the fish is just turning firm and is cooked through.

KKKKKKKKKKKKKKKKKKKKKKKKK<>>>>>>>>>>>>>>>>>>>>>>>>>

AVES
Poultry

Before the Conquest, Mexico had little in the way of poultry. Wild birds were hunted, including turkeys and a breed of large duck that now appears extinct, but none could be depended on for steady nourishment. The introduction of the domestic chicken and the domestication of the turkey proved monumental in the development of Mexican cuisine. The ancient sauces adapted brilliantly to the more easily obtainable domestic poultry.

Much of Mexican chicken cookery is based on simmering a bird slowly, using the liquid for soup, then stewing the now-tender creature in a richly spiced sauce. Chickens in Mexico need a long simmer, however, for they lead a long, full life before meeting the stew pot. You see these wiry birds everywhere, pecking around gardens, wandering down the village street, or clucking in the car park.

A simmered chicken or turkey might be rubbed with a spice paste – *moles*, *escabeches*, or *recados* – then baked or stewed until fork-tender. If a chicken is not to be simmered first, it may be combined with a selection of varied seasonings then baked slowly in the oven, where the fragrant sauce permeates the flesh of the bird. In addition to being served as a main course, chicken shows up in a wide variety of other guises: shredded and added to soups, piled into *tostadas*, stewed to make *taco* fillings, and so on.

Turkey is probably Mexico's favourite bird, its great bulk stretching to feed many mouths. It is served with the same sorts of sauces as chicken, its agreeably versatile flesh the traditional choice for the spicy sauces known as *moles*.

Duck is less common, yet its richness is offset brilliantly by the spiciness of Mexico's seasonings. Wild birds are enjoyed as well, usually marinated and grilled over a charcoal fire, the smoky

ᐊᐊᐊᐊᐊᐊᐊᐊᐊᐊᐊᐊᐊᐊᐊᐊᐊᐊᐊᐊᐊᐊᐊᐊᐊᐊᐊᐊᐊᐊᐊᐃᐅᐅᐅᐅᐅᐅᐅᐅᐅᐅᐅᐅᐅᐅᐅᐅᐅᐅᐅᐅᐅᐅᐅᐅᐅᐅᐅᐅᐅᐅ

flavour from the flames enhanced by the chilli flavours of the marinade.

As with other meats, no part of the fowl goes to waste in the Mexican kitchen. Chicken feet enrich the stock, livers are sautéed to make *taco* fillings, as are gizzards and hearts. Even the blood is made use of: that unfortunate turkey doomed to be served on Sunday as Mole Poblano will have its neck slashed, and its blood will be collected and poached into a quivering, brown, pudding-like delicacy.

Pollo Pibil
Spice-Coated Roast Chicken in Banana Leaves, Yucatecan-Style

Achiote flavours this dish with its subtle aroma, while the banana leaves keep the chicken moist. When the parcel is unwrapped it releases a fragrant steam, and the chicken inside is meltingly tender.

Achiote (see Glossary) may often be found in West Indian shops. If you cannot find it, a combination of red chilli powder and mild paprika may be used. This produces a different dish altogether, but one that is delicious nevertheless.

Pollo Pibil may be made from pork instead of chicken; *pibil* refers to the specific type of oven, called a *pib*, used for the dish. Serve accompanied by steamed rice or Arroz Blanco (page 190), black beans, a stack of warm corn tortillas and a platter of raw vegetables along with a bowl of fresh salsa. By the way, Pollo Pibil is excellent the next day, all moist and flavourful: delicious as a salad, or shredded and wrapped into *tacos*.

⋘⋘⋘⋘⋘⋘⋘⋘⋘⋘⋘⋘⋘⋘⋘⋘⋘⋘⋘⋘⋘⋘⋘◇⋙⋙⋙⋙⋙⋙⋙⋙⋙⋙⋙⋙⋙⋙⋙⋙⋙⋙⋙⋙⋙⋙

Achiote Paste

3 tablespoons achiote seeds (or substitute 1¹/₂ tablespoons each of paprika and mild chilli powder)

500 ml/16 fl oz water (omit if using paprika and chilli powder)

3 mild chillies such as ancho, New Mexico, guajillo, pasilla, etc (if using chilli powder instead of chillies and achiote, double the amount of chilli powder and paprika)

3 cloves garlic, chopped

1 to 2 medium to hot green chillies, chopped

1 tablespoon paprika

2 teaspoons cumin

¹/₂ teaspoon oregano leaves

1 teaspoon salt

3 tablespoons chopped coriander leaves

1¹/₂ teaspoons chopped fresh orange rind, or a generous pinch of dried rind

Juice of 1 orange, 1 lemon and 1 lime

Cooking and Serving

1 package banana leaves (see Glossary)

1 whole chicken, about 1.6 kg/3¹/₂ lb

3 to 4 spring onions

3 to 4 rashers streaky bacon

2 limes, cut into wedges for garnish

12 g/¹/₂ oz whole coriander leaves

1. Prepare the seasoning paste: combine the achiote seeds with 250 ml/8 fl oz of the water and bring to the boil. Reduce the heat and simmer over a low heat for 5 minutes, then cover and leave to soak for at least 2 hours, preferably overnight.
2. Half an hour before you grind the achiote seeds prepare the chillies: lightly toast each mild chilli by holding over an open flame or in an ungreased frying pan. Tear into pieces and cover with the remaining water, which should be hot. Cover and soak for 30 minutes to 1 hour.
3. Purée the achiote seeds and chillies together with the soaking liquid in a liquidizer. The bright colouring of the achiote

◀◀◀◀◀◀◀◀◀◀◀◀◀◀◀◀◀◀◀◀◀◀◀◀◀◀◀◀▶▶▶▶▶▶▶▶▶▶▶▶▶▶▶▶▶▶▶▶▶▶▶▶▶

seeds will, alas, stain the goblet, but will fade in time.

4. When puréed as smoothly as possible (it will still have some texture), put the paste through a sieve, pushing against the sieve to extract all the goodness from the ingredients, leaving behind the skins and other hard bits.

5. Combine the strained achiote-chilli paste with the garlic, fresh green chillies, paprika, cumin, oregano, salt, coriander, orange rind, and citrus juices.

6. Rub the achiote paste all over the chicken, both inside and out. Heat each banana leaf briefly over a flame to soften, then wrap the chicken in about 2 thicknesses of banana leaves. Place the wrapped chicken in a baking dish, cover with foil loosely, and marinate overnight in the refrigerator.

7. Next day, remove from the refrigerator. Partially unwrap the chicken, just enough to insert the whole spring onions into the cavity, and top the chicken with the streaky bacon. Rewrap the chicken in the leaves, then wrap tightly in foil and bake in the oven at 180°C/350°F/gas mark 4 for 2 to 2¹/₂ hours.

8. Unwrap the leaves and place the chicken on a serving platter. Garnish with the lime wedges and coriander leaves. Serve with warm flour or corn tortillas or soft warm naan or similar breads.

VARIATION

Puerco Pibil: prepare according to the basic recipe but increase the cooking time for pork accordingly. Choose a boned loin or shoulder cut, and cut into chunks about 5 cm/2 in in size.

Pollo en Escabeche de Valladolid
Chicken Breasts Coated with Spices, in a Sauce of Onions, Vinegar and Stock

While variations of this dish are eaten all over the Yucatán, it is particularly associated with the hot and dusty town of Valladolid, where chicken dishes of all sorts are a speciality.

◁◁◁▷▷

This particular dish is called *escabeche*, or pickled, in honour of the vinegar used in the sauce. Its piquant presence is somewhat reminiscent of French sauces in which the pan is deglazed with vinegar – could this dish be a souvenir of the brief French occupation?

Traditionally, the dish is prepared with a whole bird which is simmered for a long time. I like the delicacy, however, of white chicken flesh, cooked only until tender, then paired with the tangy vinegar and onion sauce. Serve Pollo Valladolid in shallow soup bowls, accompanied by crusty bread or warm corn tortillas.

4 large or 8 small chicken breasts, with or without bones
Stock (or stock cube and water) to cover
Recado (page 40)
4 small to medium onions, sliced lengthwise
100 ml/4 fl oz vegetable oil, or as needed
$^1/_2$ to 1 medium to hot fresh green chilli, seeded and
    chopped, or 3 to 4 mild fresh chillies such as Italian or
    Hungarian wax peppers
75 ml/3 fl oz cider vinegar or sherry vinegar
Pinch of cumin seeds (optional)
50 g/2 oz flour, for dredging chicken

1. Place the chicken breasts in a saucepan with stock to cover.
   Bring to the boil, reduce the heat, and simmer for 5 minutes
   (if using boned chicken breasts, cook for only 2 or 3 minutes).
   Remove from the heat and let cool in the stock. (The dish
   may be prepared ahead up to this point and kept once cool in
   the refrigerator for up to 2 days.)
2. Remove the chicken from the stock (you should have about
   750 ml/1$^1/_4$ pints stock; add water and a stock cube if needed).
   Reserve the stock.
3. Dry the chicken, remove the skin, and the bones, if necessary.
   Smear the meat with two-thirds of the spice paste. Leave at
   room temperature for 30 to 45 minutes.
4. Brown the onions and chilli in a tiny bit of the oil until
   softened; pour in the vinegar and cumin seeds, if using, let
   cook down a bit, then add the stock and the remaining spice

KKKKKKKKKKKKKKKKKKKKKKKKKKKKKK>>>>>>>>>>>>>>>>>>>>>>>>>>>>>>

paste. Boil until reduced in volume and richly flavoured. Set aside and keep warm.

5. Dredge the chicken in flour. Heat the remaining oil in a heavy frying pan and fry the chicken pieces until lightly browned and somewhat crusty. Remove from the pan and serve immediately, each portion topped with some of the onions and swimming in a small pool of the stock.

VARIATION

Substitute fish for the chicken; adjust the cooking time accordingly.

Pollo a la Mérida
Chicken in an Orange, Olive, Almond, Raisin and Caper Sauce, Yucatán-Style

The sauce is strongly Mediterranean accented, with its olives, raisins, capers, orange, and olive oil. Cinnamon adds a Moorish touch, with a scattering of the ubiquitous Mexican chopped chilli and coriander.

Serve with rice, black beans and a salad of shredded Cos lettuce and sliced red onions.

1.1 to 1.4 kg/2½ to 3 lb chicken, cut into serving pieces
2 limes
1 to 2 onions, coarsely chopped
1 red, yellow, or green pepper, or a little of each, diced
2 tablespoons olive oil
8 tomatoes, peeled, seeded and diced (tinned is fine)
2 tablespoons capers
1½ tablespoons raisins
15 blanched almonds, coarsely chopped
15 pimiento-stuffed green olives, coarsely chopped
500 ml/16 fl oz orange juice (squeezed from fresh oranges is best)
100 ml/4 fl oz chicken stock
¼ teaspoon ground cinnamon

᚛᚛᚛᚛᚛᚛᚛᚛᚛᚛᚛᚛᚛᚛᚛᚛᚛᚛᚛᚛᚛᚛᚛᚛᚛᚛᚛᚛᚜᚛᚜᚜᚜᚜᚜᚜᚜᚜᚜᚜᚜᚜᚜᚜᚜᚜᚜᚜᚜᚜᚜᚜᚜᚜

Salt and pepper to taste

$^1/_2$ to 1 medium-hot fresh green chilli, diced or coarsely chopped

2 teaspoons chopped coriander leaves.

1. Place the chicken in a shallow pan or bowl and squeeze the lime juice over. Leave for 30 to 60 minutes.
2. Lightly sauté the onions and pepper in half the olive oil until softened, then add the tomatoes, capers, raisins, almonds and olives. Cook until the liquid has evaporated and the mixture is beginning to brown.
3. Add the orange juice then remove from the heat.
4. Wipe the lime juice off the chicken and brown in the remaining olive oil over a high heat in a heavy frying pan, adding more oil if needed.
5. Pour off any fat, then add the sauce plus the stock. Reduce the heat and simmer, covered, until the chicken is tender, about 35 minutes.
6. Season with the cinnamon, salt and pepper, then serve immediately, sprinkled with the chopped chilli and coriander.

VARIATION

Pescada en Naranja: fish fillets are delicious in this spicy citrus-olive sauce. Prepare the sauce without the chicken, then serve spooned over sautéed fish fillets in a baking dish or frying pan. Heat together for 10 minutes or so, long enough to meld the flavours. Serve sprinkled with chopped chillies and coriander, accompanied by wedges of lime.

Chicken Breasts with Chilli Paste and Guacamole

Not a traditional dish, rather the sort of simple, highly spiced food that is becoming a modern classic in America's Southwest. The tender, flat medallions of chicken are superb lightly marinated in the mild and tangy spice mixture accented with a squeeze of tart lime. A dollop of guacamole brings it all to life.

◁◁◁◁◁◁◁◁◁◁◁◁◁◁◁◁◁◁◁◁◁◁◁◁◁◁◁◁◁◁◁◁▷▷▷▷▷▷▷▷▷▷▷▷▷▷▷▷▷▷▷▷▷▷▷▷▷▷▷▷▷▷▷

4 chicken breasts, bones and skin removed, pounded lightly
   to an even 1.25 cm/¹/₂ in thickness
Recado Rojo Enchilado (page 43)
1 lime, cut into wedges
1 quantity Guacamole con Jitomates (page 50)

1. Coat the chicken breasts in the spice mixture and leave for
   about 30 minutes.
2. Grill quickly or sauté in a lightly greased pan, or brush with
   olive oil and grill over an open fire. Be careful not to
   overcook the chicken.
3. Serve the chicken accompanied by wedges of lime and
   spoonfuls of guacamole.

VARIATIONS

Try stuffing the grilled chicken breasts into crusty pan-grilled
rolls, *torta*-like, and dressing the plump sandwich with the guacamole.

Poc Chuc: in the Yucatán region of Mexico, thin flat strips of
pounded steak are marinated in a spicy chilli and citrus paste,
then grilled. Authentically the meat should be venison, but beef
is equally good. Serve with rice and marinated cabbage, as well as
a chilli salsa, following a first course of Sopa de Frijole Negro y
Tortillas (page 70).

Pollo de Plaza
Chicken in Chilli-Tomato Sauce with Enchiladas,
Michoacán-Style

The picturesque village of Pátzcuaro nestles in a valley in the
lush Michoacán region, next to the lake also called Pátzcuaro.
The area is mild and fertile, well known throughout Mexico for
its white fish from the lake and its fragrant, sweet strawberries,
and known in California for its illegal smoke.
   Life in Pátzcuaro, as in most other villages, centres around the

⊲⊲⊲⊲⊲⊲⊲⊲⊲⊲⊲⊲⊲⊲⊲⊲⊲⊲⊲⊲⊲⊲⊲⊲⊲⊲⊲⊳⊳⊳⊳⊳⊳⊳⊳⊳⊳⊳⊳⊳⊳⊳⊳⊳⊳⊳⊳⊳⊳⊳⊳

plaza where the marketplace thrives by day, and food vendors and social gatherings are the focus in the evening. Dusk is filled with the enticing aroma of simple foods quickly cooking over a charcoal brazier, ready to be wrapped into *tacos* and devoured along with shots of tequila.

One of the town's specialities is the following dish of chicken served with *enchiladas*. Traditionally the chicken is jointed, pan-fried and seasoned with only a little sauce. In my less traditional version a whole chicken is coated with sauce, then roasted along with a handful of whole garlic cloves; lightly cooked potatoes and carrots are tossed into the pan at the end.

The whole robust platter of chicken, vegetables and *enchiladas* makes a festive, hearty Sunday lunch.

Sauce

   1 onion, coarsely chopped
   1 tablespoon vegetable oil
   1 tablespoon cumin seeds or 2 teaspoons ground cumin
   50 g/2 oz mild chilli powder, or mild chilli powder and
      paprika mixed
   2 cloves garlic, chopped
   250 ml/8 fl oz chicken stock
   6 ripe tomatoes, diced or coarsely chopped (tinned is fine)
   25 ml/1 fl oz tomato purée
   250 ml/8 fl oz orange juice

1. Sauté the onion in the oil. When softened, add the cumin and heat through, toasting slightly, then add the chilli powder and lightly toast.
2. Purée the onion and spice mixture along with the garlic, adding the chicken stock to smooth it. Continue to purée, then add the tomatoes, tomato purée and orange juice.

◁◁◁◁◁◁◁◁◁◁◁◁◁◁◁◁◁◁◁◁◁◁◁◁◁◁◁◁◁▷▷▷▷▷▷▷▷▷▷▷▷▷▷▷▷▷▷▷▷▷▷▷▷▷▷▷▷▷▷

Chicken

> 1.4 kg/3 lb chicken, whole
> 2 heads garlic, broken into cloves but left unpeeled
> 3 to 4 spring onions
> 250 ml/8 fl oz orange juice
> 8 to 10 small to medium potatoes, preferably waxy ones
> 4 to 6 carrots, cut into halves widthways
> 2 tablespoons vinegar

1. Place the chicken in a roasting tin. Stuff several cloves of garlic inside it, then dip the spring onions into the sauce and put these inside the chicken as well.
2. Pour half the sauce over the chicken, letting it run down into the bottom of the tin. Reserve the remaining sauce for the *enchiladas*. Scatter the remaining whole garlic cloves throughout the bottom of the pan.
3. Roast in the oven at 180°C/350°F/gas mark 4 for 1 hour, adding orange juice to the tin so that there is always an inch or two of gravy.
4. Meanwhile, prepare the vegetables: boil the potatoes until half tender, then add the carrots and continue cooking until both vegetables are just tender. Drain and toss with the vinegar. When cool enough to handle, cut into bite-sized pieces and set aside.
5. When the chicken is just tender, add the potatoes and carrots to the pan and toss with the gravy and garlic. Return to the oven and cook slowly for another half-hour or so while you make the *enchiladas*.

Enchiladas

> 12 corn tortillas
> Oil for frying
> 175 g/6 oz Cheshire cheese, crumbled (or fresh Pecorino; both are similar to the slightly creamy, slightly salty cheese that would be used in Mexico)
> 1 onion, chopped

◁◁◁◁◁◁◁◁◁◁◁◁◁◁◁◁◁◁◁◁◁◁◁◁◁◁◁▷▷▷▷▷▷▷▷▷▷▷▷▷▷▷▷▷▷▷▷▷▷▷▷▷▷▷

1. Dip each tortilla into the reserved warm sauce, then lightly fry for a moment or two in the hot oil. Quickly transfer to a plate, sprinkle with crumbled cheese and onion, then roll up and place in a baking dish. Repeat until all the tortillas are used up. If the sauce threatens to run low, add a little stock. (Note: the tortillas that I have found in Britain tend to be quite fragile; they may be easier to handle if first heated in the oil then dipped in the sauce.)
2. Pour any remaining sauce over the rolled tortillas, cover with foil and place in the oven for about 10 minutes to heat through.
3. To assemble: place the chicken on a platter and surround with the sauce-cloaked vegetables. Accompany with the *enchiladas*. Serve with lots of chilled beer.

Mole Poblano de Guajalote
Puebla-Style Turkey

Perhaps the single greatest festive dish of Mexico, Mole Poblano is often thought of outside the country as a curiosity: turkey with chocolate sauce?

Don't, however, expect a chocolate pudding sauce slathered over the bird, not unless it is badly made. A *mole* is a complex layered sauce of toasted and ground nuts, crushed raisins, soaked and puréed chillies, spices, and a little semi-sweet chocolate added at the end. There is not enough chocolate to make it sweet, only enough to set off the rest of the spicy and rich ingredients.

Though the nuns of the seventeenth-century Puebla convents are often given credit for the creation of this dish, it is more likely to have originated in ancient times in the state of Chiapas, once a part of the Mayan empire. There they have a tradition of chillied stews seasoned with chocolate; as with other chocolate dishes the women were forbidden to taste it. The men who could eat it were limited to the emperor, military nobility, important merchants, and clergy. Though the name is usually indicated as a Spanish derivative of *moler*, which means to grind, it could also reflect the Aztec word *molli*, meaning chillied foods.

◁◁◁◁◁◁◁◁◁◁◁◁◁◁◁◁◁◁◁◁◁◁◁◁◁◁◁◁◁◁◁◁◁◁◁▷▷▷▷▷▷▷▷▷▷▷▷▷▷▷▷▷▷▷▷▷▷▷▷▷▷

Mole Poblano is often sold in Mexico as a thick paste, ready to be mixed with stock to transform the dark, reddish-blackish paste into a rich sauce. Sometimes it is very good this way, other times not. Traditionally Mole is served with unfilled *tamales*, though I prefer corn tortillas to roll up into little *tacos*, or flour tortillas to make big plump *burritos*. Serving Mole Poblano with a bowl of steamed rice and a selection of fresh vegetable condiments – coriander, radishes, onions, tomatoes, fried plantains – and salsa makes a deliciously festive presentation.

The list of ingredients is long, but the preparation is easy. You merely need to simmer, soak, toast, then grind it all together and simmer it merrily to meld the flavours.

$^1/_2$ smallish turkey, or 1 whole chicken
2 bay leaves
2 onions
2 cloves garlic
3 or 4 stock cubes

Mole Sauce

8 dried pasilla chillies (smooth-skinned, dark-red ones)
6 dried negro or ancho chillies (wrinkly-skinned, dark ones)
2 dried New Mexico chillies (smooth-skinned, lightish-red ones) (optional)
25 g/1 oz raisins
35 g/1$^1/_2$ oz unblanched almonds
25 g/1 oz sesame seeds
25 g/1 oz shelled pumpkin seeds
1 large slice French bread or crusty wholewheat bread, torn into bite-sized pieces
1 corn tortilla, broken or cut up
12 g/$^1/_2$ oz roasted peanuts
1 onion, chopped
4 cloves garlic, chopped
325 g/12 oz tomatoes, chopped (tinned is fine)
3 tablespoons vegetable oil or lard
Pinch of fennel seeds
$^1/_4$ teaspoon ground cloves

◁◁◁◁◁◁◁◁◁◁◁◁◁◁◁◁◁◁◁◁◁◁◁◁◁◁◁◁◁▷▷▷▷▷▷▷▷▷▷▷▷▷▷▷▷▷▷▷▷▷▷▷▷▷▷▷▷▷

$1/_2$ teaspoon ground cinnamon, more if needed

35 g/1$1/_2$ oz semisweet chocolate (Bournville or similar is fine)

Several drops of vanilla essence (optional)

Salt and black pepper to taste

Toasted sesame seeds for sprinkling

1. Place the turkey or chicken in a large pot with the bay leaves, onions and garlic and fill the pot with water. Add the stock cubes.

2. Bring to the boil, skim the scum that rises to the surface, and reduce the heat. Simmer on a low heat for 2 to 3 hours or until the bird is tender and the soup rich.

3. Pour hot stock from the simmering turkey over the chillies to cover. Place a plate over the bowl and leave for about an hour, or until the chilli flesh is completely soft.

4. Meanwhile, pour about 100 ml/4 fl oz hot stock over the raisins in a bowl and leave them to plump up.

5. Place the almonds, sesame seeds, pumpkin seeds, bread chunks and tortilla pieces on a baking sheet. Bake in the oven at 180°C/350°F/gas mark 4 for 15 minutes, or long enough to lightly toast it all. You will probably need to toss it several times with a spoon.

6. When the mixture is lightly toasted grind in a liquidizer with the peanuts until it is a mealy consistency. Set aside.

7. When the raisins are tender, purée along with their soaking liquid. Set aside.

8. In a liquidizer or food processor blend the onion and garlic, then add the tomatoes and whirl together into a sauce. Set aside.

9. When the chillies have softened, cut open, saving their liquid for the sauce, and scrape the tender flesh away from the tough skin, using a blunt knife; if the chillies have softened well enough, the flesh should pull away relatively easily. Add the flesh to the tomato mixture and purée, then combine this with the puréed raisins and ground nuts mixture.

10. Heat the oil or lard in a heavy frying pan, then add the sauce. Let the mixture fry-simmer, then add the reserved

chilli soaking liquid to thin it out a bit. Simmer for about 10 minutes, then add the fennel seeds, cloves, cinnamon and chocolate, and the vanilla essence if using, and continue to cook for another 10 minutes or so.

11. As with so many complex simmered dishes, Mole is best at least a day after making. Joint the turkey or chicken and reheat either by simmering it or by browning it in a heavy frying pan. Heat the sauce separately, ladle it over the hot turkey or chicken, and serve immediately, sprinkled with sesame seeds.

VARIATION

Burritos de Mole Poblano: cut or tear the simmered chicken or turkey into bite-sized bits. Brown them in a frying pan, using a little of the fat from the stock. Add several ladlefuls of the *mole* sauce and simmer a minute or two to heat through, then roll up in warmed flour tortillas, along with shredded lettuce and spring onions.

Pollo Estilo Mazatlán
Mazatlán-Style Chicken

Umbrella-shaded tables are set out under the broiling Mexican sun in the open-air marketplaces of Mazatlán where tourists and locals alike tuck into platters of chicken with cooked and raw vegetables, all splashed with a mild salsa. The weather is sultry and the chicken is usually tepid rather than piping hot, somewhat like a warm salad. Beef is served the same way, and I suspect any cooked and tender meat would be a good candidate. While it is an easy dish to prepare you really do need a good homemade salsa. But frozen homemade salsa, defrosted, would work fine here, since it is to be mixed with tomatoes for a milder sauce.

It is a simple but hearty platter, enchanting in its flavour and lack of pretensions. In Mazatlán it is likely to be served with a *cazuelita* of creamy refried beans and a stack of warm corn tortillas.

◁◁◁◁◁◁◁◁◁◁◁◁◁◁◁◁◁◁◁◁◁◁◁◁◁◁◁◁◁◁▷▷▷▷▷▷▷▷▷▷▷▷▷▷▷▷▷▷▷▷▷▷▷▷▷▷▷▷▷

1 kg/2¼ lb ripe tomatoes, peeled and diced (tinned, with
   their juice, is fine)
Several spoonfuls homemade hot salsa such as Salsa de
   Chiles y Ajo (page 23) or Salsa de Chile Güero (page 24)
1 cooked chicken, cut into serving pieces
Oil for frying
Salt and black pepper to taste
4 large, waxy potatoes, boiled and cooled in their skins
½ teaspoon oregano leaves, crumbled
3 large courgettes, sliced or cut into large dice, cooked,
   then tossed with a few shakes of wine vinegar
175 to 225 g/6 to 8 oz just-tender cooked green beans
Shredded lettuce
1 avocado, peeled and sliced
Radish roses or slices
1 onion, chopped
2 tablespoons chopped coriander leaves or parsley

1. Purée the tomatoes with several spoonfuls of salsa. Reserve
   the rest of the salsa to serve separately.
2. Brown the chicken in a little oil; sprinkle with salt and pepper
   and place on a platter to keep warm.
3. Brown the potatoes, adding a little more oil if needed.
   Sprinkle both potatoes and chicken with oregano.
4. Arrange the potatoes on the platter with the chicken and add
   the courgettes, green beans and shredded lettuce. Splash the
   tomato-salsa over it all, as desired.
5. Serve garnished with the avocado, radishes, chopped onion,
   and coriander or parsley and with extra salsa on the side.

Pato con Naranja y Yerba Buena
Red Chilli-Seasoned Roast Duck with Oranges and Mint

Fresh mint has an amazing affinity with mild chilli, especially
when combined with the classic duck and orange.

This duck is worthy of a place in a celebration meal. For a
traditional Mexican *comida*, start with the lush and invigorating

◁◁◁▷▷▷▷▷▷▷▷▷▷▷▷▷▷▷▷▷▷▷▷▷▷▷▷▷▷

Sopa de Frijole Negro y Tortillas (page 70), and follow with
Arroz Verde (page 191). A salad of *nopales* sprinkled with Feta or
goat's cheese would be a good accompaniment to the duck and,
of course, a stack of corn tortillas and salsa of choice.

1 medium-sized duck
Salt and black pepper to taste
1 orange, cut in half
1 head garlic, left intact
2 tablespoons mild chilli powder (or ancho chilli powder)
2 tablespoons paprika (or New Mexico chilli powder)
2 tablespoons tequila
300 ml/10 fl oz orange juice
3 cloves garlic, chopped
2 to 3 tablespoons coarsely chopped fresh mint leaves

1. Cut off excess fat from the neck of the duck and reserve it to
   make crackling. Prick the duck all over with a fork, then place
   in a roasting tin (putting the duck on a rack will give it an all-
   over crispness; letting it sit in its own juices won't). Sprinkle
   with salt and pepper, then stuff it with the orange halves and
   garlic.
2. Roast the duck in the oven at 230°C/450°F/gas mark 8 for 30
   minutes, then remove from the oven and let cool. This
   preliminary roasting may be done the day before, if preferred,
   so you can lift the fat from the dripping when it is cool and
   solidified.
3. Meanwhile, make the chilli paste. Combine the chilli powder
   and paprika with the tequila, 50 ml/2 fl oz orange juice
   (enough to make a paste), and the chopped garlic. Rub well
   on to the duck.
4. Roast the chilli-coated duck in the oven at 180°C/350°F/gas
   mark 4 for 40 to 50 minutes or until it is tender, its skin
   crispy and not fatty, with juices that run clear when a fork is
   inserted in the fleshy part of the leg.
5. Transfer the duck to a platter and keep warm. Spoon off the
   fat from the bottom of the tin, then pour in the remaining
   orange juice. Over a high heat stir the juice into the pan
   drippings, taking care to get the brown bits mixed well.

Cook over a high heat until reduced to about 75 ml/3 fl oz.
6. Serve the duck with this intensely flavoured sauce, the whole
   thing sprinkled with the chopped mint.

VARIATION

Dice any leftover chilli-coated duck and toss it into cooked rice,
along with sautéed pineapple chunks, slices of fresh, ripe red
chillies and a sprinkling of coarsely chopped toasted peanuts.

A FEW SIMPLE MEXICAN POULTRY DISHES

Take simmered or boiled chicken or turkey thighs, breasts, or
other chunks of meat. Rub with Recado Rojo Enchilado (page
43) or mild chilli powder mixed with paprika, garlic, oregano,
cumin, salt, and beer or orange juice. Roast in a hot oven for 15
minutes or just long enough to heat through and give a crispy
edge. Serve sprinkled with coriander leaves.

Coat uncooked chicken thighs with Recado Rojo Enchilado
(page 43); add quartered potatoes and a drizzle of oil and roast
until both are almost tender. Add a handful of green olives and
finish baking.

Top lightly sautéed boneless chicken breasts with a layer of fairly
mild homemade salsa, then a layer of grated or thinly sliced
cheese. Grill until bubbly.

Pollo en Mole Colorado, from Oaxaca: combine mild Salsa Verde
(page 26) with puréed rehydrated ancho chillies, season with garlic and cumin and heat in a little oil to concentrate the flavours.
Add a simmered chicken to this sauce and heat through.

Add a dash of salsa and pineapple juice to your favourite marinade for charcoal-grilled chicken. Serve sprinkled with coriander
and chillies, and offer tortillas to wrap up the chicken in.

CARNES
Meat

Meats of all sorts figure prominently in the Mexican kitchen, though often in tiny amounts, and combined with vegetables, starches or fruits.

Pork is probably the most common meat on the Mexican table, but beef is the meat of choice in the northern regions, as it is in Texas, Arizona and New Mexico. Lamb is popular in the central regions, especially for a barbecue or in a *birria* (spicy stew); so is *cabrito*, or roast kid. Rabbit is occasionally eaten, usually stewed in chilli-based sauces such as *adobo*, or in sauces also used for cooking chicken. Other, more exotic meats appear as well: wild deer (a favourite in the Yucatán), iguana (Guerro), giant terrapin (on the South Pacific coast), armadillo (in the northern desert regions; coyly said to give 'vigour' to men), and others.

As in all peasant kitchens and great cuisines alike, no part of the animal is wasted. A whole or half pig's head seasons the traditional stew called *pozole*. The trotters are prized, especially in Jalisco, where they top *tostadas*. The fat of the pig is rendered into lard, the main ingredient that transformed Indian food into Mexican food as we now know it. Even the skin and blood are used: the skin to make huge sheets of crisp *chicharrones*, the blood for *morcilla*, a mint-and-coriander-scented blood pudding. Brains, especially beef and sheep's, are *muy Mexicana*, doted on with a passion probably inherited from the French occupation; they make delicate fillings for *tacos* or *quesadillas*. Throughout the land tripe is stewed into *menudo*, a hearty soup, and livers are spiced vigorously and sautéed into rich, brown stews, then rolled up in thin, warm tortillas. Oxtail is sliced and simmered with pink beans for a favourite soup, and if you happen to be at a cowboy-style barbecue the choicest bits of meat are the unmentionable ones.

ⵕⵕ

Whichever beast or cut of meat is chosen, the choice of seasonings and cooking methods is nearly endless. Often it is rubbed with spices and slow-roasted whole over an open fire. In the central regions, where maguey plants abound, great pits are dug and filled with hot rocks, then maguey-leaf-wrapped parcels of meat are left to cook slowly over the hot embers. Sometimes beef, lamb, or pork are pounded, coated with a spicy marinade, then grilled quickly over an open fire, barbecue style, called *carne asada*. Or chunks of meat may be sautéed, baked, roasted, or simmered with a variety of vegetables, beans, herbs, etc. However, the most common way to prepare meat, regardless of the spicing, is as it is with poultry: simmer until it is tender, then either brown or roast it and serve shredded or diced in small amounts. This gives two dishes from one piece of meat: first soup, then the meat course. Roasting, it is often implied, is wasteful, 'a cooking method for rich people'.

Carnitas a la Casera
Crispy, Tender Bits of Pork

Carnitas, meaning 'little meats', make wonderful fillings for *tacos*, *enchiladas*, *burritos*, *tortas*, and so on. In the marketplaces *carnitas* are simmered in great vats, the fat rendered out of the meat almost in the same way as in the French *confit*. The whole pig is usually prepared this way, and often the chunks of meat are served on a large round of crackling, or *chicarrón*, as a rich and crisp edible plate. It is traditionally eaten sprinkled with a dusting of mild pasilla chilli (or a mild chilli powder) and guacamole, fresh salsa, and a bowl of barely minutes-old warm corn tortillas.

Homemade *carnitas* are slightly different. To prepare the *carnitas*, homestyle, first simmer a large joint of pork, then place it in the oven and roast until tender. A bonus to this process is a large pot of broth for next day's soup.

Serve the succulent meat with a selection of salsas: a rich mild pasilla or ancho one, a feisty raw one, a tart tomatillo salsa, and a lip-searing fresh chilli mixture.

◁◁◁◁◁◁◁◁◁◁◁◁◁◁◁◁◁◁◁◁◁◁◁◁◁◁◁◁◁◁▷▷▷▷▷▷▷▷▷▷▷▷▷▷▷▷▷▷▷▷▷▷▷▷▷▷▷▷▷

1 pork leg joint, about 1 kg/2¼ lb (or use 1.4 kg/3 lb meaty
   spare ribs)
1 onion, cut into halves
2 cloves garlic
1 teaspoon salt
½ teaspoon oregano leaves, crushed
½ teaspoon cumin
Salt and pepper, and mild chilli powder to taste

1. Place the meat in a large pot and add the onion, garlic, salt,
   oregano, cumin, and water to cover.
2. Bring to the boil, then reduce the heat and simmer, covered,
   for 2 hours.
3. Drain the meat, reserving the stock for another use (add a
   stock cube or two to boost the flavour and you have the basis
   for a delicious soup). Place the meat in a baking tray and
   sprinkle evenly with salt, pepper and mild chilli powder.
4. Bake in the oven at 180°C/350°F/gas mark 4 for 45 minutes.
   Remove from the oven and, when still warm, shred with a
   fork.

VARIATION

Duck or Lamb Carnitas: duck, especially the dark-fleshed thigh
and leg with their rather fatty quality, takes readily to *carnitas*
preparation as does the rich meat of lamb. The fat is drained
away, leaving a succulent, lean meat. The tender yet crisp pieces
of duck or lamb are delicious shredded and added to *tostadas*,
tacos, salads, *tortas*, and the like.

   Follow the recipe above but use a very small amount of water
in the initial cooking (about 2.5 cm/1 in deep), and decrease the
initial cooking time to 40 minutes and the second one to 30 minutes or so. For a new-wave presentation, serve the shredded duck
or lamb on a bed of mixed salad leaves, with a vinaigrette
enhanced with Salsa Verde (page 26).

◄◄◄◄◄◄◄◄◄◄◄◄◄◄◄◄◄◄◄◄◄◄◄◄◄►►►►►►►►►►►►►►►►►►►►►►►►►►►

Carnitas en Otro Estilo
Fragrant Marinated Pork

Marinating the pork in lots of garlic, onions, bay leaves and herbs gives an almost Mediterranean scent to this dish. The meat is coated with a layer of fat before it is marinated. Traditionally this fat is seasoned lard, but I use a bland vegetable oil for health reasons and find that it produces a lovely dish, especially because pork is so lean these days that it benefits from a little delicate fat. (Note: since you simmer the meat after it has been browned, the fat can easily be skimmed from the chilled stock.)

Use this fragrant meat to layer on top of *tostadas* or *masa antojitos*, to grind and stuff into *tacos*, to shred and use inside *tortas* and so on. Or you could serve the meat on a platter, accompanied by chopped onions, coriander leaves, several salsas and a stack of soft warm tortillas for D-I-Y *tacos*.

450 g/1 lb boneless pork of choice, cut into larger than
   bite-sized pieces
Salt and pepper to taste
2 heads garlic, left whole, but each clove lightly crushed to
   remove the skin
3 onions, sliced
5 bay leaves
5 sprigs of fresh oregano or marjoram
Pinch of dried thyme or several sprigs of fresh thyme
50 ml/2 fl oz vegetable oil
750 ml/1¼ pints stock and water mixed (or water plus 1 or
   2 stock cubes)

1. Place the pork in a non-corrosive pot or bowl. Mix with the salt, pepper, garlic, onions, bay leaves, oregano or marjoram, thyme and vegetable oil, and marinate for at least 2 hours, preferably overnight in the refrigerator.
2. Heat a heavy pan and brown the meat together with the garlic, onion and seasonings in the marinating oil. When browned in parts, add the stock and water. Bring to the boil, then reduce the heat and cover, cooking at a low simmer until tender.

◁◁◁◁◁◁◁◁◁◁◁◁◁◁◁◁◁◁◁◁◁◁◁◁◁◁◁◁◁◁◁◁◁◁◁◁▷▷▷▷▷▷▷▷▷▷▷▷▷▷▷▷▷▷▷▷▷▷▷▷▷▷▷▷

3. Serve the meat chopped into small pieces, as desired. Reserve
   the stock for soups or sauces (skimming off the excess fat if
   needed). The stock may be diluted with a little water if it is
   too strong.

VARIATION

Tacos de Mercado: sauté diced potato, onion and courgettes (or
carrots, peas, green beans etc). Process some of the meat from
the above recipe in a liquidizer, along with enough of the stock
to make a paste and as many bits of tender onion and garlic as
you can fish out. Add this meat paste to the browned vegetables,
season with mild chilli or a little fiery/smoky chipotle chilli marinade, and roll up into warm corn tortillas, sprinkled with a little
chopped onion if desired.

Lengua
Tongue

In Mexico, tongue is considered among the choicest of cuts. To
be at its best, however, the tongue must first be simmered until
tender. It may then be sauced as desired: chopped into a Picadillo
(page 180), where the slightly sweet raisins enhance its bland,
mild nature; simmered into a rich chillied *adobo*, tossed into a
tinga, or julienned and enjoyed cool, dressed in a vinaigrette,
salpicón-style. Salsa Verde (page 26) is particularly good with
tongue, either as a condiment or simmered together as a sauced
dish. Tongue is good, too, sliced and reheated in Salsa Ranchera
(page 32) with or without a little smoky chipotle chilli.

Combine a fresh beef tongue with 1 onion, 5 to 10 cloves garlic, several bay leaves, and water to fill the pot. Bring to the boil,
then reduce the heat and simmer for about 3 hours, or until tender. Let the tongue cool in the stock, then remove and use as
desired.

◁◁◁◁◁◁◁◁◁◁◁◁◁◁◁◁◁◁◁◁◁◁◁◁◁◁▷▷▷▷▷▷▷▷▷▷▷▷▷▷▷▷▷▷▷▷▷▷▷▷

Mancha Manteles
'Tablecloth Stainer'

How this got its name is not certain; likely it is the red-hued, soupy chilli-fruit sauce that tends to splash around, much to the detriment of the tablecloth.

The dish is a classic, with a number of variations. It may be prepared from chicken, pork, or a mixture of the two; it always has a selection of fruit, though exactly which fruit are included varies according to each recipe – and the marketplace. Chorizo is sometimes included for a spicier and more chilli-redolent, richer sauce, and sometimes avocado is used as a garnish. The nuts included can vary too – some use almonds or even walnuts rather than peanuts.

    1 onion, diced
    2 cloves garlic, coarsely chopped
    2 tablespoons vegetable oil
    1 to 2 medium-hot fresh green chillies such as jalapeño,
        seeded and diced
    $1/_4$ to $1/_2$ green pepper, diced
    325 g/12 oz tomatoes, seeded and diced (tinned is fine)
    1 teaspoon cinnamon
    1 tablespoon mild chilli powder (or ancho chilli powder)
    1 tablespoon paprika (or New Mexico red chilli powder)
    5 cloves, whole, or a generous pinch of ground cloves
    1 tablespoon sesame seeds
    50 g/2 oz roasted peanuts
    350 ml/12 fl oz stock of choice
    450 g/1 lb lean stewing pork
    $1/_2$ chicken, jointed
    1 bay leaf
    2 small Cox's apples, sliced
    $1/_2$ orange, sliced or diced
    250 ml/8 fl oz pineapple juice

1. You can make this either by simmering the meat first then layering it with the sauce and simmering or baking to meld the flavours, or you can simply layer the sauce with the meat

⫷⫷⫷⫷⫷⫷⫷⫷⫷⫷⫷⫷⫷⫷⫷⫷⫷⫷⫷⫷⫷⫷⫷⫷⫷⫷⫷⫷⫷⫷⫷⫷⫷⫸⫸⫸⫸⫸⫸⫸⫸⫸⫸⫸⫸⫸⫸⫸⫸⫸⫸⫸⫸⫸⫸⫸⫸⫸

and bake until tender. If presimmering, cut down on the amount of stock in the sauce.

2. Prepare the sauce: in a heavy pan sauté the onion and garlic in the vegetable oil to soften, then add the chillies, green pepper, tomatoes, cinnamon, chilli powder and paprika, cloves, and sesame seeds and cook together for about 10 minutes until a sauce is formed. Add the peanuts and stock and purée until it reaches a smooth consistency.

3. Return the sauce to the pan and add the pork, chicken, bay leaf, apples, orange and pineapple juice. Cover tightly and simmer over a low to medium heat or bake in the oven at 180°C/350°F/gas mark 4 for about 2 hours or until the meat is fork-tender. If using presimmered pork and chicken cook over a low heat for about 20 minutes.

VARIATIONS

Add a diced plantain or banana, allowing 15 minutes' cooking time for the plantain, only a minute or two for the banana.

Pollo con Frutas: prepare the sauce, omitting the meat. Add a diced banana and a handful of green seedless grapes for just a few minutes at the end of cooking. Serve as a sauce alongside a chicken that has been seasoned with a generous amount of mild chilli and stuffed with whole garlic cloves and bay leaves, then roasted to tender succulence.

Santa Fe Chile Verde
Green Chilli and Pork Stew, New Mexico-Style

Santa Fe is a charming small town, not much larger than a village, in austerely beautiful northern New Mexico. It seems incongruous that this place of eerie *mesas* silhouetted against black night sky, of *adobe* architecture and Native American Indian culture is in fact part of the United States. It feels like another world.

The region has maintained its culinary heritage well, steadfastly resisting chain-store sameness. Now the rest of America is

ᐊᐊᐊᐊᐊᐊᐊᐊᐊᐊᐊᐊᐊᐊᐊᐊᐊᐊᐊᐊᐊᐊᐊᐊᐊᐊᐊ◊ᐳᐳᐳᐳᐳᐳᐳᐳᐳᐳᐳᐳᐳᐳᐳᐳᐳᐳᐳᐳᐳᐳᐳᐳᐳᐳᐳ

rediscovering and encouraging regional cuisines, especially spicy ones, and chic restaurateurs have been flocking to the Southwest, offering provocative new interpretations of traditional foods.

Luckily, the traditional dishes have not been lost. Great, spicy, sloppy stews still reign, able to feed a large family and stretch to include any last-minute guests by adding a handful of beans, an extra stack of tortillas, etc.

This green chilli and pork stew is one of my favourites. It is delectable, especially served in shallow soup bowls, accompanied by tortillas. When making stews like this, make a big pot, then any left over can be used in *enchiladas*, *tostadas*, *tortas*, etc.

1 to 1.4 kg/2¼ to 3 lb pork shoulder, cut into
    1.25 to 2.5 cm/½ to 1 in dice
Flour for dredging
Oil for sautéing
3 onions, diced
5 cloves garlic, chopped
10 fresh large green chillies (or 5 green peppers with 3 to 5
    medium chillies), roasted (see Glossary), seeded, peeled
    and cut into strips
500 ml/16 fl oz chicken, pork, beef or vegetable stock
25 g/1 oz coriander leaves, coarsely chopped
675 g/1½ lb tomatoes, chopped (tinned, with juice, is fine)
Generous pinch of oregano, crumbled
Cayenne pepper to taste
Salt if needed
Chopped radishes and soft warm flour tortillas, to serve

1. Dredge the meat with flour. Brown in a little oil, then add the onions and garlic and cook until the onions are translucent and softened.
2. Add the chillies (or peppers and chillies), stock, coriander, tomatoes, oregano, cayenne, and salt if necessary. Simmer over a low heat, covered, until the meat is very tender, adding more water or stock if needed.
3. Serve the tender meat in shallow soup bowls or on plates, with lots of sauce, accompanied by chopped radishes and soft warm flour tortillas.

◁◁◁◁◁◁◁◁◁◁◁◁◁◁◁◁◁◁◁◁◁◁◁◁▷▷▷▷▷▷▷▷▷▷▷▷▷▷▷▷▷▷▷▷▷▷▷▷▷

Puerco con Verdolagas
Pork with Purslane

Native to Europe, purslane grows widely in North America and Mexico. It is delicious raw, and its slightly acidic flavour is good in a simple tomato salad, dressed with olive oil and studded with salty black olives.

In Mexico it is frequently served cooked, as in the following pork stew, which combines the piquancy of the herb with the equally piquant tomatillos and spicy chillies.

  4 pork chops or 450 g/1 lb boneless pork stewing meat (or
      meaty spareribs or other meat and bone cuts – allow
      extra weight for the bones)
  1 small to medium onion, chopped
  3 garlic cloves, chopped
  750 ml/1¼ pints light chicken or vegetable stock
  8 to 10 tomatillos (or a handful of raw gooseberries or
      shredded sorrel, if tomatillos are unavailable)
  3 medium-hot fresh chillies, chopped (for a milder, subtler
      flavour, roast, peel, seed and chop chillies before using)
  Vegetable oil for sautéing
  450 g/1 lb purslane (it sounds like a lot, but much of that is
      thick stems that you will discard)

1. Place the pork, onion and garlic in a heavy pan with the stock. Cover and simmer for about 30 minutes, or until the pork is quite tender.
2. Remove the pork from the stock and set aside.
3. Add the tomatillos and chillies to the stock. Bring to the boil, then simmer until tender, about 5 minutes. Purée to make a sauce and set aside.
4. Remove the tender, succulent leaves and small stems from the large stems of the purslane. Discard the big stems.
5. Sauté the reserved pork in a little oil until well browned and crispy. Add the reserved sauce and the purslane and bring to the boil, cooking over a medium-high heat for 5 to 10 minutes or long enough for the sauce to thicken a bit.
6. Serve immediately, accompanied by warm corn tortillas or unfilled *tamales*.

◄◄◄◄◄◄◄◄◄◄◄◄◄◄◄◄◄◄◄◄◄◄◄◄◄◄◄◄◄◄◄◄◄►►►►►►►►►►►►►►►►►►►►►►►►►►►►►

Puerco con Piña
Pork in Pineapple Juice with Peppers and Prunes

Moorish influences echo in this spicy-sweet stew, with its sprinkling of sesame seeds as a contrast of taste and texture to the rich,
deeply flavoured sauce. Traditionally the sauce in this dish would
be puréed, but I like the interest the texture provides: the strands
of sweet onion, the tiny bits of prune, the sweet bites of red pepper, all awash in the spicy pineapple sauce.

Though the recipe calls for pork, this would be equally good
prepared with turkey thigh or even, I think, a vegetarian alternative such as *tofu*.

2 onions, sliced
3 cloves garlic, coarsely chopped
450 g/1 lb pork chops, boned and cut into bite-sized pieces
2 tablespoons vegetable oil, or as needed
1 red pepper, roasted, peeled and cut into strips
1 to 1¹/₂ tablespoons pure mild chilli powder such as ancho
    or pasilla, or use a mixture of mild chilli powder and
    paprika
3 small to medium tomatoes, coarsely chopped
3 to 4 prunes, pitted and diced
350 ml/12 fl oz pineapple juice
25 g/1 oz toasted sesame seeds

1. Brown the onions, garlic and pork in the vegetable oil.
2. When browned in parts, add the roasted red pepper, chilli
   powder, tomatoes, prunes and pineapple juice.
3. Bring to the boil, then reduce the heat, cover and simmer
   until the meat is tender, about an hour. Remove the lid and
   cook further to evaporate and concentrate the sauce, if
   needed.
4. Serve sprinkled with toasted sesame seeds.

ᐊᐊᐊᐊᐊᐊᐊᐊᐊᐊᐊᐊᐊᐊᐊᐊᐊᐊᐊᐊᐊᐊᐊᐊᐊᐊᐊᐊᐊᐊᐊ▷▷▷▷▷▷▷▷▷▷▷▷▷▷▷▷▷▷▷▷▷▷▷▷▷▷▷▷

Chile Colorado
Red Chilli Stew, Sonora-Style

This is a classic 'bowl of red', a simple stew rather than its tarted-up descendants. You'll find Chile Colorado in many guises throughout the Southwest and into the northern state of Sonora. It is typical *charro*, or cowboy fare, a combination of Spanish beef with Indian chilli stewing. Note that there are no tomatoes or other elaborations – this should taste as austere and direct as a night spent under a desert sky, and equally as satisfying.

Serve Chile Colorado in shallow soup plates with soft flour tortillas to scoop up the meat and make impromptu *burritos* with. If *masa harina* is unavailable, whirl several broken-up *tostada* or *taco* shells in a food processor until it becomes a sort of meal or coarse flour and use that to thicken the stew.

3 to 5 pasilla chillies
3 to 5 ancho chillies
1 tablespoon ground cumin
2 small to medium onions, chopped
5 cloves garlic, coarsely chopped
2 tablespoons vegetable oil
1 kg/2¼ lb lean beef, cut into bite-sized cubes
1 teaspoon salt and/or a stock cube
350 ml/12 fl oz lager
50 g/2 oz *masa harina*
Salsa or cayenne pepper to taste

1. Pour hot but not boiling water over the chillies in a bowl and leave, covered, until they are softened. Remove the stems and purée the flesh, then put through a strainer or sieve to extract the tough bits of skin.
2. Toast the cumin in a heavy, ungreased frying pan until it smells fragrant. Remove before it burns and set aside.
3. Sauté the onions and garlic in the oil until softened, then add the meat and brown. Add the reserved puréed chillies, the salt and/or stock cube, and lager then bring to the boil. Reduce the heat, cover, and simmer over a low heat until the meat is tender, about 2 to 3 hours, adding water or stock if more liquid is needed.

◄◄◄◄◄◄◄◄◄◄◄◄◄◄◄◄◄◄◄◄◄◄◄◄◄►►►►►►►►►►►►►►►►►►►►►►►►►

4. When the meat is tender, make a paste of the *masa harina* and some of the simmering liquid, then add to the stew. Return to the simmer and cook, stirring every so often, until the stew thickens somewhat. Season to taste with salsa or cayenne and either serve right away or let cool and serve the next day. As with all long-simmered dishes, it's even better the day after making (you'll probably have to thin it with a little stock or water when you reheat it).

VARIATIONS

Texas Chile con Carne (Bowl o' Red): use coarsely minced beef instead of stewing steak, and season with a little crumbled oregano. Cooked red kidney beans could be added towards the end of cooking, but many Texans consider this a reason to go for their guns. Ditto for tomatoes. Use the above recipe as a guide, then follow your own taste for seasonings and extras.

The thing about Texas Chile con Carne as opposed to other Southwestern versions is that everyone has his or her own opinion rather than geographical straitjacket. The main rule is that almost anything goes; chilli aficionados, usually descriptively grizzly and scratchy-voiced, add some of the most alarming ingredients. You can see them in chilli cook-offs, each adding his or her 'secret ingredient': sometimes as prosaic as a splash of ketchup, other times as alarming as a jar of red ants, the ashes of three cigarettes, or the diced flesh of a snake.

Vegetarian Chilli: prepare the Texas Chile without the meat. Add about 250 ml/8 fl oz chopped tomatoes or tomato sauce, to taste, and a good sprinkling of oregano. A generous sprinkling of mild chilli powder and paprika builds a lovely layer of flavour on top of the mild chillies. Add cooked red kidney or pink pinto beans to taste and simmer for a half-hour or so, to meld the flavours.

Whichever Chile con Carne you prepare, it is at its classic best when topped with lots of chopped onion, grated Cheddar cheese and shredded lettuce, a spoonful of salsa and a splodge of soured cream. Some add diced avocado as well. Serve with corn or flour tortillas, Mexican Southwest-style, or with crisp cream crackers or water biscuits.

<⫷⫷>

Ropa Vieja
Shredded Beef

Ropa Vieja translates as 'old clothes'. Perhaps it is because the meat is shredded, as old clothes are apt to become; more likely there is no reason at all, and it is yet another example of the Mexican habit of giving rather whimsical names to dishes.

Though this is one of the simplest dishes to prepare, demanding little from the cook, it does, however, need a long simmering time. This makes it great for cook-ahead meals.

Ropa Vieja is eaten with soft flour tortillas for D-I-Y *burritos*; it also makes a great filling for *chimichangas*, or to layer with corn tortillas, then top with a mild chilli or *ranchera* sauce and a fried egg or two. Try Ropa Vieja with a handful of diced cooked potatoes added when you cook the shredded meat, or seasoning the meat with a little oregano and/or cumin. It makes a great basis for all sorts of flights of culinary fancy, yet it remains homely unpretentious fare.

1.4 kg/3 lb flank steak or beef chuck
350 ml/12 fl oz water or stock or cover
10 cloves garlic, whole
Several grindings of coarse black pepper
Salt to taste (unless using stock for cooking)
25 g/1 oz lard or 2 tablespoons vegetable oil
2 onions, sliced
4 small to medium fresh green chillies such as jalapeño, Kenya, etc, roasted (see Glossary), peeled, seeded and coarsely chopped
1 green pepper, roasted, peeled, seeded and coarsely chopped

1. Place the beef with the water or stock, 7 whole, unpeeled cloves of garlic, black pepper and salt, if using, in a heavy cast-iron or similar pan. Cover tightly, and simmer over a low heat for 2 to 3 hours or until the meat is tender and very well cooked through. It is important that the cover fits tightly or the liquid will evaporate. If you have any doubts, check and add liquid if needed.

2. When the meat is tender, remove from the heat and let it cool in its own liquid.
3. When cool enough to handle, remove the meat from the liquid. Pull it apart with your fingers, forming long shreds. Return the meat to the soaking liquid.
4. Peel and chop the remaining 3 garlic cloves, heat the lard or oil in a large heavy frying pan, then add the garlic and quickly stir it through the hot oil, taking care not to let it burn. Add the onions and sauté until softened, about 5 minutes, then add the chillies and green pepper. Add this mixture to the shredded meat.
5. Cook again, this time uncovered and over a medium-high heat, until the flavours are blended and most of the liquid has evaporated, about 10 minutes. Serve immediately.

VARIATION

Mochomos: in Chihuahua a similar dish is prepared using pork; the crisp shreds of meat are served topped with guacamole, shredded lettuce and diced tomatoes.

Albondigas y Ejotes
Meatballs and Green Beans in Broth

Green beans add a fresh counterpoint to the chilli-flavoured broth. For a main-meal soup rather than a stew, increase the stock accordingly.

Serve with fresh corn tortillas (slightly thick homemade ones are good) fried into a crispy croûton-like pieces to float in the rich broth.

◁◁◁◁◁◁◁◁◁◁◁◁◁◁◁◁◁◁◁◁◁◁◁◁◁◁◁◁◁◁◁◁◁◁◁▷▷▷▷▷▷▷▷▷▷▷▷▷▷▷▷▷▷▷▷▷▷▷▷▷▷▷

8 oz/225 g lean minced beef
1 small to medium courgette, finely chopped
2 teaspoons finely chopped coriander leaves
1 teaspoon mild red chilli powder
¼ to ½ teaspoon cumin powder
25 to 50 g/1 to 2 oz cooked rice or finely ground corn chips
500 ml/16 fl oz beef stock
175 to 225 g/6 to 8 oz green beans
Either warm corn tortillas as accompaniment, or several
   corn tortillas cut into strips and fried until golden brown
   and crispy

1. Mix together the beef, courgette, coriander, about half the
   chilli powder and cumin, and the rice or ground corn chips.
   Roll into meatballs and set aside.
2. Heat the stock with the remaining chilli powder and cumin;
   when boiling, reduce the heat to a simmer and add the
   meatballs. Cook, covered, over a medium heat for about 5
   minutes, then add the green beans and continue cooking until
   the meatballs are cooked through.
3. Serve immediately, spooning the meatballs and green beans
   into bowls along with a little broth. Accompany with warm
   corn tortillas or top with strips of golden fried ones.

LEFTOVERS

Marketplace tacos: crumble and brown any leftover meatballs in a
hot frying pan along with an equal amount of the green beans.
Add a spoonful of rice, heat together and roll up in a warm corn
tortilla. Add salsa to taste.

Picadillo
Spiced Minced Beef Hash with Raisins and Nuts, Oaxaca-Style

Versions of Picadillo, a sort of minced or shredded meat hash,
are enjoyed throughout Mexico and the Caribbean. Its name
comes from the Spanish, *picar*, to mince. The nuts, sherry and

ᐊᐊᐊᐊᐊᐊᐊᐊᐊᐊᐊᐊᐊᐊᐊᐊᐊᐊᐊᐊᐊᐊᐊ◇▷▷▷▷▷▷▷▷▷▷▷▷▷▷▷▷▷▷▷▷▷▷▷

sweet spices also reflect its Spanish heritage.

It is a dish that is eaten all over Mexico, changing from region to region. In the northern regions it is heavier on the garlic, and might have a handful of green olives stirred in. Often in the central areas diced potatoes are added to the mixture. Sometimes Picadillo is made with boiled and shredded meat rather than minced beef. Sadly, as with hash the world over, often Picadillo is simply a way of stretching a few pathetic leftovers.

This particular Picadillo is from Oaxaca, full of sweet spices, raisins and nuts. It is especially enjoyed as a filling for roasted red peppers or for crisp pastries called *empanadas*; it is good, too, in *tamales*, *burritos* and the like.

    2 onions, chopped
    2 cloves garlic, chopped
    450 g/1 lb minced beef or pork
    1 teaspoon cinnamon
    ¹/₄ teaspoon cloves
    Generous shake each: cumin, cayenne pepper, salt
    25 g/1 oz raisins
    25 g/1 oz roasted almonds or peanuts, coarsely chopped
    2 tablespoons tomato purée
    150 ml/5 fl oz dry sherry or red wine
    1 tablespoon sugar or honey
    1 tablespoon coarsely chopped coriander leaves (optional)
    1 small ripe plantain or 2 medium potatoes
    Oil for frying

1. Brown the onions and garlic in a pan with the meat, then sprinkle in the cinnamon, cloves, cumin, cayenne and salt. Pour off any fat that accumulates.

2. Add the raisins, nuts, tomato purée, sherry or wine, and sugar or honey. Simmer until the mixture has thickened, about 10 to 15 minutes. Taste for seasoning, then sprinkle in the coriander, if using.

3. Meanwhile peel the plantain or potatoes. Cut the plantain into large dice, or if using potatoes cut into small dice. Brown in the oil in a separate pan, then add to the meat mixture. Cook until the plantain or potato is tender and the liquid has nearly evaporated.

◁◁◁◁◁◁◁◁◁◁◁◁◁◁◁◁◁◁◁◁◁◁◁◁◁◁◁◁◁◁▷▷▷▷▷▷▷▷▷▷▷▷▷▷▷▷▷▷▷▷▷▷▷▷▷▷▷▷▷▷▷

BARBACOA Y CARNE ASADA
Barbecued Meats

Roasting meat over an open fire is a Mexican speciality, with many methods and meats to choose from. The English word barbecue in fact comes from the Mexican custom of laying a whole animal on the grill, *barba* (head, or beard) to *coda* (tail). The expression *barba-coda* eventually became *barbacoa* in Mexico and barbecue in the English-speaking world.

Mexican barbecues are apt to feature very simply prepared meats, but with a wide assortment of accompanying goodies. *Frijoles refritos* and tortillas are, of course, perfect partners for barbecued meat, fish or poultry. Vegetables are delicious added to the grill to roast along with the meats: corn, especially, rubbed with melting butter and sprinkled with cayenne pepper before serving. Potatoes taste delicious roasted on the open fire, and are good dipped into chilli salsa. Salads of leafy greens and herbs, a selection of salsas, and a platter of sweet, juicy fruits all provide colourful accompaniments for the roasting meats.

There are many ways of preparing, seasoning and serving the barbecued meats. In the Yucatán, pork is rubbed with a vermilion-coloured paste of achiote seeds, then wrapped in banana leaves and placed in a pit with hot stones, known as a *pib* (see *Pollo Pibil*, page 150) to cook slowly until tender.

In the central highlands, the pit is lined with maguey leaves, then stones, and a hot fire, and on top of that aromatic vegetables, a pot of stock with chickpeas and rice, and the meat – lamb, kid, or beef – on top of this. The whole thing is enclosed in more maguey leaves, a sheet of metal or wood is added and a layer of mud to keep the heat from escaping. It is somewhat like the Yucatecan *pib*, and much like the Hawaiian *luau*. When, after six hours or so, the great feast is unwrapped, it is a celebration! The meat has dripped into the stock and the vegetables. Portions of everything are served along with mountains of tortillas, lots of drink, and a *salsa borracho*, or 'drunken salsa', in which chillies, garlic and onion have been mixed with a little *pulque*. Sometimes a simple *barbacoa*, the meat roasted over an open fire, is accompanied by a smoky broth based on the drippings from the roasted meat and perhaps flavoured with smoky and fiery chipotle chillies. Lamb is delectable like this, and kid is always considered a treat, burnished with a paste of mild chillies and garlic, perhaps a dash of tequila or lime juice and roasted until crispy on the outside and meltingly tender within.

Below are several barbecue ideas of more modest proportions.

Carne Asada
Barbecued Meat Platter

Barbecues of grilled meats – steaks, chorizos, great devilled rib bones – are the basis for a Carne Asada, variations of which are eaten throughout Mexico.

The meat used is usually beef or pork, or both, and very simply seasoned: it might be marinated in a little oil and vinegar, but is more likely to be simply rubbed with salt, pepper, a squeeze of lime juice (in Jalisco it would be orange) and a smear of oil before being grilled over an open flame.

While the meat is prepared simply, it is the accompaniments that make the meal: strips of sautéed sweet and hot peppers, a piece of cheese set out on the grill, melting into a deliciously stringy mass (see Queso Fundito, page 47), plump spicy chorizo or other sausages, guacamole, creamy refried beans or simmered ones, a *cazuela* of cheese-stuffed *enchiladas*, fried bananas, a selection of salsas and relishes and, of course, the ever-present stack of tortillas. A platter of sweet tropical fruit is the perfect accompaniment, or a salad of sliced sweet oranges, red onions and mixed greens, along with icy lager to drink, or tequila mixed with fruit juice.

    4 to 8 plump chorizo sausages or other spicy cooking
      sausages
    325 g/12 oz each: beef tenderloin and pork tenderloin
    4 to 8 spring onions, trimmed (optional)
    12 corn tortillas

1. Place the sausages in a pan and cover with water. Bring to the boil, reduce the heat, and simmer until almost cooked through, about 20 minutes. Drain and let cool.

◁◁◁◁◁◁◁◁◁◁◁◁◁◁◁◁◁◁◁◁◁◁◁◁◁▷▷▷▷▷▷▷▷▷▷▷▷▷▷▷▷▷▷▷▷▷▷▷▷▷

2. Arrange the sausages and steaks over very hot coals, close
   enough to sear the meat, then move them further away so as
   not to overcook them. The pork should just lose its pink
   colour, the beef, of course, should not. Grill the onions, if
   using, and warm the tortillas. Keep any accompaniments
   warm if necessary: if your barbecue is large enough, this can
   be at the back of the grill, or wherever the heat is not so high.
3. Serve as soon as the meat is cooked through – slices of grilled
   meat and sausage flanked by any of the accompaniments
   suggested above.

Chuletas a la Parilla
Chilli Paste-Coated Pork or Lamb Chops, Pounded Flat and Grilled

This is the sort of simple Mexican fare that is so memorable. The
meat is left attached to its bone, the flesh rubbed with a mild red
chilli paste, then pounded to a thin cutlet. This not only tender-
izes the meat and flattens it to a thickness good for quick grilling,
it pushes the chilli paste into the meat so that the flavours per-
meate the flesh rather than lying on top.

Note: the rib lies at the side of the chop, so the meat may be
pounded without chaos ensuing while you try to avoid smashing
the bone.

   1 tablespoon mild chilli powder
   2 teaspoons paprika
   1 teaspoon ground cumin
   3 cloves garlic, chopped
   1 small onion, finely chopped
   2 tablespoons olive or vegetable oil
   4 pork or lamb chops, rib or loin cut, with the bone at the
     side
   Salt to taste
   1 ripe avocado, preferably dark-skinned and rich-tasting,
     sliced

1 orange and/or 2 limes, cut into wedges
Coriander leaves, chopped or whole, to garnish
Salsa of choice

1. Mix together the chilli powder, paprika, cumin, garlic, onion and oil.
2. Slash the fat around the edge of the chops at intervals so that the meat will open up as it is pounded. Spread a spoonful or two of the chilli mixture on to each side of each chop.
3. One by one place a chop between 2 sheets of plastic wrap large enough to let the meat spread by about twice its size. Using the flat side of a meat mallet, pound the meat evenly and firmly, taking care to reach the areas around the bone so that they do not remain too rare while the rest of the cutlets are overcooking. You want an even 0.6 cm/^{1}/$_4$ in thickness for the cutlets.
4. Grill over open coals, about 3 minutes on each side, until the meat is no longer pink at the bone. Sprinkle with salt.
5. Serve immediately, each chop topped with slices of avocado, wedges of orange and/or lime and a scattering of coriander. Offer salsa separately – try a simple Pico de Gallo (page 36) or offer a selection of several sauces, ranging from mild to incendiary.

VARIATION

Sabana: pound tender beef steaks until 0.6 cm/^{1}/$_4$ in thick and coat with the above chilli paste. Place a portion of mashed cooked black beans down the centre of each steak and roll up; secure with bamboo skewers. Grill over an open fire along with spring onions and serve with Arroz Verde (page 191).

◁◁◁◁◁◁◁◁◁◁◁◁◁◁◁◁◁◁◁◁◁◁◁◁◁◁◁◁◁◁◁◁▷▷▷▷▷▷▷▷▷▷▷▷▷▷▷▷▷▷▷▷▷▷▷▷▷▷▷▷▷▷▷

Fajitas
Marinated and Grilled Steak, Served with Pico de Gallo and Flour Tortillas, Rio Grande-Style

Fajitas have become THE Mexican-American dish of recent years, their fame spreading from the cattle ranches and border bars where they have been eaten for generations.

The Fajitas I have had in restaurants outside their region of origin have been no more than sautéed strips of meat, over-cooked and sizzling on a hot grill, with tortillas and every topping imaginable. And I have even seen Fajitas of chicken or fish (when the name itself means 'little belts', referring to the cut of meat). It's enough to make an old cowpoke whinge and whine.

A truly delicious Fajita should be quickly grilled over charcoal, its simple beef flavour undisguised, then it should be wrapped immediately in a warm, soft flour tortilla, along with a spoonful of crunchy chilli-peppered Pico de Gallo, and a small spoonful of guacamole added if desired. The contrast of textures and temperatures is memorable. So too should be your surroundings: ideally the paint will be peeling, you'll have downed several tequilas and limes and be surrounded with wild cowboys and college students; mariachis may be circulating through the very noisy room, adding to the general din and confusion.

To make Fajitas marinate 450 to 675 g/1 to 1½ lb tender beef, preferably the cut that comes from the belly of the beast, with the juice of 3 limes, a shot of tequila, several cloves of chopped garlic, and 1 or 2 chopped chillies. Leave at room temperature for an hour or two, or longer in the refrigerator. Grill over charcoal, then cut into thin strips and serve with warm flour tortillas, Pico de Gallo (page 36), Salsa Picante (page 31) and Guacamole con Jitomates (page 50).

ARROZ, FRIJOLES Y SOPAS SECAS DE MACARONI

Rice, Beans and Pasta Casseroles

Those of us who grew up eating Mexican-American food became aficionados of 'Spanish rice', a red concoction that tasted of tomato, mild red chilli and cheese. I ate it every Tuesday for school dinner and remember it with an embarrassing fondness.

However, this vaguely spicy dish bore little resemblance to the wealth of well-prepared, pilaf-like rice dishes that I tasted when I first visited Mexico. There rice is first sautéed, then simmered in stock with a variety of seasonings: green herbs (Arroz Verde), black bean stock (Arroz Negro), tomatoes, vegetables, and so on. Rice is never served as a hearty main course dish (except for paella which is a popular Sunday afternoon lunch dish in areas with a strong colonial tradition). Rather, rice dishes are usually served at the beginning of a meal, as a course after soup, and are called *sopa seca*, or 'dry soup'.

Sopa seca refers not only to rice, but also to pasta casseroles cooked in stock and tortilla casseroles baked with stock and zesty seasonings (see Tortillas, Tortilla Dishes and Tamales for the latter).

Beans come to the table alongside the main course, or sometimes just a few spoonfuls at the end. Indeed, it is said that 'a proper meal begins with rice and ends with beans'.

Arroz
Rice

When cooking rice, the most important thing is not to overcook it. Measure the amount of rice and liquid with care. Too much liquid and you might be tempted to continue cooking until it is absorbed; by that time the grains will be soft and mushy.

◁◁◁◁◁◁◁◁◁◁◁◁◁◁◁◁◁◁◁◁◁◁◁◁◁◁◁◁◁◁▷▷▷▷▷▷▷▷▷▷▷▷▷▷▷▷▷▷▷▷▷▷▷▷▷▷▷▷▷

Choosing the rice is important – whole grains give fluffier, lighter results; too many broken grains and you will have a stodgy potful. I particularly like the 'easy cook' rice, which is not an impostor of good rice as its names implies, but rather rice that has been treated with a steaming process that results in the grains keeping their shape when cooked. The process also retains more vitamins from the outer layer than in ordinary rice.

A heavy cast-iron pot is most suitable for cooking Mexican rice dishes: it fries the grains best, conducts the heat evenly and keeps the dish from burning. These qualities result in firmer-textured, plumper grains.

Two Simple Rice Dishes

White Rice topped with Chilli, Spring Onions, Coriander, and Lime: an invigorating dish to accompany complex, dark, spicy sauces and casseroles: top freshly steamed, lightly buttered rice with chopped spring onions, fresh green chilli, coriander leaves and diced lime.

Arroz con Jacoqui: layer steamed white rice with a generous amount of diced mild roasted and peeled green chillies (from a tin is fine), grated cheese, and soured cream. End with a layer of cheese and bake in a medium-hot oven until the cheese melts. Serve with soured cream and more chopped chillies or spring onions.

Arroz Mexicana
Mexican 'Spanish Rice'

Arroz Mexicana is the rice you will most often find with the *comida corrida*. It is ubiquitous throughout the country, rather than a regional speciality. It can be wonderful or dismal, and at its best, it is tinted with the brick-red hue of mild chilli and tomato, with brightly coloured vegetables studded throughout.

1 onion, chopped
1 tablespoon vegetable or olive oil
1 clove garlic, chopped
1 small to medium carrot, coarsely chopped
225 g/8 oz rice
2 tablespoons mild chilli powder
100 g/4 oz tomatoes, chopped (tinned is fine)
600 ml/1 pint chicken, beef or vegetable stock
100 g/4 oz peas
50 g/2 oz sweetcorn
1/4 green pepper, diced
1/4 teaspoon oregano leaves

1. Sauté the onion in the oil until softened, then add the garlic and carrot and cook for a minute or two. Stir in the rice and cook until lightly gilded, then sprinkle in the chilli powder and cook for a few more minutes.
2. Add the tomatoes, stock, peas, sweetcorn, green pepper and oregano.
3. Bring to the boil, then cover, reduce the heat and simmer over a low heat until the rice is just tender. This will take between 10 and 20 minutes, depending upon the type of rice.

VARIATIONS

Con Platanos: in the Veracruz area especially, rice is frequently enjoyed topped with bananas. Slice the bananas and add directly to the rice as a garnish, or use plantain. Slice at an angle or lengthwise and fry in a little butter or oil, then use as a garnish for the cooked rice. This may be used on plain white rice as well as Arroz Mexicana.

Con Mariscos: add a handful of seafood to Arroz Mexicana. Include a diced chorizo sausage and a sprinkle of saffron for a simple Mexican paella.

Con Chorizo: add diced Mexican or Spanish chorizo to Arroz Mexicana for a hearty rice dish.

Con Legumbres: add several cooked halved artichoke hearts, 10 or so pimiento-stuffed green olives and a spoonful of capers. Serve the dish sprinkled with coriander leaves and thinly sliced medium-hot green chillies.

Ensalata de Arroz Mexicana (Southwestern Rice Salad): splash the cooled rice with a mustardy vinaigrette – one that is heavy on the vinegar as the rice has been cooked with oil. Serve as a zesty rice salad garnished with roasted and peeled red peppers.

Arroz Blanco
White Rice

Arroz Blanco is the most basic rice dish, one that appears most often as a prelude to a *comida*. It is, however, scarcely the unadorned boiled rice we think of when we hear 'white rice'. This is pilaf-style, the grains sautéed first, often with some onion or garlic.

Arroz Blanco can be varied endlessly. Add a little achiote paste (see Pollo Pibil, page 150), or Recado Rojo Enchilada (page 43) for Arroz Amarillo, or cook it in chicken stock for a richer Arroz Blanco. Add a handful of prawns and cook the rice in seafood or fish stock and you have Arroz con Camarones, a traditional Lenten *sopa seca*.

    1 small to medium onion, chopped and/or 3 cloves garlic,
       chopped
    35 g/1¹/₂ oz lard (or butter or oil)
    225 g/8 oz rice
    600 ml/1 pint hot water or stock of choice
    Salt and pepper to taste

1. Lightly sauté the onion and/or garlic in the fat, then add the rice and cook over medium heat until the rice is golden.
2. Add the hot water or stock then reduce the heat, cover, and simmer until cooked through, 10 to 20 minutes, depending on the rice you use. Season to taste with salt and pepper.

◁◁◁◁◁◁◁◁◁◁◁◁◁◁◁◁◁◁◁◁◁◁◁◁◁◁◁◁◁▷▷▷▷▷▷▷▷▷▷▷▷▷▷▷▷▷▷▷▷▷▷▷▷▷▷▷▷

Arroz Verde
'Green Rice' with Purée of Chillies, Coriander Leaves, Roasted Onion and Garlic

A well-made Arroz Verde is one of those simple, classic dishes in which the end result surpasses its humble ingredients. Arroz Verde gets its distinctive colour and flavour from a paste of roasted, chopped mild green chillies (green peppers work just as well) and lots of fresh coriander leaves.

2 small to medium onions, cut into halves (with brown skin
   left intact)
6 large cloves garlic, unpeeled
1 green pepper
2 medium-hot fresh green chillies, or to taste
50 g/2 oz fresh coriander leaves, coarsely chopped
250 ml/8 fl oz chicken or vegetable stock
75 ml/3 fl oz vegetable oil
325 g/12 oz rice

1. In an ungreased, heavy frying pan roast the onions, garlic, green pepper and chillies until charred and blistered, turning so that they cook evenly (they could also be done under the grill or over an open fire).
2. Let cool, then peel the onions, garlic, pepper and chillies (discard the seeds) and chop finely. Place in a liquidizer and purée; when smooth, add the coriander leaves and stock, blending together.
3. Heat the vegetable oil and sauté the rice until it is glistening and lightly browned.
4. Add the vegetable purée to the rice, cover, reduce heat and cook until the rice is just tender.
5. Fork it to fluff it up and let it stand for 5 minutes or so, covered with a clean towel. Serve immediately.

VARIATION

Arroz Verde con Mariscos: fragrant green rice takes exceedingly well to the addition of seafood; it looks especially beautiful topped with red langoustines, pink-fleshed prawns, a handful of clams, unshelled mussels.

Proceed as in the above recipe, substituting fish stock for the vegetable or chicken stock. Add just a little seafood for a side dish, a large amount of varied fish and seafood for a full meal, paella-style.

Arroz con Elote
Rice with Sweetcorn

Sweetcorn and green and chilli peppers stud this gentle, flavourful dish. It is distinctively Mexican yet adaptable enough to serve with a wide variety of hearty dishes.

Preparing it with vegetable stock gives a zesty, full-flavoured vegetarian dish, good as an accompaniment to cheese-stuffed chillies. It also goes well with a spicy roasted fish and with the delicately subtle Verduras con Crema (page 211).

Since the dish is so gentle, a splash of spicy fresh salsa brings a welcome liveliness.

> 1 small to medium onion, chopped
> 2 cloves garlic, chopped
> 1 green pepper, roasted, peeled and diced or cut into strips
> 1 mild to medium green chilli, such as jalapeño, roasted
>   (see Glossary), peeled, seeded and diced
> 50 g/2 oz butter
> 225 g/8 oz rice
> 225 g/8 oz sweetcorn (frozen is fine)
> 500 ml/16 fl oz vegetable or chicken stock

1. Lightly sauté the onion, garlic, green pepper and chilli in the butter until the onion is softened, then stir in the rice and raise heat a little, cooking until the grains are lightly gilded.
2. Stir in the sweetcorn, then add the stock. Raise the heat and cook until the mixture just begins to boil, then cover and reduce the heat to a low simmer. Cook for another 5 to 15

minutes (depending upon the type of rice you are using) until rice is just cooked through.
3. Keep warm until ready to serve.

Arroz Negro
Rice Cooked in Black Bean Stock, Yucatán-Style

This comes to the table with the same startling colour as an inky black risotto, or the cuttlefish-tinted rice dishes of Spain, but in this dish the colour comes from the cooking liquid from black beans. It makes a splendid accompaniment for hearty meat or seafood stews or braises.

    2 tablespoons vegetable oil
    3 cloves garlic, chopped
    225 g/8 oz rice
    500 ml/16 fl oz cooking liquid from black beans
    100 g/4 oz tomatoes, chopped (tinned, with their juice, is
        fine)
    1 stock cube of choice
    1 bay leaf
    Pinch of mild red chilli powder
    1/4 to 1/2 green chilli pepper, seeded and chopped

1. Heat the oil and fry the garlic in it, then add the rice and cook until golden, stirring to cook evenly.
2. Add the black bean liquid, tomatoes, stock cube, bay leaf, and chilli powder, bring to the boil, then cover and reduce the heat to a simmer. Cook over a low heat until the rice is just tender (10 to 20 minutes depending on the rice you use).
3. Fluff with a fork, adding the chopped green chilli as you do so.

GARNISHES AND SERVING SUGGESTIONS FOR
RICE DISHES

Cazuela de Arroz y Carne: top rice dish of choice with mild chilli

◁◁◁◁◁◁◁◁◁◁◁◁◁◁◁◁◁◁◁◁◁◁◁◁◁◁◁◁▷▷▷▷▷▷▷▷▷▷▷▷▷▷▷▷▷▷▷▷▷▷▷▷▷▷▷▷

powder and marinated and lightly browned lamb or pork chops. Bake in a hot oven until the meat is crispy around the edges. Serve with the juice of half an orange squeezed over it all, and garnished with thinly sliced lettuce dressed in oil, vinegar and oregano, and diced cooked beets. This is a typical family-style supper dish.

Surround a platter of rice with grilled smoky meaty sausages and butter-browned banana or plantain slices.

Serve rice dish of choice topped with a fried or poached egg and a splash of tart, spicy green salsa.

Accompany Arroz Negro or Verde with garlicky *carnitas*, a coriander-lime salsa, and dollops of soured cream.

Serve Arroz con Elote as a bed for Chiles Rellenos (page 215).

FRIJOLES
Beans and Pulses

Frijoles de Olla
Basic Simmered Beans

The ever-present pot of beans simmers slowly and patiently, a portrait of tradition in its rustic clay pot. No meal in Mexico would be complete without *frijoles*, even if only a few spoonfuls. Mexican beans come in a wide variety of sizes, shapes and hues; the ancient Indians cultivated a rainbow-coloured range of beans far wider than the types we know.

Generally, certain regions favour certain types of beans: pink bayo gordo and pinto beans are the most popular in the north and central areas, with black beans favoured south from Oaxaca and the Yucatán towards Guatemala.

Beans are simmered slowly in a pot until creamy and tender.

◁◁◁◁◁◁◁◁◁◁◁◁◁◁◁◁◁◁◁◁◁◁◁◁◁◁◁◁◁◁◁◁◁◁◁▷▷▷▷▷▷▷▷▷▷▷▷▷▷▷▷▷▷▷▷▷▷▷▷▷▷▷▷▷▷

They are then served in a variety of dishes. You'll find beans in soups, stews, with vegetables and so on, but the most popular way of serving them is as *frijoles refritos*, or puréed fried beans. This rich purée may be eaten on its own, with rice and salad or a main course, or spread on to all sorts of *antojitos*. It might be stuffed into a *burrito* or green chilli, or topped with cheese and melted into a rich, deliciously unctuous mixture.

RULES FOR MAKING GOOD BEANS

Clean them and inspect for stones.

Soak overnight in cold water, or bring to the boil and leave in the hot water for 1 hour to soften in lieu of soaking.

For the most Mexican of flavours, cook them in an earthenware pot.

Beans should simmer very slowly over a low flame.

Always start with water to cover rather than drowning the beans; as liquid is absorbed, add more water (hot is best).

Add salt only when the beans are almost done as, if they are not yet tender, the salt will toughen them.

The herb epazote is often added to beans in Mexico, especially black beans. It is said to cut the gaseous effects, and it also gives a distinctive flavour. Alas, I cannot find it anywhere in London and often add several bay leaves in its place.

    225 g/8 oz beans, cleaned and soaked
    About 4.2 litres/7 pints water
    1 onion, cut in half
    2 tablespoons fat, such as lard
    Salt to taste

1. Put the beans in a pot with about half the water and the onion. Bring to the boil.

◁◁◁◁◁◁◁◁◁◁◁◁◁◁◁◁◁◁◁◁◁◁◁◁◁◁◁◁◁◁▷▷▷▷▷▷▷▷▷▷▷▷▷▷▷▷▷▷▷▷▷▷▷▷▷▷▷▷▷▷

2. After about an hour, when the skins of the beans begin to wrinkle, add the fat. Continue to simmer until the beans are tender, adding more water as needed.
3. When just about tender, add salt.
4. Use the beans for stews, soups or refried beans, or enjoy them country-style: simply spooned into bowls along with a little of the cooking liquid or other flavourful stock, seasoned with a little chopped raw onion, tomato, fresh coriander, chillies and oregano.

Note: save bean cooking liquid for rice. Arroz Negro (page 193), cooked in the liquid of black beans, is startlingly good with its ebony hue and rich dark flavour. Pinto bean liquid gives a lighter flavour, which goes well with chicken.

VARIATION

Frijoles con Puerco: combine cooked beans with a generous amount of chopped tomatoes, chopped onion, fresh coriander, and lots of diced streaky bacon. Simmer until the beans are meltingly tender, adding more liquid if necessary.

Frijoles Refritos
Refried Beans

This rich paste of mashed and fried beans is only fried once, despite its name. Any sort of bean may be used, but pink beans are the most common in most areas and black beans are favoured in the south.

Tinned *frijoles refritos* are readily available in Mexico, California, the Southwest of the USA, and these days they are easily found in London and other large cities in the UK as well as in other urban areas of Europe. Using refried beans from a tin is one of those times I do not baulk at using tinned food – they are delicious and lend themselves to preparing all sorts of dishes that would otherwise be impossible without the omnipresent pot of simmering beans on the backburner.

ᐸᐸᐸᐸᐸᐸᐸᐸᐸᐸᐸᐸᐸᐸᐸᐸᐸᐸᐸᐸᐸᐸᐸᐸᐸᐸᐸ<>ᐳᐳᐳᐳᐳᐳᐳᐳᐳᐳᐳᐳᐳᐳᐳᐳᐳᐳᐳᐳᐳᐳᐳᐳᐳ

Why make your own? The tinned ones are a bit salty, and they are also made with animal fat. Making your own enables you to control both the fat and salt content. They are more economical as well.

Frijoles de Olla (page 194)
75 g/3 oz lard or vegetable oil
Salt to taste
100 to 225 g/4 to 8 oz cheese, grated (optional)

1. Mash the beans either with a fork gradually as you add them to the pan, or by cheating and puréeing about half of them in a food processor or liquidizer, leaving the rest a bit chunky.
2. Heat about 2 tablespoons of the fat in a pan. Add a small amount of the beans, cooking them down as their liquid evaporates, then adding more fat and beans. Cook this way, until the moisture is a heavy, rather dry paste. Season with salt (beans need quite a lot).
3. If using cheese, place the hot Frijoles Refritos in a casserole or shallow baking dish. Top with cheese and bake or grill until the cheese melts and becomes bubbly.

VARIATION

Frijoles Refritos con Chorizo: add about 225 g/8 oz browned and crumbled chorizo sausage (or diced streaky bacon) to the above recipe after frying.

Frijoles Mexicana
Refried Beans with Onion and Roasted Tomato

This rich and savoury bean paste comes as a revelation even to those who have doted on refried beans for years. The seasoning paste of roasted tomatoes and raw onions, cooked in a small amount of fat (I use oil; lard is the traditional choice) until it forms a thick, highly seasoned paste, is what gives the beans their layers of complex flavour.

4 small to medium tomatoes
2 small to medium onions, peeled and cut into small pieces
2 tablespoons vegetable oil
225 g/8 oz refried beans, either homemade (page 196) or
    tinned

1. Roast the tomatoes over an open flame if you have a gas
   cooker. If not, grill under the highest possible heat. Roast
   until the skin chars and bursts, then remove from the heat
   until cool enough to handle.
2. Remove all the skin from the tomatoes, then cut them into
   halves and squeeze or cut out the seeds. Chop the flesh.
3. In a liquidizer or food processor purée the onions then add
   the tomato pieces and whirl into a purée.
4. Heat the oil in a heavy, ungreased frying pan then add the
   purée, letting it splatter and 'fry' into a dryish, well-
   concentrated purée. Add the beans and cook together until
   well mixed and heated through.

VARIATION

Season Frijoles Mexicana with mashed sardines and serve in a
roll garnished with grated cheese, avocado, radishes, crisp fried
tortilla wedges and chipotle or pickled jalapeño chilli. Or spread
the mixture on to crisp *tostadas*.

Frijoles Negroes Enchillados
Chillied Black Beans

Red chilli-seasoned black beans make an excellent filling for *burritos*, *tacos*, even pita bread. Try them spread on crisp tortillas for
the classic of the Yucatecan kitchen, Huevos Motul (page 129),
or topped with melted cheese and spread on to crusty bread
along with a fresh salsa.

Cooked, puréed black beans make an excellent addition to
sauces; freeze small amounts so that you always have them
available.

◁◁◁◁◁◁◁◁◁◁◁◁◁◁◁◁◁◁◁◁◁◁◁◁◁◁◁◁◁◁◁▷▷▷▷▷▷▷▷▷▷▷▷▷▷▷▷▷▷▷▷▷▷▷▷▷▷▷▷▷▷

2 onions, chopped
2 cloves garlic, chopped
1 tablespoon vegetable oil
1½ teaspoons cumin seeds
1½ teaspoons pure chilli powder or mild chilli powder
2 medium tomatoes, chopped
450 g/1 lb cooked black beans, with some of their liquid,
    about half the beans mashed (use a liquidizer)
Salt to taste

1. Sauté the onions and garlic in the vegetable oil until softened then sprinkle in the cumin seeds and lightly toast until they become aromatic.
2. Sprinkle in the chilli powder, cook a minute longer, then add the chopped tomatoes and cook until saucelike.
3. Add the black beans and cooking liquid to this mixture, raise the heat, and cook down to the desired consistency. Season with salt.

DISHES TO MAKE WITH BLACK BEANS

Prepare black beans and do not mash, but leave whole. Serve each bowlful with a spoonful or two of cooked hominy and garnished with wedges of lime.

Serve black beans as an accompaniment for roast duck, or mash and spread on *tostadas* and top with shreds of duck, soured cream, chillies, radishes, coriander.

Anglo-Mexican Burritos: spread warm mashed black beans thickly over warm naan; top with crumbled Feta or fresh Pecorino cheese, chopped fresh mint, coriander, chillies and a dollop of soured cream.

Black beans make a good basis for a thick zesty soup.

◁◁◁◁◁◁◁◁◁◁◁◁◁◁◁◁◁◁◁◁◁◁◁◁◁◁◁◁◁◁◁◁◁◁◁<>▷▷▷▷▷▷▷▷▷▷▷▷▷▷▷▷▷▷▷▷▷▷▷▷▷▷▷▷▷

Lentejas Costenas con Frutas
Brown Lentils Simmered with Fruit

Lentils with fruit sounds alarming. However, the surprising
thing is that the earthy, substantial pulses are nearly transformed
by cooking with the light, sweet fruit.

> 100 g/4 oz brown-green lentils
> About 700 ml/24 fl oz water
> 6 shallots or 2 small to medium onions, coarsely chopped
> 4 cloves garlic, coarsely chopped
> 2 tablespoons vegetable oil
> 1 large tart apple, diced
> 4 rings of pineapple, fresh or tinned (unsweetened), cut
>   into bite-sized chunks
> 3 small or 2 medium tomatoes, diced
> 1 almost-ripe banana, cut into bite-sized pieces
> Salt and cayenne pepper to taste

1. Place the lentils in a saucepan with the water. Bring to the
   boil, reduce the heat, and simmer until the lentils are tender
   and the water has nearly evaporated.
2. Meanwhile, sauté the shallots or onions and garlic in the
   vegetable oil until lightly browned and softened. Add the
   apple and fry until brown, then add the pineapple, sauté a
   little, and add the tomatoes. Cook down until saucelike in
   consistency.
3. Add this mixture to the lentils, and heat together for about 5
   minutes, to cook through and mingle the flavours.
4. Add the banana (gently sauté first, if preferred) to the lentils
   and fruit, and heat through a few minutes longer. Add salt
   and cayenne pepper to taste. Serve immediately, or cool and
   store in the refrigerator to heat and serve later.

SOPAS SECAS DE MACARONI
'Dry Soups' of Pasta

Savoury rice casseroles and baked tortilla dishes such as *chila-quiles* comprise the bulk of dry soup dishes, or *sopas secas*, but pasta is greatly enjoyed in Mexico too. For one thing it is filling, an important consideration when there are more mouths to feed than food to fill them.

Of all the shapes, fideos, the very thin angel-hair strands, are probably the most popular: they seem to accept good-naturedly the vibrant Mexican seasonings, and bake into thick and filling *sopa seca* casseroles without asserting their own individuality. Other shapes are favoured, too, often tossed into cooked broths for the soup course: thick strands of macaroni added to a pork and spinach broth, flat ribbons of noodles added to a garlicky tomato soup, and so forth.

Sopa Seca de Fideo
Casserole of Thin Noodles with Chorizo, Tomatoes and Cheese

This satisfying dish is eaten in one version or another through-out the Republic. Its top should be crusty and cheesy, the pasta underneath soft and yielding in the tomato sauce.

325 g/12 oz thin fideo, vermicelli, or cappellini
2 to 3 bay leaves
About 225 g/8 oz chorizo sausage (if unavailable, substitute
  minced beef or pork seasoned with mild chilli powder,
  paprika, and oregano)
2 small to medium onions, chopped
1 green pepper, chopped
1 to 2 medium-hot fresh green chillies, seeded and chopped
  (retain seeds if more heat is desired)
3 cloves garlic, chopped
250 ml/8 fl oz tomato sauce
250 ml/8 fl oz stock of choice
About 325 g/12 oz cheese suitable for melting, grated

◁◁◁◁◁◁◁◁◁◁◁◁◁◁◁◁◁◁◁◁◁◁◁◁◁◁◁◁◁◁◁▷▷▷▷▷▷▷▷▷▷▷▷▷▷▷▷▷▷▷▷▷▷▷▷

1. Boil the noodles in water with the bay leaves. When almost tender, after only a few minutes, drain the pasta and discard the bay leaves.
2. Fry the chorizos, crumbling them as they cook; when they begin to brown add the onions, pepper and chillies and cook together until the onion has softened. Add the garlic, tomato sauce and stock.
3. Combine the sauce with the cooked pasta, then place in a baking dish. Cover with a layer of grated cheese.
4. Bake in the oven at 200°C/400°F/gas mark 6 until the top is bubbly and lightly browned, and the dish is heated through. Serve immediately.

VEGETARIAN VARIATION

Omit the chorizo and increase the amount of onion. Add 1 teaspoon each of mild chilli powder and paprika to the onion as it fries, increasing the mild chilli powder if the dish needs extra flavour. Pure chilli powder would give an even brighter, truer flavour here.

ENSALADAS Y VERDURAS
Salads and Vegetables

To appreciate Mexican vegetables – and fruit – one must visit a marketplace. One comes away not just with inspiration, but inevitably with recipes from the vendors.

My first glimpse of a Mexican market was Mercado Libertad, Guadalajara, with the verdant aroma of vegetables, the sweet, slightly sickly smells of fruit in its ripest stages as it settled into an hour or more of peak flavour before sliding quickly into rottenness. All was piled high, in places artless and chaotic, at other times arranged with breathtaking precision. Next to the haphazard pile of oranges lay avocados, set out in neat star or flower designs. A wide array of chillies was mounded in great heaps: black-green poblanos, fiery habaneros, fleshy red jalapeños. A basket held *nopales*, fierce-looking but succulently delicious; another basket held some sort of squash with a distinctly prehistoric look. There were baby onions, strong green shoots pushing up from purple-white bulbs, and fronds of delicate lettuce, still dewy but beginning to wilt in the heat of the day.

There was fruit, a combination of familiar and foreign: papayas the size of big watermelons, yellow mangoes the size of a thumb and gigantic orange-red ones. Bananas ranged from tiny red nuggets, yellow eating ones, green cooking ones, to large, blackening monsters.

Because so many of the dishes in Mexico's restaurants are based on meats, as well as the fact that most of us are wary of eating raw vegetables and fruit South of the Border, the visiting diner might think that in a land with so much fresh produce there is little vegetable cuisine. Emphatically not so: no soup or stew is complete without a garden basketful of vegetables simmering in it. And while tossed green salads are not often eaten to end the meal, as they are in Europe, most dishes are garnished

◁◁▷▷▷▷▷▷▷▷▷▷▷▷▷▷▷▷▷▷▷▷▷▷▷▷▷▷▷▷▷▷▷

with shredded greens, radishes, chopped herbs, sliced chillies, and other fresh vegetables. *Tostadas* come to the table piled high with shredded raw vegetables, soups are frequently served scattered with a handful of what we would think of as salad.

Vegetables might also be puréed and used in complex sauces such as *pipiáns* or *moles*. As a separate course, served before the main meat or fish one, vegetables are prepared simply, reflecting the Mediterranean influences of the Spanish and French occupation. They might be cooked gently in cream and cheese, or braised with chillies and tomatoes; they may be hollowed out and stuffed, or breaded and fried. Large, fresh mild chillies and peppers are stuffed with cheese, meat, fish or beans, dipped in batter then fried; diced courgettes might be dressed with oil and vinegar, or tossed into a guacamole.

Vegetable relishes, *adornos*, appear frequently on the table – pickled cabbage, onions, carrots and chillies – along with fresh salsas of chopped tomato, chillies, onions, combined with radishes, garlic, spring onions, and so forth. And raw vegetables such as cucumber and jicama are often eaten as a snack, sprinkled with cayenne pepper and lime juice.

ENSALADAS
Salads

Frutas del Mercado
Street Vendor Fruit Platter

In the streetmarkets of cities, towns and villages throughout Mexico you will find snacks of fruit and hot peppers like this one. Along the road leading to many of the pyramids in the Yucatán, for instance, there are vendors selling sweet, juicy oranges that have been sprinkled somewhat alarmingly with hot red pepper. In the oppressive heat of that region, they are uncompromisingly refreshing. In Guadalajara chunks of pineapple, jicama and cucumber are skewered and sold in the marketplace or park, sprinkled with enough chilli to brighten your outlook on life or at least rouse you from a heat-induced stupor.

This platter is a more citified, civilized and sociable version, as it were, of the traditional – and ancient – fruit and chilli snack.

250 g/9 oz jicama
1 small to medium ripe, flavourful pineapple, or
   3 flavourful sweet oranges
1 cucumber, peeled and sliced
Juice of 1 to 1¹/₂ limes
Pinch of salt
Several pinches of hot chilli powder, or a pure chilli
   powder made from one type of chilli only (ancho, pasilla,
   etc), or a pinch of cayenne

1. Peel and cut the jicama and pineapple or oranges into bite-sized pieces and arrange on a platter.
2. Arrange the cucumber slices on the platter as well, then sprinkle the whole thing with lime juice, salt and chilli powder.
3. Serve immediately.

Ensalada de Nopales
Cactus Pad Salad

Nopales, or *nopalitos*, are the cactus pads of the same plant that produces the prickly pear. The pads are scraped to remove their extremely irritating prickles, then simmered until tender. They are often cut into strips for more manageability, though sometimes they are left whole and stuffed with cheese or meat.

Nopales have a flavour somewhat like green beans with a viscosity reminiscent of okra. They are delicious tucked into *tacos* along with spicy rich meat, since their own flavour is so clean and fresh. Good with seafood, or chopped and added to various *taco* and *tamal* fillings, they are also a classic scrambled with eggs, chillies and tomatoes. Occasionally *nopales* are left whole and stuffed with cheese or meat, then simmered until tender and served with a mild, ancho chilli-based sauce.

Nopales are one of the few vegetables that I do not find

⫷⫷⫷⫷⫷⫷⫷⫷⫷⫷⫷⫷⫷⫷⫷⫷⫷⫷⫷⫷⫷⫷⫷⫷⫷⫷⫷⫷⫷⫗⫗⫗⫗⫗⫗⫗⫗⫗⫗⫗⫗⫗⫗⫗⫗⫗⫗⫗⫗⫗⫗⫗⫗⫗⫗⫗

objectionable when preserved in a bottle; in fact, the spiced brine often adds flavour. If using bottled *nopales*, simply drain (and rinse if desired).

As a salad, the combination of tangy *nopales* with either the delicately bland hard-boiled egg or rich and nippy cheese is superb.

> 450 g/1 lb cooked *nopales* (see Glossary), drained
> 2 ripe tomatoes, cut into thick slices (optional)
> 1 small onion, chopped
> 25 g/1 oz coriander leaves, chopped
> 2 tablespoons vegetable oil
> 1 tablespoon mild vinegar or lime juice
> 1/2 mild green chilli, thinly sliced (optional)
> Salt to taste
> Either: 1 hard-boiled egg, diced, or 50–75 g/2 to 3 oz
>   Caerphilly or Cheshire cheese, crumbled, or 50 g/2 oz
>   cooked prawns

1. Arrange the *nopales* on a platter. Garnish with the tomatoes if using, sprinkle with the onion and coriander, then drizzle with the oil and vinegar or lime juice.
2. Sprinkle with the chilli if using, a little salt, and either the diced hard-boiled egg, crumbled cheese, or cooked prawns. Serve immediately.

Ensalada de Calabaza y Jitomate
Courgette and Tomato Vinaigrette

Almost Mediterranean in style, this simple salad makes a lovely dish for a languid summer afternoon or evening.

> 450 g/1 lb small to medium courgettes, cut into large dice
> 3 medium to large ripe, sweet and flavourful tomatoes,
>   peeled, seeded and diced
> 50 ml/2 fl oz olive oil
> 1/2 medium-sized medium-hot fresh green chilli, seeded and
>   chopped

◁◁◁◁◁◁◁◁◁◁◁◁◁◁◁◁◁◁◁◁◁◁◁◁◁◁◁◁◁◁◁◁▷▷▷▷▷▷▷▷▷▷▷▷▷▷▷▷▷▷▷▷▷▷▷▷▷▷▷▷▷▷▷

3 spring onions, thinly sliced
1 tablespoon finely chopped coriander leaves
35 ml/1¹/₂ fl oz wine vinegar
Salt and black pepper to taste
1 or 2 hard-boiled eggs, shelled and diced

1. Cook the diced courgettes in boiling water to cover for about 5 minutes or until just tender. Drain.
2. Place the courgettes in a bowl and toss with the tomatoes, then dress with the olive oil, chilli, spring onions, coriander leaves, wine vinegar, salt and pepper.
3. When ready to serve, garnish with the diced hard-boiled egg.

A FEW SIMPLE MEXICAN SALADS

Mexican salads are vibrant and full of flavour, yet informal and unfussy. Precise measurements are unimportant; spirit and flavour, all.

Palmitos en Vinegreta (Hearts of Palm Salad): hearts of palm are seldom available fresh, even in Mexico. Take directly from the tin and dress in a sprightly vinaigrette. Garnish with diced tomatoes, green olives and lots of parsley.

Coliflor con Guacamole (Cauliflower with Guacamole): serve cauliflower, steamed just tender (not mercilessly boiled until nasty and grey), dressed with a simple vinaigrette, then spoon guacamole over (page 50). Garnish with sliced, lightly pickled beetroot and shredded lettuce.

Ensalada de Piña con Pimientos Morrones (Salad of Pineapple and Red Peppers): the vibrant colours and sweet flavour of red peppers with pineapple is enticing. No dressing is necessary.

Avocado and papaya with chopped coriander, a squeeze of lime juice, and a pinch of red pepper.

Orange, watercress and red onion.

◁◁◁◁◁◁◁◁◁◁◁◁◁◁◁◁◁◁◁◁◁◁◁◁◁◁◁◁◁◁▷▷▷▷▷▷▷▷▷▷▷▷▷▷▷▷▷▷▷▷▷▷▷▷▷▷▷▷

Mango with lime juice, a pinch of red pepper, and coarsely chopped peanuts.

From Uxmal, Yucatán: sliced avocado, grated carrot and julienne of beetroot, arranged on a bed of lettuce and dressed with a mustardy vinaigrette.

Mixed Greens and Chilli Salad: add roasted, peeled and lightly marinated green peppers or mildish chillies to a salad of mixed lettuce. Garnish with lightly pickled onion slices or chopped raw onion.

Ensalada de Noche Buena: on Christmas Eve the traditional salad is a gaudy mixture of fruit, scattered with nuts and even hard sugar sweets. On a bed of sliced or shredded lettuce, arrange chunks of tart apple, pineapple, orange, jicama and cooked beetroot and dress it all with a honey-laced vinaigrette. Scatter with roasted peanuts and either pomegranate seeds or raw cranberries.

Tortilla or Taco Salad: add crushed tortilla chips to a salad of mixed greens, much as one might add croûtons. For a full-blown *taco* salad, Southwestern-style, add diced avocado, grated cheese, cooked kidney beans, and a little hot browned minced beef or chorizo sausage.

Bean Salad, Guanajuata-style: cook mixed beans, including black beans, chickpeas and pinto beans. When tender, drain and dress in a vinaigrette, along with just-tender cooked green beans (and yellow wax beans if available). Garnish with strips of mild chilli, diced tomato and onion. In Guanajuata legend has it that the more types of beans used in this dish, the better your luck will be.

◄◄◄◄◄◄◄◄◄◄◄◄◄◄◄◄◄◄◄◄◄◄◄◄◄◄◄◄◄◄◄◄◄◄◄►►►►►►►►►►►►►►►►►►►►►►►►►►►►►►►►►►►►►

LEGUMBRES Y VERDURAS
Vegetables and Greens

Enchilado de Col
Chilli-Braised Cabbage

Mild chilli flavours and tomatoes make a delicious braising mixture for cabbage.

2 small to medium onions, diced
$1/4$ to $1/2$ medium-hot fresh green chilli, seeded and chopped
2 tablespoons vegetable oil
$1/2$ head of cabbage, cut into large dice
4 to 5 small to medium tomatoes, diced (seed and peel only
   if you wish)
$1/2$ teaspoon mild chilli powder
$1/2$ teaspoon paprika
175 ml/6 fl oz stock of choice
Juice of $1/2$ lime
Salt and pepper to taste, if needed

1. Lightly sauté the onions and chilli in the oil until softened
   and the onions begin to brown. Add the cabbage and
   continue to sauté, then add the tomatoes, chilli powder and
   paprika and continue to cook. When the tomatoes are
   saucelike pour in the stock.
2. Cook over a medium-high heat until the cabbage is cooked
   through and the liquid has almost evaporated, about
   15 minutes.
3. Season with a squeeze of lime juice, and salt and pepper
   if needed.

Note: leftovers make the basis of a good freewheeling vegetable
soup. Add diced cooked potatoes, stock and a squeeze of lime
juice, and serve topped with a spoonful of soured cream.

◁◁◁◁◁◁◁◁◁◁◁◁◁◁◁◁◁◁◁◁◁◁◁◁◁◁◁◁◁◁▷▷▷▷▷▷▷▷▷▷▷▷▷▷▷▷▷▷▷▷▷▷▷▷▷▷▷▷▷

Legumbres Enchilados
Mixed Vegetables with Chilli Spicing

Throughout the Republic, artlessly informal mixtures of vegetables are quickly tossed in a little chilli and other spices then served as a garnish for nearly anything: *enchiladas*, *tostadas*, grilled meats, eggs, and so on. The mixture, of course, varies according to what is available. Sometimes the vegetables are tossed in a little oil and vinegar with a pinch of oregano, other times served warmed with chilli.

1 onion, diced
2 carrots, steamed but firm, diced (or use raw and cook a
    little longer)
3 tablespoons vegetable oil
4 cold boiled potatoes, diced (peeled or unpeeled,
    according to taste)
50 to 100 g/2 to 4 oz peas or green beans
2 teaspoons mild chilli powder
Generous pinch of cumin seeds or ground cumin
Salt and pepper to taste
2 teaspoons coarsely chopped coriander leaves

1. Sauté the onion and carrots in the oil until lightly browned, then add the potatoes, peas or green beans, chilli powder, and cumin seeds or ground cumin. Season with salt and pepper.
2. Serve sprinkled with the coriander.

VARIATION

Instead of sautéing with cumin and chilli, simply toss with a little vinegar or vinaigrette.

Verduras con Crema
Spinach with Cream

A most delicious version of creamed spinach, with the haunting
flavour and elusive warmth of roasted green chillies. Not really
spicy hot: it is flavour rather than force that comes wafting
through. Particularly good paired with Arroz con Elote (page
192), its suave flavour is equally at home with European fare as
with Mexican.

    1 small to medium onion, chopped
    3 cloves garlic, chopped
    2 jalapeño-type chillies, roasted (see Glossary), peeled,
       seeded and diced
    12 g/¹/₂ oz unsalted butter
    150 ml/5 fl oz soured cream
    225 g/8 oz spinach (fresh or frozen), cooked, squeezed dry
       and chopped
    Salt and pepper to taste
    Chopped spring onions (optional)

1. Combine the onion, garlic and chillies in a liquidizer or food
   processor and blend until they form a fine mixture or a near
   paste (take care – food processors for some mysterious
   reasons can turn onions bitter).
2. Heat the butter in a heavy frying pan and when melted add
   the onion-garlic-chilli mixture. Cook until soft and golden
   then add a spoonful or two of soured cream and cook down to
   a paste.
3. Stir in the spinach, cook for a minute, then add the remaining
   soured cream and continue to cook for a few minutes or until
   it thickens up. Serve hot or tepid. Season with salt and pepper
   and sprinkle with chopped spring onions if desired.

◁◁◁◁◁◁◁◁◁◁◁◁◁◁◁◁◁◁◁◁◁◁◁◁◁◁◁◁◁◁◁◁◁◁◁◁◁◁▷▷▷▷▷▷▷▷▷▷▷▷▷▷▷▷▷▷▷▷▷▷▷▷▷▷▷▷▷▷▷▷▷▷▷▷▷▷

Legumbres en Pipián
Vegetables in Pumpkin Seed Sauce

While *pipián* (a spice paste of ground toasted pumpkin seeds) is enjoyed throughout much of Mexico, it is especially favoured in the Yucatán Peninsula. This taste of ancient Mexican tradition is virtually the same as the sauce served by the pre-Columbian tribes. When Cortés's men were fêted by Montezuma – before the latter's tragic downfall – *pipián* was on the menu (though the modern name is derived from *pepita*, the Spanish word for pumpkin seed).

Pale green in colour, with a nutty spiciness mysteriously reminiscent of Southeast-Asian *saté* sauces, *pipián* is traditionally served with duck, roast turkey, thin grilled steaks, roast fish and the like. With a generous amount of lime juice it makes a good dip for flour tortillas or crusty bread. Though it is delicious eaten in these traditional ways I find its richness particularly suited to vegetables. Tomatillos add a tangy quality to the sauce; if they are unavailable, a handful of gooseberries, cooked and unsweetened, can apparently lift a Mexican sauce with the same tart quality.

Serve Legumbres en Pipián on its own as a vegetarian meal, or as an accompaniment for roast duck or other hearty meats.

1 onion, chopped

2 cloves garlic, chopped

10 tomatillos or several spoonfuls mild Salsa Verde (page 26); or try a handful of gooseberries, squeeze of fresh lime, or shredded sorrel leaves

35 ml/1½ fl oz vegetable oil

100 ml/4 fl oz stock

1 quantity Pipián (page 35)

4 medium potatoes, and 4 carrots, both boiled, cooled, and tossed with a teaspoon or so of vinegar

2 or 3 courgettes, boiled, drained, and diced

75 g/3 oz cooked peas

75 g/3 oz cooked sweetcorn

2 teaspoons chilli powder

Salt and pepper to taste

◁◁◁◁◁◁◁◁◁◁◁◁◁◁◁◁◁◁◁◁◁◁◁◁◁◁◁◁◁◁▷▷▷▷▷▷▷▷▷▷▷▷▷▷▷▷▷▷▷▷▷▷▷▷▷

Salsa of choice
Warm corn tortillas (optional)

1. Whirl the onion and garlic in a liquidizer or food processor to chop, then add the tomatillos (or Salsa Verde or other substitutes), 1 tablespoon vegetable oil and stock and whirl to a sauce consistency.
2. In a heavy pan combine this mixture with the Pipián sauce and heat until it thickens and comes to the boil. Remove from the heat and keep warm.
3. Sauté the vegetables in the remaining oil and when hot sprinkle with the chilli powder and continue to brown. Add half the sauce, and continue cooking until thickened and no longer liquidy. Season to taste.
4. Serve hot or at room temperature with hot salsa and the remaining Pipián sauce on the side, and with warm corn tortillas, if liked.

Chayote
Delicate Squash

Chayote is the most elegant member of the squash family, with a flavour reminiscent of courgettes, but gentle and sweet. Its elusive mild taste lets it pair good-naturedly with a variety of other flavours.

In appearance the chayote resembles a pale, shiny avocado. It is available in many supermarkets throughout the UK, especially in areas and shops that cater to West Indian populations.

Botanically a fruit, the chayote is generally eaten as a vegetable. Dipped in flour, then battered and fried, it is delicious. It is even good simply boiled, then mashed and served buttered, with a dab of salsa.

4 chayotes, cut into quarters
35 g/1^1/$_2$ oz butter
2 small to medium onions, chopped
^{1}/$_2$ small hot chilli, finely chopped (optional)
Salt and black pepper to taste

◅◅◅◅◅◅◅◅◅◅◅◅◅◅◅◅◅◅◅◅◅◅◅◅◅◅◅◅◅◅▻▻▻▻▻▻▻▻▻▻▻▻▻▻▻▻▻▻▻▻▻▻▻▻▻▻

1. Place the chayotes in a saucepan with water to cover. Cover the pan and bring to the boil, cooking gently until the chayotes are just tender, about 20 minutes.
2. Drain and cool. Remove the stones with a paring knife, then peel gently, taking care not to remove too much flesh, only the paper-thin skin. Cut the chayotes into large dice.
3. Melt the butter in a frying pan and sauté the onions, and chilli if using, until softened and lightly browned in parts. Add the chayote and toss with the onions.
4. Season with salt and pepper.

VARIATION

Chayotes con Queso: top the above dish with about 100 g/4 oz grated white cheese. Cover and cook for about 5 minutes, or long enough to melt the cheese.

Chayotes Rellenos
Tomato-Onion Stuffed Chayotes

The flavours and presentation of Chayotes Rellenos are much like those of Middle Eastern dishes. Doubtless it is a direct descendant, courtesy of the Spanish colonists.

Serve as a first course, followed by a roasted meat dish, or as a vegetarian main course, accompanied by Arroz Verde or Negro (pages 191 and 193) and a tangy salad.

2 large chayotes, cut into halves lengthwise
2 small to medium onions, coarsely chopped
12 g/¹/₂ oz butter
¹/₂ medium-hot, small, fresh chilli, chopped (remove the seeds for less heat, if preferred)
2 medium tomatoes, seeded and diced
2 cloves garlic, finely chopped
12 g/¹/₂ oz parsley, chopped
Salt to taste
75 to 100 g/3 to 4 oz Cheddar cheese, grated

◁◁

1. Place the chayotes in a saucepan with water to cover. Bring to the boil, then reduce the heat and simmer, covered, until tender when pierced with a fork or thin sharp knife, about 30 to 40 minutes. Drain and cool.
2. Remove the stones then scoop out the flesh with a sharp spoon and paring knife, taking care not to pierce the skin. Reserve the shells and dice the flesh.
3. In a large frying pan melt the butter and sauté the onions until softened and golden. Add the chilli, then the tomatoes and cook until the tomatoes are no longer raw. Stir in the garlic, reserved chayote flesh, and half the parsley. Add salt to taste.
4. Pile the reserved shells high with the stuffing mixture, then mix the cheese with the remaining parsley and sprinkle it over the tops of the stuffed chayotes, patting it down to make it stick if need be.
5. Bake in the oven at 180°C/350°F/gas mark 4 until the cheese is melted and the chayotes heated through, about 20 minutes.

Chiles Rellenos
Stuffed Mild Green Chillies

Ubiquitous throughout not only Mexico but also the Mexican-American regions of the United States, Chiles Rellenos can vary from inspired to ordinary. Together with *tacos* and the like, they tend to be lumped into the combination plate syndrome in restaurants and arrive looking tired, soggy and defeated. To be honest, even nondescript Chiles Rellenos are pretty good. But freshly made, with a zesty filling of spiced meat or melted cheese, a crisp batter coating and a fresh tomato sauce, they are exceptional.

Traditionally Chiles Rellenos are made with poblano chillies – lush and large mild green chillies that have a lovely pepper/vegetable flavour as well as a little chilli heat. In most areas of the United States, Chiles Rellenos are prepared using tinned mild green chillies, firstly because poblanos are not always available and secondly because the tinned chillies are already roasted and peeled, making the whole process easier. Since poblanos are seldom available in the UK I usually use green peppers roasted and peeled, then left to marinate with a few shakes of cayenne pepper. Mild green chillies are often found in tins in British supermarkets. Use them if you like, though they are narrower than large green peppers and hence are more difficult to stuff.

Serve a cheese or seafood-filled Chile Relleno as a hearty starter, or enjoy the meat-filled one as a main dish, accompanied by Arroz Negro (page 193) and a scattering of lightly vinegared lettuce, radishes, coriander, etc.

4 green peppers, roasted, peeled and seeded (leave the stem on, simply make a slit in the pepper and cut out the seeds and core)
Generous sprinkle of cayenne pepper or other ground hot chilli
325 g/12 oz mild meltable cheese, cut into fingers
or
Picadillo (page 180)
or
Prawn filling for Tacos de Camarones (page 93)
2 eggs, separated
25 g/1 oz flour, plus extra for dusting the chillies
Salt to taste
Oil for deep frying
Salsa Ranchera (page 32)
Lightly vinegared shredded lettuce (optional)

1. Take the roasted, peeled and seeded peppers and sprinkle judiciously with cayenne pepper. Leave for at least 30 minutes; best if wrapped and refrigerated overnight.
2. Fill the cavity of each pepper with the filling you have chosen. Set aside.
3. Make the batter: beat the egg whites until almost stiff, then in a separate bowl lightly beat the yolks and add the flour to make a light paste. Combine both mixtures and add salt to taste.
4. Heat the oil in a frying pan. Dust the stuffed peppers with flour, then shake off any excess, dip the chillies in the batter,

and fry. I find the best way of coating the peppers is to spoon some batter into the pan of hot oil, then top with the pepper and spoon some batter over it. It seems to work better this way than dipping it in batter and hoping for the best.

5. Fry each pepper until golden brown, then remove from the pan and serve blanketed in or resting in a puddle of Salsa Ranchera. I like a scattering of thinly shredded lettuce, lightly vinegared, atop the pepper, as the heat of the pepper lightly wilts the lettuce.

VARIATIONS

Burritos de Chiles Rellenos: leftover Chiles Rellenos make great *burritos*: gently warm flour tortillas and spread with hot refried beans. Put a warm cheese-stuffed pepper on the bean-spread tortilla, sprinkle with onion and salsa, and roll up.

Red peppers or mild chillies are also good for stuffing: fill roasted and peeled red peppers with Picadillo, mild green chillies with fresh goat's cheese or a seafood stuffing. Don't fry, simply heat in a baking dish in a medium-hot oven, moistened with a little stock.

Chiles en Nogada: with the red, green and white colours of the Mexican Republic's flag, this dish is prepared on Mexican Independence Day. Prepare Picadillo-stuffed peppers and serve with the traditional creamy nut sauce made by grinding 150 g/5 oz walnuts then blending them with 225 g/8 oz cream cheese and 250 ml/8 fl oz soured cream until a smooth creamy sauce is formed. Season with salt. Garnish with ruby red pomegranate seeds and green coriander leaves. To further the colour theme, use a combination of red and green peppers rather than all green.

Chiles Rellenos con Frijoles: stuff cayenne-sprinkled roasted and peeled peppers or poblano chillies with refried beans, then cover the slit in the pepper with lots of grated cheese. Grill until the cheese is melted and bubbling.

◁◁◁◁◁◁◁◁◁◁◁◁◁◁◁◁◁◁◁◁◁◁◁◁◁◁◁◁◁◁◁▷▷▷▷▷▷▷▷▷▷▷▷▷▷▷▷▷▷▷▷▷▷▷▷▷▷▷▷▷▷

Cebollitas Asadas
Grilled Spring Onions

Order *carne asada* (charcoal-grilled meats) nearly anywhere in Mexico, but especially in Mexico City, and they will come accompanied by grilled whole spring onions. The open-fire roasting gives a sweet edge to their assertive flavour.

The best onions for this dish are the ones that have grown beyond infancy, with little bulbs already well formed.

    8 to 12 large spring onions
    Vegetable oil
    Salt to taste
    Lime juice to taste

1. Prepare a charcoal fire and let it burn until medium hot. Cut off the roots of the onions, as well as trimming the greens down.
2. Brush the onions with a little oil, then lay them on the hot grill. You may like to place a piece of foil under the green parts as they are more tender, cook quicker, and are more apt to burn. The onions should take 5 to 10 minutes to cook, depending on the size.
3. Serve sprinked with salt and lime juice.

Ejotes con Pimientos Morrones
Green Beans with Red Peppers

This is a popular combination in Mexico. Not only do the peppers bring out the fresh sweetness of the beans, but the combination of red and green appeals to the Mexican passion for bright colours.

    450 g/1 lb green beans, cut into bite-sized lengths
    2 to 3 cloves garlic, chopped
    1 to 2 tablespoons olive oil
    2 red peppers, stems and seeds removed, cut into strips or
        large dice

◁◁◁◁◁◁◁◁◁◁◁◁◁◁◁◁◁◁◁◁◁◁◁◁◁◁◁◁◁◁◁▷▷▷▷▷▷▷▷▷▷▷▷▷▷▷▷▷▷▷▷▷▷▷▷▷▷

Salt to taste
Dash of lemon juice, balsamic vinegar, or sherry vinegar

1. Cook the green beans in boiling water for about 3 minutes or until crisp-tender. Drain and either rinse with cold water or toss a few ice cubes around the hot beans to stop the cooking and chill them immediately. This helps retain the bright colour and crisp texture.
2. Heat the garlic and olive oil for a minute in a frying pan, then toss in the red peppers and quickly sauté.
3. Add the reserved green beans and toss together. Season with salt and a dash of lemon juice or vinegar and serve either warm or at cool room temperature.

Hongos
Mushrooms

During the rainy season, beginning around July, the market-places in Mexico abound with mushrooms and fungi. Few are familiar, many alarmingly exotic, most are seldom seen outside the region they grow in. Pick your way through baskets of small brown ones, large, fleshy, orange-yellow-hued ones, brick-red, or dusty white – the colours seem to include half the spectrum.

In general, fungi in Mexico are prepared rather simply – a quick jump through the sauté pan with a little chipotle chilli or a spoonful of tomato sauce, and a dose of the requisite chopped onions and garlic. Prepared like this, you might find them adorning a grilled steak, *enchiladas*, or a piece of casseroled chicken.

One of the stranger fungi is *huitlacoche*, a pearly blue-white fungus that grows on the kernels of corn, deforming them to monstrous knobbly proportions. When cooked, the *huitlacoche* exudes a black, inky liquid. It is amazing that anyone was ever brave enough to taste it for the first time and discover how delicious it is. If you should be lucky enough to come by *huitlacoche*, it should be cooked simply, with chillies and seasonings; combined with courgettes and corn; or simmered into soup *Huitlacoche* is a prized *quesadilla* or *taco* filling, the mysterious flavour a perfect pairing for the soft, dry-corn flavour of the tortilla.

◁◁◁◁◁◁◁◁◁◁◁◁◁◁◁◁◁◁◁◁◁◁◁◁◁◁◁◁◁◁◁◁◁◁◁◁◁◁◁◇▷▷▷▷▷▷▷▷▷▷▷▷▷▷▷▷▷▷▷▷▷▷▷▷▷▷▷▷▷▷

Gorditas Aztecas
Plump, Peanut-Topped Potato, Cheese and Courgette Cutlets

These rather fetching cutlets are crisp on the outside and soft inside. With a splash of tangy green salsa and a scattering of crunchy peanuts, their simple potato taste is elevated to one of lively sophistication.

Serve as a pleasing snack or substantial appetizer. Partnered with a bowl of clear broth filled with vegetables and/or meat, they also make a memorable lunch.

4 large potatoes, peeled, boiled and mashed
225 g/8 oz Cheshire or Lancashire cheese, crumbled
2 cloves garlic, chopped
25 g/1 oz *masa harina*
1 or 2 courgettes, coarsely chopped
1 egg, lightly beaten
Salt, black pepper and oregano to taste
Vegetable oil for frying
Green salsa to taste
50 g/2 oz roasted peanuts, coarsely chopped

1. Combine the mashed potatoes with the crumbled cheese, garlic, *masa harina*, courgettes, and egg. Mix well, then season with salt, pepper and oregano.
2. Form into cutlets about 10 cm/4 in long, 7.5 cm/3 in wide, and 2 to 2.5 cm/³/₄ to 1 in thick.
3. Heat enough oil to reach a depth of about 2.5 cm/1 in. When hot, brown the cutlets on both sides until crisp and golden.
4. Serve the cutlets hot, drizzled with a spoonful or two of green salsa and a sprinkling of crunchy peanuts.

POSTRES Y PANES
Desserts and Baked Goods

The ancient Mexican kitchens of the Aztec, Maya, and other nations had no tradition of desserts. Without wheat flour, milk, cream, butter or sugar, their sweets were limited to fresh tropical fruits, fruity *tamales*, honey-scented *atoles*, and fruit pastes known as *ates*.

The tradition of modern Mexico's desserts originated in the colonial convents. It reflects the Moorish-influenced Spanish penchant for sugary, egg yolk-rich sweets, which became a favourite of the convents since the painters of that era used egg whites to 'fix' the colours of the tempera paints in their frescoes. The leftover yolks were sent to the convents for the sisters to put to good use.

The New World nuns made full use of Spanish-transplanted foods and introduced hen's eggs in place of the strong-flavoured wild bird's eggs. While the nuns favoured cloves, cinnamon and nutmeg they ignored the native vanilla, pecan and allspice – and, surprisingly, chocolate. However, this was probably due to its dubious reputation for inciting other hungers, and the fact that in pre-Conquest Mexico chocolate was forbidden to women.

Other influences helped shape Mexico's sweet tooth: the brief French occupation left a penchant for rich pâtisserie fare and those crisp rolls, *bolillos*, that are as good as any you might find in France; the German-Jewish immigration around World War II has left its imprint in the form of hearty European-style baked goods; and cakes and pies reflect the proximity and influence of the United States.

With sweltering heat and weather that begs for refreshment, flavoured ices and ice-creams are enjoyed everywhere. Montezuma is said to have been the first to enjoy ice-cream, sending runners high into the mountains for ice which was mixed

◁◁◁◁◁◁◁◁◁◁◁◁◁◁◁◁◁◁◁◁◁◁◁◁◁◁◁◁◁◁◁◁◁◁◁◁◁◁◇▷▷▷▷▷▷▷▷▷▷▷▷▷▷▷▷▷▷▷▷▷▷▷▷▷▷▷▷▷▷▷▷▷▷▷▷▷▷

with sweet flavourings for him. Modern refrigeration opened the way for a wealth of iced desserts, prepared with the same vivacity that other foods are: brilliantly coloured and flavoured ices of tropical fruits, sweet milk, spicy chocolate and so on. There are *paletas*: intensely refreshing ice-lollies made from chunky lightly puréed fruit, in flavours such as watermelon, strawberry, cantaloupe, coconut, lime, mango, papaya, guava, cactus fruit, almond and so on. *Helado* is the Mexican equivalent of the Italian *gelato*, a rich ice-cream based on luscious tropical fruits.

Rice puddings, custards (flans), and other egg-based puddings are immensely popular throughout the Republic. The French *îles flottantes* reappear in Mexico as fluffs of pink and green meringue cosseted in a creamy custard sauce. Jellied desserts in shimmering garish hues are doted on as well.

In the Yucatán honey, intensely fragrant with the aroma of the jungle, is the traditional sweetener. In the rest of the country *piloncillo* is favoured. A fragrant, dark-brown unrefined sugar that tastes of molasses, it is sold in semi-hard cones and makes delicious nibbling.

Many of the sweets found in Mexico are heavy or gaudy, and too sweet for contemporary Euro-American tastes. There are sweet fruit pastes and concentrated goat's-milk fudges, desserts made from sweet potato paste, sugary cakes of sweetcorn or carrots, and nut pastes fashioned into gaily coloured shapes. Cakes, confectionery and sturdy puddings are based on puréed chickpeas or pinto beans, sweetened and formed into hefty treats. They can taste almost excruciatingly sweet.

Mexican baked goods are too wide and varied to do justice to here. Instead I have chosen only a few of the most representative baked goods that seem to fit best within the scope of this book. There are so many more: king's bread, studded with candied fruit, and 'bread of the dead', with its sugar-coated crossbones topping, are among the most outstanding.

The desserts in this book comprise traditional ones as well as contemporary ideas using regional ingredients, and were chosen for their appeal to modern tastes.

<<<<<<<<<<<<<<<<<<<<<<<<<<<<<><>>>>>>>>>>>>>>>>>>>>>>>>>>>>>

Naranjas y Fresas
Oranges and Strawberries, with Lime and Orange flower Water

The lush, verdant region of Michoacán grows the sweetest, most fragrant strawberries in Mexico. Often they are made into aromatic, delectable preserves, which are spooned on to a buttered *bolillo* (roll), accompanied by a mug of *café con leche*, and enjoyed in the still-cool early morning.

This recipe is a contemporary idea made with traditional ingredients. It makes a fresh beginning to a spicy weekend breakfast, and a refreshing finish for a lavish meal.

> 3 ripe, sweet and juicy oranges, peeled and cut up into bite-sized pieces
> 225 g/8 oz strawberries, hulled and sliced
> Rind and juice of $1/_2$ lime
> 1 tablespoon orange flower water, or to taste
> Sugar to taste

1. Combine the oranges and strawberries, then toss with the lime rind and juice and the orange flower water. Add sugar to taste.
2. Chill and serve.

Naranjas Náhuatl
Aztec Oranges

Inspired by drinks such as tequila sunrise, margarita, etc, this is a perky fruit compote to begin a robust *huevos rancheros* brunch.

> 6 ripe juicy oranges, peeled and sliced
> 25 ml/1 fl oz each: tequila, lime juice, and orange-flavoured liqueur or grenadine
> 1 tablespoon sugar, or to taste

1. Toss the oranges with the remaining ingredients.
2. Chill until ready to eat.

◁◁◁◁◁◁◁◁◁◁◁◁◁◁◁◁◁◁◁◁◁◁◁◁◁▷▷▷▷▷▷▷▷▷▷▷▷▷▷▷▷▷▷▷▷▷▷▷▷▷

VARIATION

Tunas y Piña a la Mexquitic (Prickly Pear and Pineapple Compote, Morelia-Style): prickly pears, with their neon pink-red colour and distinctive flavour, are doted on in Mexico. You can find them sold on the street, the sharp prickles removed, the fruit peeled and ready for eating. As with all fruit desserts, make sure that the fruit used for this recipe is ripe and full of tropical flavour.

Substitute sliced ripe pineapple and prickly pears for the oranges. Omit the grenadine or orange liqueur.

Mangos con Salsa de Frambuesa y Fresa
Mangoes with Mixed Berries and Berry Sauce

A purée of berries enhanced with lime juice makes a vibrantly coloured and flavoured sauce to puddle around fruit, especially mangoes and whole berries. For a Fauvist-inspired presentation, add slices of green kiwi, along with a handful of blueberries and a few leaves of mint.

   225 g/8 oz strawberries, cleaned and picked over
   225 g/8 oz blackberries or raspberries, cleaned and picked
     over
   Dash of lime juice or balsamic vinegar
   Sugar to taste
   2 medium-sized ripe flavourful mangoes
   Fresh mint for garnish (optional)

1. Purée about two-thirds of the berries with lime juice or balsamic vinegar and sugar to taste. Blend until a saucelike consistency is formed. Set aside.
2. Peel and slice the mangoes.
3. Pour a puddle of sauce on each plate and arrange the mango slices and reserved berries on top. Serve immediately, garnished with mint, if using.

Plátanos al Horno
Leah's Baked Bananas with Melted Chocolate

This decadent little combination of two ingredients (not count-
ing any whipped cream or coffee ice-cream you might want to
dollop on top and let melt in) is included not because it is an
authentic Mexican dish but because both the ingredients are
Mexican and it tastes so awfully good following a spicy, robust
meal. Also, it is very simple to prepare this rich and gooey sweet,
even if the rest of the meal leaves you too exhausted even to pick
up a whisk.

This is a contribution from my daughter, Leah (it is one of the
only dishes known to lure her into the act of food preparation).

Serves 1

   1 banana, unpeeled
   About 6 squares of milk or plain chocolate
   Whipped cream or coffee ice-cream (optional)

1. Make a slash lengthwise in each banana, cutting through the
   skin into the flesh inside.
2. Tuck as many chocolate squares as will fit into the cavity of
   the banana. Wrap the stuffed banana up in foil.
3. Bake in the oven at 200°C/400°F/gas mark 6 for about 10
   minutes, or long enough to melt the chocolate. Serve
   immediately, with a drift of whipped cream or coffee ice-
   cream on top, if liked, the banana pulled open slightly to
   accommodate it.

Plátanos al Horno con Naranja
Bananas Baked with Orange Juice and Cinnamon

Baked bananas are one of those dishes that seem too simple to be
so good. They are fiesta food, sold at holiday times from street
vendors, buttery and sweet, often scented, as this one is, with
orange juice. Amounts need not be specific – adjust them to suit
your taste.

◄◄◄◄◄◄◄◄◄◄◄◄◄◄◄◄◄◄◄◄◄◄◄◄◄◄◄◄◄◄►►►►►►►►►►►►►►►►►►►►►►►►►►►►►►►

4 bananas, peeled and left whole
Several tablespoons of dark demerara sugar
2 teaspoons ground cinnamon
Unsalted butter
75 to 100 ml/3 to 4 fl oz orange juice
Whipped cream, to serve

1. Arrange the bananas in a baking dish and sprinkle with sugar
   and cinnamon, then dot with butter and pour the orange juice
   all around.
2. Bake in the oven at 180°C/350°F/gas mark 4 for 30 minutes
   or until the bananas are soft, the sugar slightly caramelized,
   and a sauce has formed. Serve immediately, topped with a
   drift of lightly whipped cream.

VARIATION

Use rum, instead of orange juice. Heat first in a small pan to
cook off the alcohol (keep your face and any curtains or cloths
away from the pan as it might ignite) so that the rum will not
catch fire in the oven.

Calabaza Enmielada
Pumpkin with Dark Demerara Sugar

This is a simple sweet, probably prepared since ancient times
when honey rather than the Spanish-imported sugar was used for
sweetening. The simplest and most spectacular presentation is a
grand one: use a whole pumpkin, the Hallowe'en-lantern type.
Bake the whole sugar-stuffed pumpkin in a baking dish with a
little water at the bottom until the flesh is tender.

In Mexico, this soft sweet pumpkin is scooped out into a deep
bowl, then doused with milk and enjoyed for breakfast.

1 kg/2¼ lb pumpkin, or other orange-fleshed squash, seeds
   removed, and cut into large pieces
Dark demerara sugar to taste
About 75 ml/3 fl oz water, more if necessary

◁◁◁◁◁◁◁◁◁◁◁◁◁◁◁◁◁◁◁◁◁◁◁◁◁◁◁◁◁◁▷▷▷▷▷▷▷▷▷▷▷▷▷▷▷▷▷▷▷▷▷▷▷▷▷▷▷▷▷▷

1. Pack the sugar on to each piece of pumpkin, then place in a baking dish.
2. Pour the water around, cover tightly, and cook on the stove top or bake in the oven at 180°C/350°F/gas mark 4 until tender, about 1 hour.

Chimichangas de Frutas
Fruit-filled 'Chimichangas'

Chimichangas are parcels of flour tortillas wrapped around a filling, then fried to a golden crispness. They are Southwestern in origin rather than Mexican. While they are usually prepared with savoury fillings, they make a delectable sweet stuffed with fruit and blanketed with sugar and cream. I got the idea from the London restaurant Down Mexico Way, where I believe the *chimichanga* rested in a pool of mango purée. My fruit *chimichangas* sometimes do and sometimes don't – the filling, too, varies according to whatever fruit is in season.

4 flour tortillas
Oil for frying

Fruit filling

1 banana, diced
1 kiwi fruit, diced
1 nectarine, peach or mango, diced
1 small apple, diced
A handful of berries

Sugar for sprinkling
Ice-cream or whipped cream for topping
Mango or strawberry purée, seasoned with sugar and lime juice (optional)

1. Soften the flour tortillas one at a time in a very lightly oiled frying pan.
2. Place several spoonfuls of the fruit filling down the centre of

◄◄◄◄◄◄◄◄◄◄◄◄◄◄◄◄◄◄◄◄◄◄◄◄◄◄◄◄◄◄◄◄►►►►►►►►►►►►►►►►►►►►►►►►►►►►►►

each tortilla then roll up to enclose the filling, parcel-style.
3. When all 4 parcels have been assembled, fry in hot oil about
   1.25 to 2.5 cm/¹/₂ to 1 in deep.
4. Drain on absorbent paper and serve immediately, sprinkled
   generously with sugar, topped with ice-cream or whipped
   cream, and, for the ambitious, lying in a puddle of fruit purée.

Arroz Chocolatl
Chocolate Rice Pudding

After the Conquest, Mexico took readily to rice: sweet and
creamy rice puddings have been well loved since then. The following recipe is particularly nice since it includes cocoa.

50 g/2 oz shortgrain rice
250 ml/8 fl oz milk
2 tablespoons sugar
Tiny pinch of salt
35 g/1¹/₂ oz cocoa powder
¹/₄ teaspoon cinnamon
¹/₂ teaspoon vanilla essence
Cream and soured cream, to serve

1. In a coffee grinder or liquidizer grind the rice into a fine
   meal.
2. Combine the ground rice with the milk, sugar and salt. Bring
   to the boil, reduce the heat, and simmer over a very low heat
   until thickened, 5 to 10 minutes.
3. Add the cocoa, cinnamon, and vanilla essence. Serve cool,
   topped with a spoonful or two of *crema Mexicana*, a mixture of
   half cream and half soured cream.

◁◁◁◁◁◁◁◁◁◁◁◁◁◁◁◁◁◁◁◁◁◁◁◁◁◁◁◁◁◁◁▷▷▷▷▷▷▷▷▷▷▷▷▷▷▷▷▷▷▷▷▷▷▷▷▷▷▷▷▷▷

Flan de Café
Coffee Custard

Flan, or crème caramel, is as ubiquitous in Mexico as it is in
Spain where it originated. Often in Mexico you'll find the
creamy delicate egg custard combined with the strong flavour of
New World seasonings such as coffee.

Syrup

   25 ml/1 fl oz strong brewed coffee
   50 g/2 oz sugar

Custard

   75 g/3 oz sugar
   6 eggs, lightly beaten
   500 ml/16 fl oz milk
   1 teaspoon vanilla essence

1. Heat the coffee with the sugar and bring to the boil. Cook for
   5 minutes or until syrupy.
2. Pour the syrup into a large dish or smaller custard cups,
   twirling around to coat both bottom and sides. Set aside.
3. Make a hot-water bath for the custard by setting a large
   baking dish half filled with hot water in the oven at
   180°C/350°C/gas mark 4.
4. Beat together the sugar, eggs, milk and vanilla essence. Pour
   into the prepared dish or custard cups then place in the hot-
   water bath.
5. Bake for about 25 minutes. Test by pressing the back of a
   spoon on to the custard. It should make a crevice about 1.25
   cm/$^1/_2$ in deep.
6. Remove from the hot water and cool, then chill in the
   refrigerator.
7. To serve, loosen round the edge of the custard with a knife,
   then invert on to a plate. The coffee caramel on the bottom
   will form a thin sauce.

⊲⊲⊲⊲⊲⊲⊲⊲⊲⊲⊲⊲⊲⊲⊲⊲⊲⊲⊲⊲⊲⊲⊲⊲⊲⊲⊲⊳⊳⊳⊳⊳⊳⊳⊳⊳⊳⊳⊳⊳⊳⊳⊳⊳⊳⊳⊳⊳⊳⊳⊳⊳

Dulce de Coco
Coconut Fudge or Jam

Somewhere between a pudding and a sweet, this is an intensely
sweet concoction of caramelized coconut and coconut milk, light
brown in colour. Its flavour conjures up Mexican sweet shops,
where the sugary smell is woven into the languid air. It is delicious in tiny spoonfuls with a cup of black unsweetened *café de
olla* alongside. In Mexico this sweet is prepared more in a fondant
style, the resulting macaroon-like sweets tinted bright green or
pink.

175 g/6 oz desiccated coconut
400 ml/14 fl oz (1 tin) unsweetened coconut milk
250 g/9 oz sugar
Pinch of salt
Juice of ¹/₄ lime or lemon

1. Combine the coconut, coconut milk, sugar and salt in a
   saucepan.
2. Slowly bring to the boil, then reduce the heat and simmer,
   letting it bubble away, stirring every so often, until very thick
   (about 15 to 30 minutes). It should have turned light golden
   brown and caramelized. Stir as often as you can, as the
   coconut will settle, and if you are not careful it will burn.
   When stirring, use a long spoon, if possible, to prevent it
   splattering on to your hand.
3. Add the lemon or lime juice and spread over the bottom of a
   large baking dish or on to a large plate to cool.
4. Chill. When cold, roll into balls or serve by the spoonful.
   Accompany with strong, unsweetened coffee or a glass of
   brandy.

Helado de Chocolatl
Chocolate-Cinnamon Ice-Cream

If you choose only one dessert to prepare from this book, choose
this one. Deep and dark, with the exotic aroma of cinnamon, it is

◁◁◁◁◁◁◁◁◁◁◁◁◁◁◁◁◁◁◁◁◁◁◁◁▷▷▷▷▷▷▷▷▷▷▷▷▷▷▷▷▷▷▷▷▷▷▷▷

an extraordinary ice-cream. Like an Italian *gelato*, it is so richly chocolatey it is almost chewy.

Since it is so rich, serve only small portions and follow, perhaps, with strong, black, unsweetened coffee.

Makes about 1.2 litres/2 pints

600 ml/1 pint whipping cream
500 ml/16 fl oz milk
150 g/5 oz sugar
4 cinnamon sticks plus 1 teaspoon ground cinnamon
200 g/7 oz semi-sweet plain chocolate
4 egg yolks
35 g/1 1/2 oz unsweetened cocoa powder

1. In a heavy saucepan combine the whipping cream, milk, sugar and cinnamon. Cook over a medium heat until the sugar is dissolved and the mixture is quite hot, stirring every so often. Remove from the heat.
2. Break up the chocolate and add to the hot cream mixture. Leave for about 5 minutes, or until the chocolate softens and melts.
3. Meanwhile, beat the egg yolks.
4. When the chocolate has softened, stir or beat well to mix and dissolve it into the milk; don't worry if tiny bits of chocolate remain – they will melt later. Gradually add a cup of this hot chocolate mixture to the egg yolks, beating with each addition, then stir the egg mixture into the hot chocolate.
5. Make a thinnish paste of the cocoa, using a cup of the hot chocolate mixture, then add this to the hot chocolate.
6. Cook gently over a low heat, stirring occasionally. When the mixture is hot and slightly thickened – enough to coat the back of a spoon – remove from the heat.
7. Let cool, then remove the cinnamon sticks. Freeze, either in an ice-cream maker or in a baking tray, to be forked up every so often, granita-like.

◁◁◁◁◁◁◁◁◁◁◁◁◁◁◁◁◁◁◁◁◁◁◁◁◁▷▷▷▷▷▷▷▷▷▷▷▷▷▷▷▷▷▷▷▷▷▷▷▷▷

Helado de Yerba Buena, con
Tostadas de Chocolatl
Fresh Mint Ice-Cream with Chocolate Tostadas or Tostaditas

Fresh mint ice-cream is a revelation to those who have tasted
only the garishly green stuff made from overly strong mint
essences. Fresh mint is mildly bracing, and the flavour varies
depending on the type you use. I like to use a combination of
peppermint, fragrant tiny leaves of Corsican mint, pungent gin-
ger mint, and a little sweet spearmint. (By the way, *yerba buena*
means good herb, the name once given by the Native American
Indians to what is now San Francisco, probably because of the
wild mint that grew on its hillsides.)

250 ml/8 fl oz double cream
250 ml/8 fl oz milk
75 g/3 oz sugar
3 tablespoons finely chopped fresh mint of choice
4 flour tortillas, whole or cut into wedges
Bland vegetable oil for frying
200 g/7 oz dark chocolate, broken, chopped, or coarsely
    grated

1. Place the double cream, milk and sugar in a saucepan. Heat
    over a medium heat until the sugar melts and dissolves.
2. Remove from the heat, add the chopped mint leaves, and let
    cool.
3. Freeze in an ice-cream maker, an ice-cube tray or any other
    shallow, freezer-proof dish.
4. When ready to serve, fry the whole tortillas or tortilla wedges
    in hot oil until golden. Drain on absorbent paper and quickly
    sprinkle generously with the chocolate. The heat from the
    tortillas should melt the chocolate nearly immediately. If not,
    place them briefly in a moderately hot oven.
5. Serve the mint ice-cream garnished with the chocolate-
    topped *tostadas* or *tostaditas*.

◁◁◁◁◁◁◁◁◁◁◁◁◁◁◁◁◁◁◁◁◁◁▷▷▷▷▷▷▷▷▷▷▷▷▷▷▷▷▷▷▷▷▷▷▷

Nieve de Frutas
Fruit Blizzard

Fresh fruit, frozen then whirled into a sweet and tangy froth, makes a most refreshing end to a meal, especially if the meal is spicy and the weather outside as hot as the food.

Freeze any sliced, juicy, ripe fruit: strawberries, pineapple, mango, nectarines, watermelon, cactus fruit, papaya, cantaloupe, blackberries, etc. Whirl the frozen fruit in a food processor with sugar to taste, enough fruit juice or tequila to make a sorbet-like consistency, and a dash of lime or lemon juice for balance if needed.

Nieve de Mango con Fresas Borrachas
Frozen Ice of Mango with Strawberries in Liqueur

The variety of slightly sweetened tropical fruit drinks available in the shops makes preparing frozen ices easy and accessible. Simply freeze a carton of mango juice, then when ready to serve peel the paper box off, hack the frozen juice into pieces and whirl it to a froth in a liquidizer with a little citrus or pineapple juice. Serve topped with fresh strawberries and a dash of any liqueur. It makes a thoroughly refreshing way to end a chilli-laden meal, and any other type of fruit juice and fruit can be substituted.

PASTRIES AND BAKED GOODS
La Panadería

Many visitors to Mexico find it a surprise that bread in Mexico is so good, and so much a part of the diet. Rather than overtake the tortilla, Mexico has created a separate tradition of baking. *Bolillos* and *virotes*, crusty rolls similar to those found in France, are a legacy from the brief reign of Maximilian and Carlota. There is a wide variety of sweet breads and rolls, often with iced sugary frostings that attract the attention not only of customers, but of a

◄◄◄

handful of flies and the odd bee or two.

Mexican bakeries entice with the same excitement as French pâtisseries, with their wide range of colours, shapes and textures. There might be *gaznates* (fried cakes made with rum), *empanadas* filled with candied sweet potatoes or pineapple, *polvorones* (sugar-coated shortbread), meringues and so on. Many pastries are local, particular to each region, town, village. In Zacatecas they favour syrup-dipped cinnamon doughnuts. Fiestas demand their own breads: my favourite is the *crokadillo*, the slightly sweet dough fashioned into tiny spikes and the finished bread decorated with sugar icing features. I have celebrated even the most ordinary days with loaves of this bread.

Mexican sweets are very sweet indeed. They are often vibrantly coloured, in pastel-brights of pink, green, blue and yellow. Confections may be made from simmering milk (usually goat's) into thick fudge, or by grinding and shaping coconut, squash seeds and nuts, as well as candied fruits, often sweetened with brown-black *piloncillo* sugar.

Churros
Crisp Long Fluted Fritters

Freshly fried in huge cauldrons of viciously hot oil, *churros* are crispy golden on the outside, airily tender and nearly hollow on the inside, served blanketed with a flurry of sugar.

An authentic *churria*, or *churro* shop, is a scrap of daily Mexican City life. Peer in the window and watch the constant motion of squeezing the curls of dough into oil, fishing out the golden snakelike fritters, shaking on the sugar. Order a plate with a cup of dark rich chocolate or *café con leche*, then find a stool and sit back to savour the sweet treat as you observe the drama of life in Mexico unfold around you.

Churros are easy to make at home, but to obtain the characteristic fluted shape you'll need a pastry bag fitted with a star tip. An unusual aspect of these fritters is that the oil used for the frying is flavoured by adding a lemon or lime half to it when hot; by the time the moisture from the lemon or lime pulp has evaporated

⊲⊲⊲⊲⊲⊲⊲⊲⊲⊲⊲⊲⊲⊲⊲⊲⊲⊲⊲⊲⊲⊲⊲⊲⊲⊲⊲⊲⊲⊲⊲⊲⊳⊳⊳⊳⊳⊳⊳⊳⊳⊳⊳⊳⊳⊳⊳⊳⊳⊳⊳⊳⊳⊳⊳⊳⊳⊳⊳⊳⊳⊳⊳⊳

the oil is lightly perfumed with citrus. Lemon extract added to
the batter instead makes a handy shortcut.

Churros make a memorable breakfast accompanied by a mug of
hot chocolate or *café con leche*. They're good, too, as a late-night
snack, accompanied by a glass of brandy or rum.

> 2 teaspoons aniseed
> 75 g/3 oz caster sugar
> 250 ml/8 fl oz water
> Pinch of salt
> 1 teaspoon sugar
> 100 g/4 oz butter or margarine
> 100 g/4 oz flour
> 4 eggs
> $1/_4$ teaspoon lemon essence, or half a lemon or lime
> Oil for deep frying

1. Whirl the aniseed and caster sugar in a liquidizer. Set aside.
2. In a saucepan combine the water, salt, 1 teaspoon sugar, and
   butter or margarine. Heat until the butter melts, then bring
   to the boil.
3. When it reaches a rolling boil, add the flour all at once,
   remove from the heat, and beat the mixture with a wooden or
   other heavy spoon until it becomes a thick, shiny paste that
   comes away from the side of the pan.
4. Add the eggs one at a time, beating well after each addition
   until the paste is smooth and shiny. Add the lemon essence, if
   using.
5. Fill a pastry bag with the dough.
6. Heat enough oil to reach a depth of 5 to 7.5 cm/2 to 3 in. If
   not using lemon essence in the dough, add a lemon or lime
   half to the oil. It will sputter a bit as the moisture in it
   evaporates.
7. Discard the lemon or lime half. Start squeezing the dough
   into the oil until you have a ribbon of paste about 17.5 to 22.5
   cm/7 to 9 in long. You can fry several lengths at a time.
8. Cook until browned and crisp, then drain on absorbent paper.
9. Serve immediately, sprinkled with the aniseed-scented sugar.

◁◁◁◁◁◁◁◁◁◁◁◁◁◁◁◁◁◁◁◁◁◁◁◁◁◁◁◁◁◁▷▷▷▷▷▷▷▷▷▷▷▷▷▷▷▷▷▷▷▷▷▷▷▷▷▷▷▷▷▷

Buñuelos
Fried Crisp Dough Puffs

These crisp rounds of dough coated with cinnamon and sugar are especially popular at Christmas. They are cherished by children, the sugary sweets clenched in little hands. In Oaxaca a Christmas Eve tradition is a *buñuelo* feast, accompanied by a smashing of plates the fritters have been eaten off. It is meant to bring good luck. The next morning the town is nearly ankle deep in broken crockery.

Cinnamon sugar

> 225 g/8 oz sugar
> 1 tablespoon cinnamon

Dough

> 4 eggs
> 225 g/8 oz sugar
> 225 g/8 oz flour
> 1 teaspoon baking powder
> 1 teaspoon salt
> Vegetable oil for deep frying

1. Combine the sugar and cinnamon. Set aside.
2. Beat the eggs together with the sugar until thick and golden. Stir together the flour, baking powder and salt and slowly add to the egg mixture.
3. Turn out on to a board and knead until the dough is smooth and no longer sticky, about 5 minutes.
4. Divide the dough into 16 pieces. With floured hands shape each piece into a ball and place in a bowl or on a board. Cover with a towel or waxed paper and leave to rest for about 30 minutes.
5. On a floured board, roll each ball out to make a flat, thin circle.
6. Heat about 5 cm/2 in of oil in a heavy pan and fry the dough circles, one or two at a time, until golden brown.
7. Remove the doughnuts from the hot oil and drain on

◁◁◁◁◁◁◁◁◁◁◁◁◁◁◁◁◁◁◁◁◁◁◁◁◁◁◁▷▷▷▷▷▷▷▷▷▷▷▷▷▷▷▷▷▷▷▷▷▷▷▷▷▷▷

absorbent paper, then toss them in the cinnamon-sugar mixture to coat lavishly. Serve immediately.

Cinnamon Buñuelo Stars with Ice-Cream, Caramel Sauce and Bananas

This is a Southwestern dessert inspired by traditional South of the Border ingredients and dishes. Cutting the tortillas into star shapes may seem like no more than whimsy, but in fact the crisp and browned points make a particularly delicious contrast to the rich sauce and ice-cream.

Buñuelo Stars

2 tablespoons cinnamon
75 g/3 oz sugar
4 flour tortillas
Bland vegetable oil for deep frying

Caramel Sauce

225 g/8 oz sugar
750 ml/1¼ pints whipping cream
Pinch of baking powder
1½ teaspoons good vanilla essence

600 ml/1 pint dark rich chocolate ice-cream, or flavour of choice (such as coffee, banana, walnut, pecan, caramel swirl or praline, etc)
2 bananas, sliced

1. Make the *buñuelo* stars: mix the cinnamon and sugar and set aside. Cut the flour tortillas into star shapes (save the scraps to fry and enjoy powdered with sugar and cinnamon as sweet nibbles). Heat the oil until hot enough to brown the tortillas lightly almost immediately. Add the stars a few at a time, pressing down to cook until golden, about 1 minute. Drain on absorbent paper, and sprinkle with the cinnamon-sugar mixture. Set aside.

2. Make the caramel sauce: place the sugar in a large, heavy saucepan and heat over a medium-high heat until it turns golden, 5 to 8 minutes. Remove from the heat and add about 100 ml/4 fl oz water, taking care that it does not splatter you. Return to the heat, stirring to dissolve the caramel as it heats. Add the cream and baking powder, and simmer, stirring every so often, until the sauce thickens and turns a golden caramel colour; this should take about 30 minutes. Remove from the heat and add the vanilla essence. Set aside, stirring every so often as it cools.
3. To assemble: spoon the warm caramel sauce on to dessert plates. Top with a scoop of ice-cream, and decorate informally with slices of banana and *buñuelo* stars. Serve immediately.

VARIATION

The *buñuelo* stars make lovely biscuits or accompaniments for fruit puddings.

Suspiros
Chocolate Meringues

These are delicately textured, with a crisp-edged exterior and a soft chocolate centre. *Suspiros* means sighs, and I think that might be more descriptive than any explanation I can give here.

Though the recipe calls for leaving the meringues in the turned-off oven for 3 hours, I find that sometimes they are still a little soft and fudgy at that stage, because of the chocolate. It also depends on the weather and the individual oven. To be honest, they are rather good this way, topped with a dollop of whipped cream. For a crisper texture, simply reheat the oven and crisp the meringues up for 10 minutes or so, then turn the oven off and let them sit to dry a little.

Makes 2 to 3 dozen meringues, depending on size

◁◁◁◁◁◁◁◁◁◁◁◁◁◁◁◁◁◁◁◁◁◁◁◁◁◁◁◁◇▷▷▷▷▷▷▷▷▷▷▷▷▷▷▷▷▷▷▷▷▷▷▷▷▷▷▷▷

4 egg whites at room temperature
Pinch of salt
1 teaspoon vanilla essence
175 g/6 oz sugar
2 teaspoons ground cinnamon
100 g/4 oz semi-sweet plain chocolate, grated

1. Whip the egg whites until foamy. Add the salt and whisk until very stiff, then whisk in the vanilla essence.
2. Whisk in the sugar, a small amount at a time, whipping as you add it until the meringue is shiny and stiff. This should take about 3 minutes by hand.
3. Whisk in the cinnamon and grated chocolate, then spoon the meringues on to an ungreased baking sheet lined with baking parchment.
4. Place in the oven preheated to 180°C/350°F/gas mark 4 and immediately turn off the heat. Leave the meringues in the oven for 3 hours. DO NOT OPEN THE OVEN DOOR until that period of time has passed. I often prepare them the night before and leave them in the oven overnight.
5. Remove from the baking sheets. If they are too moist and soft, reheat and leave to dry in the oven.

Torta de Cielo
Flat Almond Sponge

The sweet scent of almond in this cake is enticing. flat, dense, and slightly chewy it sits on the bakery shelf, looking plain next to the tarted-up beauty-contestant gaudiness of the more extravagant offerings.

But do not be misled, for what this cake lacks in appearance it makes up in flavour. Serve as an accompaniment to tea, coffee or a glass of brandy, or as a sweet course at the end of a meal – and if it still seems too plain, serve it in a pool of puréed and lightly sweetened berries or tropical fruit, topped with a dollop of sweet, cool, whipped cream.

<<<<<<<<<<<<<<<<<<<<<<<<<<<<<<<<>>>>>>>>>>>>>>>>>>>>>>>>>>>>>>>>

175 g/6 oz raw almonds, preferably with skins
100 g/4 oz unsalted butter, at room temperature
225 g/8 oz sugar
3 medium eggs, lightly beaten
1 teaspoon pure almond essence
Pinch of salt
25 g/1 oz flour

20 x 20 cm/8 x 8 in square or round baking tin, buttered

1. In a food processor or grinder grind the almonds into a mealy consistency. If your liquidizer can do this, use it. Set the ground almonds aside.
2. Cream the butter and sugar together until smooth. Add the eggs, ground almonds, almond essence and salt. Mix until smooth.
3. Stir the flour into the mixture and mix only until the flour has been incorporated.
4. Pour or spoon into the buttered baking tin and bake in the oven at 350°F/180°C/gas mark 4 for 40 to 50 minutes or until firm. Remove from the oven and cool.

BEBIDAS Y REFRESCOS
Drinks

In a land that simmers in the bondage of an unrelenting heat, cooling and refreshing drinks form as important a part of the cuisine as do the savoury and spicy foods. Walk down any street and, alongside stalls selling all manner of enticing *tacos* and skewers, fruits and spicy nibbles, you will find others selling a wide variety of cooling, invigorating, gaily coloured drinks.

In the street, vendors whip up cold *licuados de frutas* (fruit milkshakes) on the spot – a splash of milk or rice-milk is added to the fresh purée of fruit then the whole thing is poured into your glass ready to be drunk eagerly. The fruit is sweet and perfumed; it exquisitely slakes your parched throat.

Huge glass crocks of rainbow-tinted fruit drinks known as *aguas de frutas* line street stalls, ready to be ladled into glasses. Made from sugared fruit – or even ground nuts, rice or seeds – and water, they refresh against the merciless heat. Made for the typical Mexican sweet tooth they are often too cloying for my tastes; however, you can adjust the sugar in homemade versions to suit your own preferences.

There are warm drinks too: corn *masa*, the foundation of the Mexican kitchen, is thinned with water or milk and heated to make *atole*, a thick gruel-like drink, often flavoured with vanilla, strawberries, pineapple, chocolate, etc.

Mexican coffee is strong, frequently seasoned with cinnamon or stirred with a cinnamon stick; hot chocolate is also fragrant with cinnamon and scented almond. Both invigorating drinks date back to pre-Hispanic times when they were served as royal potions to the Aztec rulers. Tea in Mexico is usually herb, and often drunk as a medicinal or curative brew, with specific healing powers attributed to each herb.

The liquid refreshment almost synonymous with Mexico is

◁◁◁◁◁◁◁◁◁◁◁◁◁◁◁◁◁◁◁◁◁◁◁◁◁◁◁◁▷▷▷▷▷▷▷▷▷▷▷▷▷▷▷▷▷▷▷▷▷▷▷▷▷▷▷▷

tequila and the wide variety of drinks made from that zesty firewater, especially margaritas. Mexico also brews excellent beers; indeed, even for those who seldom drink these brews, the combination of hot sultry weather and bracingly refreshing beer is difficult to beat. There is also mezcal, like tequila, distilled from the maguey, with its little worm curled up at the bottom of the bottle, and *pulque*, the slightly sour, foamy alcoholic drink of the Aztecs. There is a small but thriving wine industry in Baja California. Some of the wine is rather rough, though some of it good. There are also a number of speciality drinks: liqueurs, rum, brandies.

Aguas Frescas
Fruit 'Waters'

Almost any fruit can be used to make *aguas* – from the familiar strawberry or mango, to the exotic guava, sour tamarind, or scarlet hibiscus flowers. They are so very refreshing. They make a perfect accompaniment to a summer lunch, a children's party or spicy brunch, or for a fiesta or Mexican party-celebration when a non-alcoholic drink is called for in addition to the tequila drinks.

1 of the following:
3 mangoes, peeled and sliced
About 450 g/1 lb fresh strawberries, hulled
675 g/1$\frac{1}{2}$ lb guavas, sliced or diced
1 kg/2$\frac{1}{4}$ lb ripe, sweet cantaloupe, red or yellow
    watermelon, or honeydew melon, sliced or diced

2 litres/3$\frac{1}{2}$ pints cool water
Sugar to taste
Juice of $\frac{1}{2}$ a lemon or lime if using mango or melon
Fruit or fresh mint for garnish

1. Blend the fruit of choice with about 500 ml/16 fl oz of the water in a liquidizer. Let stand for an hour, then strain.
2. Combine with the remaining water, sugar to taste (and lemon

◁◁◁◁◁◁◁◁◁◁◁◁◁◁◁◁◁◁◁◁◁◁◁◁▷▷▷▷▷▷▷▷▷▷▷▷▷▷▷▷▷▷▷▷▷▷▷▷

or lime juice if using mango or melon) and serve over ice.
Garnish with matching fruit: strawberries for strawberry
agua, mango slices for mango, and so forth – or put a sprig of
fresh mint into each glass.

VARIATION

Agua de Granada: squeeze 10 ripe pomegranates or whirl the
seeds in a liquidizer, then strain to obtain the juice. Add to 3
litres/5¼ pints water and sweeten to taste. Chill and serve with
ice.

Tamarindo
Tamarind Cooler

Tamarind originated in Asia where it is still used a great deal as a
tart-sour but earthy flavour in curries, sauces, desserts and so on.
Tamarind pods look intimidating to deal with – filled with rock-
hard bean-like seeds and a sticky pulp – but they are not as
difficult as they appear. They yield their sour flavour readily.
Sometimes a liquid tamarind can be found, at other times a block
of pressed tamarind flesh. Both deliver fine flavour and are easier
to work with.

Tamarindo is more refreshing and less cloying than other
fruit-based drinks. It makes a good non-alcoholic alternative to
beers, its refreshing lightness well suited to spicy and smoky
foods.

225 g/8 oz tamarind, either the pods, lightly crushed, or
    the already crushed and pressed chunk, or syrup
500 ml/16 fl oz boiling water
2 litres/3½ pints water
Sugar (start with 150 g/5 oz and add more to taste)

1. Mix the tamarind with the boiling water and let stand
   overnight.
2. Strain and mix with the water and sugar to taste. Serve over
   ice.

◁◁◁▷▷▷

Limonada
Limeade

Often in Mexico this sprightly refreshment will be tinted with an artificial-looking green food colour to denote its lime flavour. I find it much more aesthetic, as well as more flavourful, to add slices of lime to the crock or pitcher. If you are serving it in individual glasses, make a cut in each lime slice and fasten it on to the glass rim.

    10 large and juicy limes
    2 litres/3¹/₂ pints water
    Sugar to taste

1. Squeeze 8 of the limes into the water, adding one or two of the lime halves as well (or grate the rind off one or two of the discarded halves).
2. Slice the remaining limes, discard the pips, and add to the liquid, or save some slices to decorate the glasses with.
3. Sweeten with sugar to taste. The limes are very tart; they may need a lot of sugar.

VARIATIONS

Mexican limeade, with its strong lime flavour, welcomes a jolt of vodka or tequila.

Use sparkling or soda water in place of still water in the basic limeade.

Limonada de Oaxaca: in Oaxaca, the rinds of very green and fragrant limes are finely grated to add colour and scent to this drink. In the central marketplace Indian women grind the lime peel with *molcajetes* to extract the fragrant green oils that both flavour and tint the drink. Often the juice is not added at all, since it bleaches out the colour the green lime imparts. However, the tangy tart citrus juice makes a much more refreshing drink, to my taste.

◄◄◄◄◄◄◄◄◄◄◄◄◄◄◄◄◄◄◄◄◄◄◄◄◄◄◄◄◄►►►►►►►►►►►►►►►►►►►►►►►►►►►►►►

Agua de Jamaica
Hibiscus Drink

Hibiscus flowers have a startlingly tart flavour and a bright, trop-ically scarlet colour. This drink quenches thirst with vigour and its colour is so vivid, so bright, that a glassful adds an inexplicable festivity. Agua de Jamaica is sometimes combined with dry, fruity light red wine and a little fresh lime juice for a lively sangría, or served with a shot of tequila.

Since this is a popular drink throughout the Caribbean as well, you can often find dried hibiscus blossoms sold in West Indian markets. Accentuate its exotic appearance, if you like, by garnish-ing the glasses or punch bowl with gaily coloured, edible unsprayed blossoms.

225 g/8 oz hibiscus flowers
500 ml/16 fl oz boiling water
3 litres/5¼ pints cool water
Sugar to taste

1. Steep the hibiscus blossoms for 30 minutes in the boiling water.
2. Strain and combine with the cool water and sugar to taste.
3. Serve over ice.

VARIATION

Mix equal parts of Agua de Jamaica, sparkling mineral water and well-chilled rosé wine. Serve garnished with thinly sliced citrus fruit.

◁◁◁◁◁◁◁◁◁◁◁◁◁◁◁◁◁◁◁◁◁◁◁◁◁◁◁◁◁◁◁◁◁◁◁◁◁◁◇▷▷▷▷▷▷▷▷▷▷▷▷▷▷▷▷▷▷▷▷▷▷▷▷▷▷▷▷▷▷▷▷▷▷▷▷▷▷▷

Chicha de Frutas
Mixed Fruit Punch

25 g/1 oz mint leaves
100 g/4 oz sugar
1 litre/1³/₄ pints pineapple juice
500 ml/16 fl oz orange juice
Juice of 2 lemons, plus 1 lemon cut into thin slices
Juice of 2 limes, plus 1 lime cut into thin slices
¹/₄ cucumber, unpeeled, cut into thin slices
Crushed ice or large block of ice

1. Mix the mint with the sugar and muddle the leaves a little in
    the sugar. Add the remaining ingredients and let the ice chill
    the drink as you serve it.
2. If you are not going to serve it in a large punch bowl with ice
    melting in, thin the punch down (the lime and lemon will be
    quite strong and tart) with plain or sparkling water.

VARIATION

Though one of the delights of this punch is its non-alcoholic
nature, it is also good with a shot of vodka or tequila.

Leche con Fresas
Strawberry Milk

Every marketplace and bus station throughout Mexico has at
least one stall devoted to this drink, with several liquidizers lined
up, whirling away and serving up various concoctions of frothy
fruit and milk.

This makes a delicious brunch or breakfast drink. As with
other simple foods, the quality of raw ingredients makes all the
difference in the world. Highly perfumed, sweet fruit will make a
memorable drink, indifferent fruit will not.

◁◁◁◁◁◁◁◁◁◁◁◁◁◁◁◁◁◁◁◁◁◁◁◁◁◁◁◁◁◁◁◁◁▷▷▷▷▷▷▷▷▷▷▷▷▷▷▷▷▷▷▷▷▷▷▷▷▷▷▷▷▷▷▷▷

750 ml/1¼ pints cold milk
225 g/8 oz strawberries, hulled
1 teaspoon cinnamon, or several drops of vanilla essence
Sugar to taste
Several cubes of crushed ice

1. Place all the ingredients in a liquidizer and whirl until frothy.

VARIATIONS

In the streets of Mexico the vendors have an egg basket next to
the blending machine, to toss a raw egg into the whirling sweet
milk.

Leche con Plátanos: use 2 ripe bananas in place of the strawberries;
sweeten with honey instead of the sugar.

Licuado de Fruta: use water or fruit juice instead of milk with
acidic juicy fruits: pineapple, cantaloupe, watermelon, or mango.
Strain and serve with chunks of the fruit floating in it, bobbing at
its surface, and pour over crushed ice if desired.

Tropical fruit and yogurt drink: I like the combination of half milk,
half fruit-flavoured yogurt combined with tropical fruits such as
mango, banana, strawberries, etc. Add enough ice to chill and
give consistency and whirl into a chilly froth.

Bebidas de Coco, Limón y Frutas
Coconut-Lime-Fruit Drinks

Creamy coconut milk pairs beautifully with tart fresh lime juice;
add any of a range of tropical fruit juices to this mixture and you
have a taste of Mexico. For a lazy afternoon cocktail, add a dose
of rum to the concoction.

‹‹‹

500 ml/16 fl oz coconut milk (use unsweetened so that you
   can add sugar to taste)
100 ml/4 fl oz fresh lime juice
500 to 750 ml/16 to 25 fl oz tropical fruit juice as desired:
   mango, papaya, guava, passion fruit, or any mixture
Sugar to taste
Ice
Rum (optional)

1. Combine the coconut milk, lime juice, fruit juice and sugar to
   taste.
2. Serve poured over ice, with or without rum.

Agua de Arroz
Rice Cooler

It seems curious – a drink based on steeping ice overnight, then
sweetening and straining. It is, however, extremely refreshing,
with an edge of pleasing chalkiness that soothes as the climate
scorches.

Agua de Arroz is also known as *horchata* in the Yucatán and in
regions that lie close to Guatemala. Variations of this drink are
quite popular throughout Central America, the Caribbean, Spain
and other areas of the Mediterranean as well as Mexico.
Commercial *horchata* is often based on rice powder and con-
densed milk and is very rich and sweet, like Thai tea. This recipe,
however, is light and refreshing. It separates slightly upon stand-
ing, so stir it up before drinking.

450 g/1 lb white rice (uncooked)
100 g/4 oz ground almonds
3 tablespoons ground cinnamon
2 litres/3½ pints hot water or half water and half milk
150 g/5 oz sugar, or to taste
1 teaspoon almond essence or vanilla essence
Ice cubes

◁◁◁◁◁◁◁◁◁◁◁◁◁◁◁◁◁◁◁◁◁◁◁◁◁◁◁◁◁◁▷▷▷▷▷▷▷▷▷▷▷▷▷▷▷▷▷▷▷▷▷▷▷▷▷▷▷▷▷▷

1. Rinse the rice to rid it of any talc. In a large bowl combine the rice, almonds and cinnamon with the hot water or water and milk and let soak for at least 6 hours or overnight in the refrigerator. Strain, reserving both the liquid and the solids.
2. Purée the solids, adding 500 ml/16 fl oz of the liquid. Whirl it in a liquidizer until it is as smooth as possible.
3. Strain this combination of solids and liquid through several layers of dampened cheesecloth, squeezing well to extract all of the milky liquid. Now discard the solids.
4. Sweeten with sugar and season with almond or vanilla essence.
5. Chill and serve over ice cubes.

VARIATIONS

Chocolatl: add 25 to 50 g/1 to 2 oz cocoa powder, to taste, to the strained rice and almond mixture. To prevent lumpiness, blend the cocoa powder into a paste first with a little water or milk.

Fresa: combine the prepared drink with crushed strawberries.

Add a splash of brandy, Kahlua, or other favourite firewater.

For a bright, nearly neon colour and refreshing fruitiness, add several crushed prickly pears to the drink; strain before serving.

Café de Olla
Mexican Coffee

As with much of the world, the first taste of the day in Mexico is a cup of steaming-hot and strong coffee with warm, soothing milk. Coffee is indigenous to the Americas, and was drunk by the ancient Aztecs to give strength and vigour. The best Mexican coffee is grown in Uruapan in the state of Michoacán, the highlands of Chiapas, Cordoba, Veracruz and Oaxaca. A darkish roast, though not quite as black and oily as Italian or French roast, is preferred, with lighter roasts reserved for the better-quality beans, darker roast for the lower-quality ones.

◁◁◁◁◁◁◁◁◁◁◁◁◁◁◁◁◁◁◁◁◁◁◁◁◁◁◁◁◁◁◁◁◁◇▷▷▷▷▷▷▷▷▷▷▷▷▷▷▷▷▷▷▷▷▷▷▷▷▷▷▷▷▷▷▷▷

Traditional Mexican coffee is brewed without the aid of a coffee pot, simply by boiling it with sugar and spices then letting it steep. Sometimes it is strained through a cheesecloth (or clean sock), other times an eggshell or lump of coal is added to the pot to help settle the grounds. Since the grounds are heavy and sink to the bottom anyway, I find that just letting it sit for a few minutes eliminates most of the heavy grounds. If that is not acceptable, you could use a tiny strainer.

In Mérida, in the Yucatán Peninsula with its large Lebanese population, Greco, or Greek-style coffee is served in tiny cups as it is throughout the Middle East.

1 litre/1³/₄ pints water
50 g/2 oz brown demerara sugar
2 to 3 cinnamon sticks
4 cloves
4 tablespoons ground dark-roasted coffee beans

1. Heat the water, sugar, cinnamon and cloves over a medium heat until the sugar has dissolved.
2. Add the coffee and bring to the boil. Remove from the heat, cover, and let stand for 15 minutes before serving.

VARIATION

Café con Leche (Coffee with Milk): this is the equivalent of *café au lait*. Heat 500 ml/16 fl oz milk in a pan while the coffee is steeping, then pour into cups at the same time as the coffee. Add extra sugar to taste, if desired.

Chocolatl Mexicano
Mexican Hot Chocolate

Chocolate is yet another edible gift bequeathed to the world by Mexico. It was said to impart virility, strength and power, and during pre-Hispanic times it was reserved for royalty and people of high position. Bernal Diaz Castillo, one of Cortés's men who chronicled the Conquest, tells of the gold filigree gourds filled

◁◁◁◁◁◁◁◁◁◁◁◁◁◁◁◁◁◁◁◁◁◁◁◁◁◁◁◁◁◁◁◁◁◁◁▷▷▷▷▷▷▷▷▷▷▷▷▷▷▷▷▷▷▷▷▷▷▷▷▷▷▷▷▷▷▷▷▷

with the strong bitter drink that Montezuma downed as an aphrodisiac before visiting his wives.

Its name is said to come from the Indian Náhuatl words *xoto*, meaning bitter, and *atl*, meaning water, though some say it is derived from a Mayan word for hot water.

While many Mexicans buy chocolate in bars as we do, many still prepare their own chocolate much as we might do coffee, by selecting, roasting and grinding the beans. Watch a *chocoltera* at work: smell the heady, bitter scent of the beans as they roast, sputtering and crackling as they are ground into an oily brown paste.

The traditional way to prepare chocolate is with a *molinillo* in a jug over an open fire. The *molinillo* is a strange-looking carved wooden beater that is rolled between the hands and whips the chocolate into a warm froth. While a whisk or liquidizer in theory does as good a job, of course nothing makes hot chocolate as distinctively Mexican and delectable as that *molinillo*.

Mexican chocolate is dark and deep, seasoned with cinnamon and often cloves and almond. To approximate it, use semi-sweetened chocolate with a heady dose of cinnamon added; include a pinch of cloves and almond if you like.

> 100 g/4 oz bittersweet plain chocolate, broken into small pieces (use a baking chocolate from France, or Cadbury's Bournville)
> 1 teaspoon ground cinnamon
> 1 litre/1³/₄ pints milk
> Pinch of cloves (optional)
> Almond essence (optional)
> Extra sugar to taste, if needed (this will depend on the chocolate)

1. Gently heat the chocolate with the cinnamon and milk, stirring constantly until the chocolate is melted. Add the cloves and almond essence, if using.
2. Blend in a liquidizer or whip into a froth with either a whisk or a *molinillo*.
3. Serve immediately.

⊲⊲⊲⊲⊲⊲⊲⊲⊲⊲⊲⊲⊲⊲⊲⊲⊲⊲⊲⊲⊲⊲⊲⊲⊲⊲⊲⊲⊲⊲⊲⊲⊳⊳⊳⊳⊳⊳⊳⊳⊳⊳⊳⊳⊳⊳⊳⊳⊳⊳⊳⊳⊳⊳⊳⊳⊳⊳

Note: 100g/4 oz cocoa powder may be used in place of chocolate; add sugar and vanilla essence to taste.

VARIATIONS

Leah's Café Mocha con Crema: rich and invigorating, this near-
dessert drink of cream- and chocolate-topped Café Mocha is my
daughter's favourite concoction, inspired by Aztec flavours. Pour
half to two-thirds Mexican hot chocolate into a mug and fill with
hot strong coffee. Top with whipped cream, a sprinkling of cinnamon, and a heavy grating of milk chocolate.

In the Southeast of Mexico, Mayan tradition still dictates pre-
colonial honey to sweeten the chocolate rather than sugar.

Prepare Mexican chocolate using all water. Serve hot and frothy,
or let cool and serve chilled, over crushed ice. This is a modern
version of an ancient Aztec drink. When iced, it is good with a
slosh of Kahlua and/or brandy.

Té
Tea

Mexican teas are not the cups of bracing, milk-laced tea that we
drink; rather they are herbal teas, or tisanes, in the French manner. Many people take them as curatives, and the seller will help
you decide on the appropriate tea for your ailment.
   Prepare as you would any herbal tea, by pouring boiling water
over the leaves and letting them steep. Below are listed some
popular teas and their supposed healing powers:

Anis (anise) – to soothe the stomach; this is often given, cooled,
   to help settle colicky babies
Asafetida – for bad tempers
Azahar (orange blossoms) – for both the stomach and nervous
   system
Boldo – for the gall bladder
Borage – for fever

◁◁◁

Canela (cinnamon) – for coughs
Cedar – for the stomach
Clavo (cloves) – for toothaches
Jamaica (hibiscus) – for bad temper
Jazmín (jasmine) – to soothe the nerves
Limón (lemon) – to help with pain
Maiz (cornsilk) – for the kidneys
Manzanilla (camomile) – for nausea
Naranja (orange leaf) – for the nerves
Yerba buena (mint) – a cure-all that helps against stomach upsets

Chia
Cold Chia Seed Tea

Chia seeds produce a strange and gelatinous liquid, a traditional Mexican beverage. The unusual consistency is somewhat jelly-like and makes a remarkably thirst-quenching drink. Unfortunately, this drink is more a curiosity than a practicality: chia seeds are not easily found in the UK.

Simply steep several tablespoons of chia seeds per glass of cold water until the seeds swell and become gelatinous; this will take only a few minutes. Sweeten with sugar or honey and season with lemon or lime juice. Do not strain the seeds; their strange consistency is part of the drink's charm.

Atole
Sweet Thick Warm Drink

Atoles are sweet, gruel-like drinks based on *masa harina*, the same corn flour that forms the base of tortillas, *tamales*, and so on. They are traditionally drunk as an accompaniment to sweet *tamales*.

Passed down from generation to generation through the millennia, *atoles* probably date back to the very beginnings of civilization, pre-dating the great and ancient cultures. Father Sahagun, who chronicled Cortés's conquest of the Aztec nation, mentions that at a great banquet the women were given *atoles* to drink when the men were drinking the more provocative chocolate.

Atole may possibly be one of those foods that one needs to have grown up on to appreciate fully. I confess that I don't: it is too sturdy, substantial, and sweet for my tastes. Yet, each time I am faced with a mug of this nourishing brew I grow to like it a bit more.

Atole can be made with water and/or milk; it can be flavoured with vanilla and cinnamon, with almonds, with fresh or dried and soaked fruit, or with fruit preserves. Chocolate-flavoured *atole* is called *champurrado* and is traditionally eaten for fiestas, such as Christmas Eve, accompanied by *tamales* and/or *buñuelos*. Replace the sugar with dark-brown demerara sugar, and whisk in several spoonfuls of cocoa or bittersweet chocolate. In the Pacific coastal area of Chiapas *champurrado* is served cold, thinned with water and ladled over ice, and is known as *taxcalate*. In Sonora and northwards into New Mexico *atoles* are made with blue corn *masa*, giving a steely, distinctive flavour to the drink.

Atole is classically quite thick, like an American milkshake, but I like it thinned with water and less rich and gruel-like.

2 tablespoons *masa harina*
3 to 4 tablespoons sugar, or to taste
250 ml/8 fl oz milk
500 ml/16 fl oz water
1 teaspoon cinnamon
1 teaspoon vanilla essence

1. Mix the *masa harina* with the sugar, milk, half the water, and the cinnamon. Use a whisk to dissolve the *masa* well.
2. Bring to the boil over a gentle heat, adding the remaining water to thin the mixture.
3. When hot and thickened, season with the vanilla essence, and add more sugar if needed. Serve in small cups.

<<<<<<<<<<<<<<<<<<<<<<<<<<<<<<<>>>>>>>>>>>>>>>>>>>>>>>>>>

VARIATION

Atole de Fresa, Frambuesa, Zarzamora, Piña, etc: add crushed fruit such as strawberries, raspberries, blackberries, guava, or pineapple when you add the second batch of water to thin it out. Prunes, soaked, pitted and puréed, are sometimes added to *atoles*, and any dried fruit could be used instead. The amount of fruit you use depends upon taste and availability. The *atole* could be merely flavoured with fruit, or it could be more of a fruit drink flavoured with the *atole* mixture.

COPITAS
Alcoholic Drinks

'*Salud, dinero, y amor . . . y tiempo para gustarlos.*' (Health, money and love . . . with the time to enjoy them all) – a Mexican drinking toast.

Tequila, a spirit distilled from the agave plant, is probably the best known of Mexican drinks; many consider eating *tacos* and salsa an excuse to bring out the tequila bottle. Walk through the swinging doors of any *cantina*, be it in a city, small town or village, and you're in tequila country, where life's troubles and cares are exchanged for a shrug of the shoulders and a full glass.

To *gringos*, or foreigners, there is something mysterious and evocative about this potent brew – no doubt enhanced by its drinking ritual: a wedge of lime, a tiny pile of salt on the hand, and the bottle. Take a tiny taste of the salt, a swallow of the fiery tequila, then sink your teeth into the lime wedge. Suddenly your conversation seems livelier, your companions ever so much more pleasant, your meal, no matter how humble, is more delicious, and the world in general more tolerable.

Most tequila is produced in the town of Tequila, a dusty place with unpaved streets and mud-brick houses not far from Guadalajara. (They offer tours for visitors.) The nearby hillsides are covered in meticulous rows of millions of blue agave plants, their profusions of spiny leaves looking almost prehistoric.

◁◁◁◁◁◁◁◁◁◁◁◁◁◁◁◁◁◁◁◁◁◁◁◁◁◁◁◁◁◁▷▷▷▷▷▷▷▷▷▷▷▷▷▷▷▷▷▷▷▷▷▷▷▷▷▷▷▷

Each agave plant takes eight to twelve years to reach maturity, then they are harvested and the *cabezas*, or the pineapple-like bases, are split, steamed and juiced. The resultant liquid is fermented then distilled to 80° to 100° proof. It is clear-coloured and mighty harsh at this stage, but some tequilas are aged in wood until they have a golden hue and are as smooth as good brandy or whisky. A similar, though stronger-flavoured, drink is mezcal, also distilled from agave, though a different variety, and notable for the well-pickled maguey worm lying at the bottom of every bottle.

Yet tequila – and mezcal – is not all the agave is good for. The large, pointed leaves may be used to line barbecue pits, the membrane-like skin to wrap spiced meat. The thick maggots that feed on the plant, maguey worms, are fried into a crispy appetizer or tucked into *tacos*.

In addition to the salt-lime ritual, tequila is sometimes drunk with a chilli-tomato chaser, sangrita. In the *cantina* the chaser might be beer – a jigger of tequila, glass and all, placed at the bottom of a beer mug and a bottle of beer poured over it.

Drunk down simply, tequila's tart yet smooth jolt seems as close to perfection as drink can be. However, its ability to mix socially with a wide variety of other ingredients has helped transport it North of the Border to the USA and eastward to Europe. Most notable of these drinks is the margarita, but there are also the tequila sunset, tequila sour, or even a martinez, which is a martini with tequila substituted for gin. A wonderful juice to mix with tequila is grapefruit – so refreshing, so vivacious. Orange juice is very good too.

Despite its current popularity, tequila did not exist before the Conquest. *Pulque* was the Aztec alcoholic drink, prepared from the fermented sap of the spiky maguey plant. Ancient murals at the site of the Great Pyramid of Cholula show *pulque* drinkers carousing in AD 200; *pulque* cups are common pre-Columbian archaeological finds. Milky in colour and slightly foamy, *pulque* is sold in *pulquerias*, small bars, where the drink is cured with various fruits and flavourings to disguise its sourish taste.

Mexico produces some excellent rums, and its coffee-flavoured liqueur, Kahlua, is the definitive coffee liqueur enjoyed throughout the world. A luscious liqueur, little known outside Mexico, is

◁◁◁◁◁◁◁◁◁◁◁◁◁◁◁◁◁◁◁◁◁◁◁◁◁◁◁▷▷▷▷▷▷▷▷▷▷▷▷▷▷▷▷▷▷▷▷▷▷▷▷▷▷▷

rompope, a rich concoction based on raw egg yolks, sugar and brandy, much like the Dutch advocaat. Aguardiente (literally, 'firewater') is brandy, and is often homemade; in Veracruz it is made from sugar cane and used to macerate fresh fruit. Then there is xtabentun, the Yucatecan firewater traditionally brewed from fermented honey and flavoured with aniseed to make a Pernod-like drink, available in *seco* (dry) or *crema* (sweet).

To Drink Tequila

When tequila is drunk straight, aged (*anejo*) is best, although white tequila will do. White unaged tequila is generally used for mixed drinks.

Salt
Tequila
Lime wedges

1. Make an L-shape with your hand, then lightly lick the spot between your index finger and thumb where your hand makes a well and put a pinch of salt on it (licking the spot makes the salt stick). Have several wedges of lime ready and tequila poured in small glasses.
2. Take a lick of the salt, a swallow of the tequila, and sink your teeth into the lime wedge, sucking enough of the tart juice to take the edge off the firewater.

VARIATION

While lime is classic, other fruits and vegetables may also be used: pieces of white jicama, limed and salted, lime-rubbed cucumber, or wedges of orange are all authentic tequila accompaniments.

◁◁◁◁◁◁◁◁◁◁◁◁◁◁◁◁◁◁◁◁◁◁◁◁◁◁◁◁◁◁▷▷▷▷▷▷▷▷▷▷▷▷▷▷▷▷▷▷▷▷▷▷▷▷▷▷▷

Piña Borracha
Tequila-Pineapple Punch

Literally 'drunken pineapple', Piña Borracha is a combination of
equal parts of pineapple and tequila. Any other soft sweet fruit
can be substituted for pineapple – strawberries, melon, peaches,
guavas, etc. Prickly pears are exotically good this way – add a
pinch of cloves, cinnamon and black pepper.

  1 large, ripe, strongly perfumed pineapple, peeled and
     crushed
  1 bottle tequila
  100 g/ 4 oz sugar

1. Blend the pineapple, tequila and sugar in a liquidizer. Leave,
   tightly covered, in the refrigerator for 2 to 24 hours then
   strain and serve well chilled.
2. If preferred, the mixture can be steeped in the refrigerator for
   3 weeks then strained and drunk icy cold.

Classic Margarita

  Lime or lemon peel
  Coarse salt for rim of glass
  35 ml/1$\frac{1}{2}$ fl oz tequila
  35 ml/1$\frac{1}{2}$ fl oz orange liqueur such as triple sec, curaçao,
     etc
  35 ml/1$\frac{1}{2}$ fl oz fresh lime or lemon juice
  Cracked ice

Serves 1

1. Moisten the rim of a cocktail glass with lime or lemon peel,
   then salt the rim by pouring a small amount of salt on to a
   saucer and twirling the moistened rim in it.
2. Combine the tequila, orange liqueur and lime or lemon juice
   with the cracked ice in a cocktail shaker or a liquidizer, then
   shake or blend until well mixed.

3. Strain (if using a liquidizer you will not need to) into the salt-rimmed glass and serve immediately.

VARIATION

Sopresa de Durazno: for this frozen peach margarita, omit the salt and substitute 1/2 sliced frozen peach for the ice. Blend until frothy, as above. Frozen mango or mango juice may be used in place of the peach. Rum instead of tequila and orange liqueur makes a mango daiquiri.

Tequila del Sol
Tequila Sunrise

The layers of orange and crimson run into each other, resembling a vivid tropical sunrise, presumably after a night of debauchery and tequila-drinking.

Serves 1

2 teaspoons grenadine
Crushed ice
2 teaspoons lime juice
50 ml/2 fl oz tequila
50 ml/2 fl oz orange juice

1. Pour the grenadine over crushed ice in a tall glass.
2. Mix the lime juice, tequila and orange juice together, then pour over the grenadine.

VARIATION

Tequila Sunset: omit the orange juice; combine all the ingredients, using 100 ml/4 fl oz crushed ice, then blend in a liquidizer until well mixed and serve immediately.

ᐊᐊᐊᐊᐊᐊᐊᐊᐊᐊᐊᐊᐊᐊᐊᐊᐊᐊᐊᐊᐊᐊᐊᐊᐊᐊᐊᐅᐅᐅᐅᐅᐅᐅᐅᐅᐅᐅᐅᐅᐅᐅᐅᐅᐅᐅᐅᐅᐅᐅᐅᐅ

Sangre de María
Tequila Bloody Mary

Recipe for a summer evening: sunny rooftop garden; good friends; Vivaldi; a pitcherful of Sangre de María.

Serves 2

>   350 ml/12 fl oz tomato juice
>   Juice of ¹/₂ lime
>   Dash of Worcestershire sauce
>   Generous dash of hot red pepper sauce
>   ¹/₂ teaspoon finely minced or grated onion
>   Large pinch of salt
>   100 ml/4 fl oz tequila
>   Cracked ice
>   Finely chopped coriander leaves to garnish
>   Fresh chilli (optional)

1. Combine the tomato juice, lime juice, Worcestershire sauce, hot red pepper sauce, onion and salt. Add the tequila.
2. Serve over cracked ice, sprinkled with a little chopped coriander. For a ferocious garnish, cut a slice of fresh chilli and fit it over the side of the glass, as you would a slice of lemon or lime.

VARIATION

Part of the tomato juice may be replaced by orange juice.

<<<<<<<<<<<<<<<<<<<<<<<<<<>>>>>>>>>>>>>>>>>>>>>>>>>>

Sangrita, Jalisco-Style

Sangrita (literally, 'little blood') is a spicy concoction drunk as a chaser to quell the fires of tequila. It is only fitting that this invigorating drink comes from Jalisco, the home of tequila. Serve chilled tequila in one glass, the Sangrita in another, and alternate mouthfuls as desired.

Serves 1

> 75 ml/3 fl oz tomato juice
> Dash of grenadine syrup to taste
> Juice of 1 lime or $^1/_2$ lemon
> Juice of $^1/_2$ orange
> Pinch of salt
> Crushed ice
> Chopped fresh chillies (or generous dash of red hot pepper
> sauce) and coriander leaves to taste
> 50 ml/2 fl oz tequila

1. Combine everything except the tequila.
2. Serve the Sangrita in one glass, the tequila in another, and sit back and enjoy.

VARIATION

Sangre de Viuda, literally 'blood of the widow', is Sangrita served with the tequila mixed in rather than separate.

Coco Loco

The sands on the beach at Acapulco are hot, the air sultry and thick. You lie in a beach chair under the strong sun. It is exquisitely hot, tottering between delicious and unpleasant; somehow, just when you feel closer to the latter than the former, a very young, white-jacketed waiter brings you a huge coconut filled with some of its light cooling liquid mixed with tequila. You sip and feel blissfully revived, as you run your toes through the hot sand and contemplate cooling off in the gentle sea.

◁◁◁◁◁◁◁◁◁◁◁◁◁◁◁◁◁◁◁◁◁◁◁◁◁▷▷▷▷▷▷▷▷▷▷▷▷▷▷▷▷▷▷▷▷▷▷▷▷▷

This drink is said to have originated on those Acapulco beaches: whether it did or not, it tastes best there. It is also good during a heatwave anywhere, even on a city rooftop.

Serves 1

  1 whole coconut
  1 jigger tequila
  Crushed ice (optional)

1. Punch two holes in the top of the coconut at the location of its 'eyes'. Pour off the liquid and reserve.
2. With a hacksaw, saw off the top of the coconut, leaving a cup-like shell (save for future servings).
3. Combine the coconut liquid and tequila (with crushed ice if desired) and pour into the coconut shell. Sip through a straw.

VARIATION

Tropical Madness: rum, pineapple juice and sweetened coconut milk may be added in place of the tequila.

Sangría de Guadalajara
Lime-Red Wine Float

Though it sounds unlikely, this makes an exquisitely refreshing drink, the fragrant, tangy lime perfectly balanced with the dry, slightly tannic quality of the red wine. By pouring the wine carefully into the lime cordial over the back of a spoon, two separate layers are formed. You can then either stir it, let it combine naturally, or sip it through a straw to drink it in layers.

Serves 1

  2 tablespoons lime juice cordial
  Several ice cubes
  100 to 125 ml/4 to 5 fl oz dry fruity red wine such as
    Beaujolais or simple table wine, chilled if possible

1. Pour the lime cordial over the ice cubes in a glass.
2. Over the back of a spoon carefully pour the red wine in, taking care that the wine arrives gently in the glass. It should layer with the lime cordial. If it does not, it will not look as intriguing but will still be delicious.

Toro Valiente
'Brave Bull'

Kahlua makes a delicious mixer with tequila. For a sweeter after-dinner drink than the one below, use equal amounts of Kahlua and tequila.

Serves 1

2 parts tequila
1 part Kahlua
Cracked ice

1. Combine the tequila and Kahlua and pour over cracked ice. Serve immediately.

Besito
'Little Kiss'

Also known as *beso de ángel*, or the 'kiss of an angel', this drink is a good, sweet way to end a meal or to sip as you warm yourself next to a fire.

Serves 1

Fill a liqueur glass half full with Kahlua then spoon a little whipping cream, lightly whipped if preferred, over the top. Serve immediately.

◁◁◁◁◁◁◁◁◁◁◁◁◁◁◁◁◁◁◁◁◁◁◁◁◁◁◁◁◁▷▷▷▷▷▷▷▷▷▷▷▷▷▷▷▷▷▷▷▷▷▷▷▷▷▷

Cerveza
Mexican Beers

Mexico is one of the world's major brewing nations, a result of Emperor Maximilian's introducing Viennese brewing techniques to a nation that had been brewing beer since 1544. The waves of Swiss, Bavarian and Alsatian immigrants in the 1860s also contributed to the creation of the industry.

Mexican beer, or *cerveza*, makes a superb accompaniment to the vivacious, spicy and often filling Mexican food. It has a high alcoholic content with a wide range of flavours and degrees of heaviness, though only several types are imported into Britain.

Superior is an amber-coloured and refreshing beer, while Dos XX is mellow and somewhat dark; Tres XXX is a bock-type beer available in both dark and light. Corona and Carta Blanca (sold under the name Simpático in Britain) are light and refreshing; though one might say they lack character, they are crisp partners to spicy food and best appreciated in sultry weather. Negro Modelo is a darker, fuller-bodied counterpart. In the Yucatán Carta Clara is a pilsner-type brew while Montejo is much like beer in Munich. At Christmas, rich, dark Guinness-like brews appear in the market, known as *noche buena* or Christmas Eve ('good night') beer.

A fashion that has swept through the Border towns and America's Southwest is to serve a bottle of ice-cold Corona lager, or a can of Tecate, with a wedge of lime squeezed in. Originating in rough-and-tumble Border towns, where it can be hot and desolate, this is exquisitely refreshing, if a bit short on yeasty beer character. Drunk in the right situation, when the weather simmers and you do too, accompanied by highly spiced nibbles, Mexican brew has no peers.

WAYS OF ADDING MEXICAN FLAVOURS TO EVERYDAY MEALS

Salsas: even the simplest fresh salsa gives the flavour of Mexico. If you have neither the time nor the inclination to make salsa, a plate of chopped onion, fresh chillies, tomatoes and fresh coriander is a perfect alternative.

Serve tortillas: to accompany a meal, or to wrap round chilli-seasoned roast meats or stews.

Serve wedges of lemon, lime and orange with soups, rice dishes, grilled meats, fish and poultry.

Use guacamole as a sauce for grilled or poached fish, or as an accompaniment to boiled beef dinners (include a chorizo sausage and a handful of chickpeas in the ingredients).

Cumin, mild chilli powder such as ancho, pasilla, etc, and oregano are hallmark Mexican flavours. Use them to season meat-loaves and meatballs, roasts, stews, soups, etc.

Chopped fresh coriander, especially when combined with fresh green chilli, tastes essentially of Mexico.

Roasted peanuts sprinkled with cayenne or mild chilli powder are a typically Mexican appetizer-nibble.

Fry chopped mild pasilla or ancho chillies in a little vegetable oil until crispy but not burned (the line is a fine one). Serve crumbled over rice dishes and soups.

Higado Mexicana: sautéed liver and onions is *muy Mexicano* when

◁◁◁◁◁◁◁◁◁◁◁◁◁◁◁◁◁◁◁◁◁◁◁◁◁◁◁◁◁◁◁◁◁◁▷▷▷▷▷▷▷▷▷▷▷▷▷▷▷▷▷▷▷▷▷▷▷▷▷▷

served with fresh salsa and a stack of warm corn tortillas.

Accompany any roasted or grilled meat or fish dish with black beans or *frijoles refritos*, tortillas, and a bowl of salsa, or serve *enchiladas* or *chilaquiles* with simple grilled or roasted meat.

A zesty, fresh, but not too hot salsa makes a delicious sauce for tender *al dente* noodles.

Adornos: fresh garnishes are the hallmark of Mexican cuisine. Add them to everyday fare as desired for a distinctive Mexican taste. A few suggestions:

Shredded raw cabbage tossed with vinaigrette
Sliced red onion, crumbled oregano, soured cream
Diced pineapple, shredded cabbage, sliced avocado
Julienned jicama
Chopped coriander, sliced pickled jalapeños
Diced tomatoes, onion, avocado (optional: chipotle chilli)
Thinly sliced lettuce, diced radishes, chopped spring onions, black olives
Soured cream mixed with chopped chillies or coriander

APPENDIX 1
Cooking Techniques

ROASTING

Mexico's brilliantly varied layering of flavours is due to specific techniques such as roasting and grinding. A dish might consist of nothing but tomatoes, chillies and onions, but if you roast any of the ingredients the sauce will be dramatically transformed. The smoky quality adds a whole new dimension to even the simplest of dishes.

Garlic: place the unpeeled cloves of garlic on a hot, ungreased heavy frying pan. Over a medium heat cook and turn every so often, until the garlic appears charred in places and the cloves are softish to the touch. Garlic may also be roasted a whole head at a time; each way gives a different flavour. When cool enough to handle, squeeze the soft flesh from the papery skin.

Onion: toast as for garlic. While whole onions are usually preferred, occasionally I like halved onions for the more pronounced grilled flavour. When cool enough to handle, peel and chop, or use as desired.

Tomatoes: tomatoes are often roasted for Mexican sauces, soups and stews. Sometimes I roast tomatoes by impaling them on forks then plunging them into open flames and letting them char and sputter. A less dramatic method is to grill them: place under a hot grill and cook until evenly browned, about 15 minutes. Turn occasionally for even cooking. Leave until cool enough to handle then peel, seed and chop. To make a sauce, place the grilled tomatoes in a liquidizer and blend, skins, seeds and all.

◁◁◇▷▷▷▷▷▷▷▷▷▷▷▷▷▷▷▷▷▷▷▷▷▷▷▷▷▷▷▷▷▷▷▷

GRINDING

The other technique that gives Mexican food a certain distinction is the fact that sauces are often ground – mixtures of raw
and/or roasted onions, garlic, chillies, tomatoes, and spices –
then poured into a little hot oil in a frying pan and cooked. This
intensifies the flavours and thickens the mixture, making it a
good base for stock, meat, rice, etc.

APPENDIX 2

Utensils and Cookware

CLAY

Mexican food would not look nor even taste the same without the gaily coloured clay cooking utensils, bowls, pitchers, etc. Cooking in clay imparts a certain inimitable essence to the food, with no metal pot and pan flavours to taint the ingredients.

Before cooking with clay, be sure that your pieces can withstand the heat of the fire (ask when you purchase them). Next, you must 'season' the pots, much as a wok needs to be seasoned. Rub the outside of the pots with a cut garlic clove and fill the inside with soapy water as close to the brim as possible. Place the pot on the heat, bring to the boil and boil until the water has almost evaporated. Remove from the heat and let the pot stand for at least 20 minutes. This seals the clay. Smaller pieces can be boiled in a large pot of soapy water for about an hour rather than placed on their own on top of the cooker.

MOLCAJETE AND TEJOLOTE

These are a mortar and pestle made from near-black, porous volcanic stone. They have a primitive, exotic appearance. Spices ground in a *molcajete* rather than a liquidizer are more finely textured, and sauces blended in a *molcajete* have a more intense flavour. If you do find a *molcajete* and *tejolote*, they will need to be tempered before use. First put a little rice or other grain into the *molcajete* along with a little salt. Grind and grind, with the *tejolote*, then empty the *molcajete* and repeat, continuing the process several times until the ground grain and salt are pure in colour and free of grit, pebbles or dirt.

◁◁◁◁◁◁◁◁◁◁◁◁◁◁◁◁◁◁◁◁◁◁◁◁◁◁◁◁◁◁◁◁▷▷▷▷▷▷▷▷▷▷▷▷▷▷▷▷▷▷▷▷▷▷▷▷▷▷

METATE

This is one of the oldest kitchen utensils known to Mesoamerica. It is similar to the *molcajete*, but larger and rectangular in shape with a rolling, pin-shaped stone to roll back and forth. Supported by three legs, the *metate* is used to grind *nixtamil*, or corn for *masa*. Like the *molcajete*, the *metate* needs to be tempered before using.

GLOSSARY

ACHIOTE

Also known as annatto, these are brick-red, stone-hard tiny seeds that impart a red-yellow colour and elusive, almost citrus-saffron flavour. They must be soaked overnight before use. For the basic Yucatecan achiote seasoning paste, refer to Pollo Pibil (page 150). Since the seeds need to be soaked and ground, in Mexico they are often sold ready to use in little squares, with or without additional seasonings. In Britain achiote seeds are used to colour butter and margarine. They are difficult to find in this country but can occasionally be tracked down in Caribbean markets. The small, hard seeds last nearly for ever.

AVOCADO LEAVES (*HOJAS DE AGUACATE*)

The leaves of the avocado tree, cousin of the bay laurel, are used often in Mexican cookery. They have a herby flavour, with hints of anise and bay. Unfortunately, houseplants don't have the same qualities – you really do need a large, outdoor-grown tree for the characteristic flavour and fragrance. Usually avocado leaves are toasted, then ground with other ingredients into a spicy paste; sometimes they are used whole, to line a steamer or wrap a parcel (especially a whole chicken, Veracruz-style). Bay leaves, with or without a sprinkling of anise, make the best substitute.

AVOCADOS, OR AVOCADO PEARS

Mexico raises a wide variety of avocados, from huge, melon-sized, bright green specimens to tiny, thumb-sized ones. The favourite is hass, medium-sized with dark-green to nearly black pebbly, thick skin. The flesh of these avocados is creamy and

◄◄◄◄◄◄◄◄◄◄◄◄◄◄◄◄◄◄◄◄◄◄◄◄◄◄◄◄◄◄◄◄◄◄►►►►►►►►►►►►►►►►►►►►►►►►►►►►►►►►

rich, giving itself gracefully to the flavours of chillies, tomatoes, onions, and so on. An avocado is ripe when the pointed end gives just a tiny bit when pressed; soft patches on the rest of the fruit don't indicate ripeness – they indicate spoiled spots. Once your avocado reaches the ripe stage, refrigerate it and it will keep for about ten days.

BANANA LEAVES (*HOJAS DE PLÁTANOS*)

Large, fragrant fronds of the banana palm, these are favoured throughout the tropical regions of Mexico – the southern, Yucatán, and Gulf Coastal regions – for wrapping chicken, pork, *tamales*, and so on. Banana leaves can be found in Indian grocers, or frozen in Chinese shops. Pass them over a flame to make them pliable before using.

CACTUS (*NOPALE*)

The paddles of the prickly pear-bearing cactus, *nopales* are used throughout Mexico. I often find them fresh in the UK in Caribbean markets such as London's Ridley Road. Fresh, they last for several weeks in the refrigerator.

To clean and cook: the large prickly spines will most likely have been removed. Trim the large outer edge of the paddle, including the end where the paddle was cut from the plant. Scrape or slice off the sharp bits where the spines are, or were. Cut into strips or dice and toss into a pot of salted boiling water (add an onion, a handful of coriander, and a fresh chilli, if liked), then cook for about 15 to 20 minutes. Rinse and toss with a little salt, and store in the refrigerator.

CHAYOTE

This delicate, squash-like fruit looks somewhat like a smooth avocado and tastes like a courgette that has been grown on another planet where everything tastes more delicious. Chayotes are eaten throughout the Caribbean, fried, baked, stuffed, simmered, and so on. They keep for up to about a month.

⊲⊲⊲⊲⊲⊲⊲⊲⊲⊲⊲⊲⊲⊲⊲⊲⊲⊲⊲⊲⊲⊲⊲⊲⊲⊲⊲⊲⊳⊳⊳⊳⊳⊳⊳⊳⊳⊳⊳⊳⊳⊳⊳⊳⊳⊳⊳⊳⊳⊳⊳⊳⊳⊳⊳⊳

CHEESE (QUESO)

Before the Conquest Mexico had no tradition of cheese. Since then cheese has come to be sprinkled on to a wide variety of *antojitos*, *frijoles*, soups, fruit desserts, and so on. Most of the cheese is farmhouse and regional, often rather fresh and crumbly, sometimes aged for grating.

In Mexico crumbly fresh cheese is known as *queso fresco* or *queso ranchero*, though most Mexican cheeses bear the name of the farmhouse, factory or region where they were made. Fresh Pecorino, or Feta cheese soaked in water for an hour or two to rid it of its extra salt, makes a good cheese to use wherever one would use *queso fresco*. Cheshire and Lancashire are also good; mild, milky, fresh goat's cheese may be suitable as well.

For melting, choose mild white Cheddar, or a nice mature one. Fresh Mozzarella is stringily delicious in many dishes that call for a meltable cheese, especially an Oaxaca-type one.

CHICHARRONES

Airy, crisp and nearly addictive pork cracklings. They get their distinctive texture from a double frying technique similar to that used in French cooking for souffléed potatoes and the like. The skins of freshly killed pigs are first dried in the sun for a day, then they are plunged into a great cauldron of bubbling hot oil and removed. They are allowed to cool, then the process is repeated; in the second frying the skins puff up dramatically. Because of the process they are not suitable for preparing at home.

In Mexico *chicharrones* are sold loose in nearly every market-place in the country: great slabs of golden-coloured honeycombed crispness, ready for breaking off and nibbling on, sprinkled with lime juice and fierce cayenne pepper. If you should find them, serve with guacamole and a salsa, or break them into little bits and stir them into a Salsa Verde; wrap in tortillas for *chicharrón tacos*. Alternatively, just nibble them guiltily; they're probably at their best that way.

◄◄◄◄◄◄◄◄◄◄◄◄◄◄◄◄◄◄◄◄◄◄◄◄◄◄◄◄◄◄◄<>►►►►►►►►►►►►►►►►►►►►►►►►►►►►►►►

CHILLIES

Chillies are perhaps Mexico's greatest gift to the culinary world, along with corn, tomatoes, potatoes and chocolate. To catalogue the endless variety of chillies in this small space would be an impossible task. For further information on chillies, I refer you to my book *Hot & Spicy* (Grafton Books).

Chillies, also known as *capsicum frutescens*, are amazingly rich sources of vitamins A and C. Fresh chillies are second only to beef liver in vitamin A, and in vitamin C they fall only slightly behind rose hips.

The outstanding characteristic of the chilli, its culinary fire, is due to the active ingredient 8-methyl-N-vannilyn-6-neneamide or, more simply, capsaicin. Though one can measure the heat of chillies using a measurement of Scoville units, and many cookbook writers go into elaborate detail on the subject, I don't see the point: it's not difficult to figure out that a chilli is too hot.

Then one is left to soothe the tender flesh. Do not reach for water! It may cool the singed flesh for a moment, but the pain will return, quickly and unmercifully. Better to try to absorb the volatile oils that carry the capsaicin by spooning down some soft, bland rice, corn or flour tortillas, or bread; yogurt is soothing, so is anything icy, especially tequila or vodka-laced drinks, since the alcohol adds to the painkiller effect. In Texas, salt is sworn by, but I can't recommend eating such a large amount of salt.

There are approximately 200 varieties of chillies both fresh and dried, ranging from richly mild ones to searingly hot berries no larger than peppercorns, or great, large chillies the size of a man's fist, or bigger. And in between there is a cornucopia of shapes and sizes, colours and flavours, in addition to the heat.

For practical purposes, the main two groupings of chillies are fresh and dried.

Fresh chillies are usually green, sometimes ripe yellow and red. They may be simply sliced and tossed into a dish, with their fiery, fresh flavour, or they may be roasted and peeled first, their inflammatory seeds and veins removed, leaving only a rich vegetable flavour and a small amount of heat.

To roast: over an open flame (e.g. a gas ring), or under a hot grill, or in a hot, ungreased frying pan, heat the chillies until they char, moving them so that they blacken evenly. Over an open flame, they may catch fire; don't be concerned, though do blow the flames out as too much burning will eat into the flesh of the peppers in addition to the skin. Once they are blackened, place the hot, charred chillies in a bowl or plastic bag and seal tightly. Leave for 15 to 30 minutes, then peel off the skin. The longer you leave them to sweat, the easier it will be to remove the skin – and the milder they become. This is particularly useful with chillies such as poblano, which you want to be fairly mild, but which in reality are often not.

A few of the most common fresh green chillies are:

Cayenne: the long, thin chilli often seen in Indian/Asian shops. Don't confuse it with the Thai chilli, which is needle-thin and nearly painful in intensity.

European: this is usually sold unlabelled in Europe or America, imported from Holland. It is a large, pointed and rather thick chilli, often red in colour and readily available. It may be either mild or slightly hot.

Habanero: known as Scots bonnet in Great Britain and the West Indies, this is widely available, usually in West Indian or Asian markets. It ranges from red, yellow and orange to green-yellow, and from hot to very, very hot.

Italian peppers: also known as Hungarian peppers, these are twisted and larger than the other chillies. They are very mild, with only the slightest bite.

Jalapeño: generally medium hot, but can range from piquant to incendiary. Many of the chillies found in Great Britain are variations on the jalapeño – hot but not painfully so, with enough flavour to balance the heat. Because of this the jalapeño is probably the most useful of the fresh chillies. Often it is labelled with its country of origin: Kenya, or other African/Mediterranean

ਵਵਵਵਵਵਵਵਵਵਵਵਵਵਵਵਵਵਵਵਵਵਵਵਵਵ◇▷▷▷▷▷▷▷▷▷▷▷▷▷▷▷▷▷▷▷▷▷▷▷▷▷▷▷

countries. Use in recipes that call for medium-size, medium to hot chillies.

Poblano: though these are not generally available in Great Britain, they are used much in Mexico. To approximate their flavour, roast and peel green peppers, then sprinkle with cayenne and leave to marinate.

Serrano: narrower than the jalapeño, often shorter and hotter, too. Use in recipes which call for small, fairly hot chillies.

Dried chillies come in two basic types – small, hot ones and large, mild ones. Small, hot dried chillies are sometimes very hot. They are often used for hot salsas, especially those based on vinegar, or as seasoning. There is a large variety of small dried chillies, including hontaka, árbol, tepín or pequín, japonés and bird's eye. Often, though, they are simply labelled chillies, or hot chillies. Any of them may be used in any recipe calling for small, dried, hot chillies.

Of the large, mild chillies there are many, many to choose from but two main sorts: firstly the smooth-skinned ones such as pasilla, New Mexico, Chimayo, California, Anaheim, as well as a myriad of others; they are fairly mild and give a soft, paprika-like chilli flavour. Guajillo chillies, which are not generally available in the UK, are long, narrow and light red in colour, smooth-skinned with a slightly sharper bite. The second type of large, mild chillies, the wrinkly-skinned ones, have chocolate-dark colours and rich flavours, and include the ancho, negro and pasilla. Mulato chillies are darker than the ancho, with a distinctly warmer flavour. Pasilla and ancho chillies are both available through La Mexicana and Mexicolore (see Sources). Chipotle, smoky-flavoured and full of fire, are often found dried rather than in tins.

There are several ways to use the dried mild chillies. Each recipe specifies the techniques that work best for that particular dish.

To make a mild chilli sauce, the chillies must be steeped in water to rehydrate them, then puréed and strained to rid them of the indigestible gritty bits. You can do this by tearing up the chillies and discarding the stems and seeds, then pouring hot water or stock over them and leaving them to rehydrate. To add a subtle depth of flavour, first toast the chillies lightly in an ungreased frying pan or over an open flame, only until they give off a toasted perfume, but do not colour, then pour hot water or stock over them.

When the chillies are softened, after at least thirty minutes, though they could be left for up to overnight, remove from the soaking liquid. Save the liquid for the sauce; any leftovers may be used in soups, stews, braises, etc. Purée the rehydrated chillies in a liquidizer, along with enough of their soaking liquid to make a sauce, then press through a sieve to strain away the tough bits.

For a smoother, more refined and undiluted chilli paste, take the drained and softened chillies and remove the stems and seeds. Scrape the flesh away from the tough, papery skin, using a paring knife. Discard the skin and use the concentrated chilli flesh as desired.

Another way to use mild chillies is as a garnish, cut into very thin strips and fried to a crisp. Cut with scissors, and quickly fry in hot oil, taking care not to burn them. Drain on absorbent paper.

CHILLIES, PICKLED

Chipotle Chilli: this is the smoked jalapeño chilli, usually sold either in brine or in tins in a spicy *adobo* marinade. It has both smoke and fire, in its inimitable aroma/flavour and breathtaking heat. A tiny bit of chipotle goes a long way towards creating the flavour of Mexico. When you open the tin, transfer the contents to a glass container and keep in the refrigerator for up to a month. Morita chillies have a similar flavour, though smaller in size; they may be used interchangeably with chipotles. Seldom available in the UK, chipotles can, however, occasionally be ordered from Mexicolore and La Mexicana (see Sources).

Jalapeños en Escabeche: available in jars in delicatessens, these are jalapeño chillies that have been pickled in vinegar. Really delicious ones have carrots, onion, and sometimes cauliflower added.

⊲⊲⊲⊲⊲⊲⊲⊲⊲⊲⊲⊲⊲⊲⊲⊲⊲⊲⊲⊲⊲⊲⊲⊲⊲⊲⊲⊲⊲⊲⊲⊲⊲⊲⊲⊳⊳⊳⊳⊳⊳⊳⊳⊳⊳⊳⊳⊳⊳⊳⊳⊳⊳⊳⊳⊳⊳⊳⊳⊳⊳⊳⊳⊳⊳⊳⊳⊳⊳

If available, make your own (see pages 38–9). Serrano chillies are also available *en escabeche*.

CHILLI POWDER

Mild chilli powder is sold in most supermarkets, a mixture based on mild chillies such as pasilla and ancho, with other spices and additives for flavouring. To approximate the flavour of pure chilli powder made from ancho or pasilla chillies, combine equal amounts, or to taste, of mild chilli powder and paprika. If you have whole ancho or pasilla chillies, however, you can make pure chilli powder: lightly toast the chillies on an ungreased baking sheet or in a heavy ungreased frying pan; you can do this either in the oven or on top of the stove. Toast in the oven at 200°C/400°F/gas mark 6, or over a medium heat, cooking for just long enough for the chillies to grow fragrant and slightly brittle, not to darken and develop a burnt flavour.

Let cool, then remove the stems and seeds and break the chillies into little pieces. Whirl in a liquidizer or coffee-grinder (one that you have cleaned well, or use only for grinding spices). Store in a glass jar.

CHORIZO

Pork sausage seasoned with red chilli. Selfridges in London sells a good Mexican chorizo, as do La Mexicana and Mexicolore (see Sources).

CORIANDER

Fresh, pungent green leaves grown from the coriander seed. Available in Indian or Chinese shops, and often in supermarkets. You can grow your own easily by sowing a small plot at two-week intervals (they grow quickly, then die just as quickly). However, sometimes the seeds purchased as spices are too old to germinate.

◁◁◁◁◁◁◁◁◁◁◁◁◁◁◁◁◁◁◁◁◁◁◁◁◁◁◁◁◁◁◁◁◁◁▷▷▷▷▷▷▷▷▷▷▷▷▷▷▷▷▷▷▷▷▷▷▷▷▷▷▷▷▷▷

CORN HUSKS

The outer covering of the corn, used to wrap *tamales* and other edible parcels. Often available in West African markets such as London's Ridley Road, corn husks need to be soaked in warm water for at least three hours before using. If using corn husks in which the husks, or leaves, have not been separated, cut them apart with a pair of scissors before use. I have tried drying my own husks, pulling them off corn on the cob, but once dried they are awfully small and not very suitable for even the smallest of *tamales*.

EPAZOTE

A pungent herb, also called pazote, this is known in North America as wormseed or wormweed. In Northern Mexico it is used dried, as a medicinal tea to soothe shaky nerves, or as a vermifuge; in the South it is used frequently, especially in bean dishes of all sorts. Its strong, almost unpleasant taste has the ability to round out the beans and give them a greater depth of flavour. Unfortunately epazote is not available in the UK, so I use several fresh bay leaves instead.

HOMINY

Kernels of corn that have been treated with slaked lime until they plump up, shed their skins and develop a distinctive, earthy flavour and fragrance. Hominy is often sold whole in tins in the US and is very handy. In Britain it is more often sold in West Indian shops, dried and broken into small pieces.

JICAMA

A large root vegetable rather like a water chestnut. Remove its brown skin and it is white in colour, quite sweet, and like an apple in both texture and flavour. Eat raw, as a snack, sprinkled with lime juice and cayenne pepper, or use with fruits in salads.

◁◁◁◁◁◁◁◁◁◁◁◁◁◁◁◁◁◁◁◁◁◁◁◁◁◁◁◁▷▷▷▷▷▷▷▷▷▷▷▷▷▷▷▷▷▷▷▷▷▷▷▷▷

MASA HARINA

Finely ground corn made from dry corn that has been boiled with slaked lime until the kernels swell and shake off their skins. The cooked kernels are then dried and ground into the flour, *masa harina*. In Mexico, one can often find fresh *masa* that has been ground on the *metate*, the dough fragrant with corn and the faint whiff of the stone it was ground on.

Masa harina is used for tortillas, *tamales*, *masa antojitos*, and sometimes as a thickener for sauces, such as the Chile Colorado (page 176). Quaker Oats make an excellent, white-coloured, corn-scented *masa*. As with all flour, store in a cool, dark place in a well-sealed container.

PLANTAINS (*PLÁTANOS MACHOS*)

Large, starchy bananas, used for cooking rather than for eating raw. Available in Caribbean markets and many supermarkets, plantains are ripened before use in Mexican cooking.

SEVILLE, OR BITTER, ORANGES

Sour with a sharp citrus flavour, these are a hallmark flavour of the Yucatán and other southern areas of Mexico. Seville oranges are sometimes available in markets in the UK for making marmalade; if not, orange juice can be combined with grapefruit juice and lemon or lime juice, along with a little grated grapefruit peel. The recipes in this book usually assume that Seville oranges are not available, and use combinations of other citrus juices.

SHRIMP, DRIED (*CAMARONES SECAS*)

These are tiny dried shrimp, sometimes sold crushed into a powder. They are available in Chinese or Southeast-Asian shops. Choose ones with as pink a colour as possible – a pale colour denotes old, faded shrimp. Dried shrimp are served in a variety of ways: steep in hot water, season with garlic and mild chillies and you have a simple broth. Add to Arroz Blanco (page 190) for a Lenten speciality. Crisp fried patties are made from dried shrimp, another speciality for Lent.

◁◁◁◁◁◁◁◁◁◁◁◁◁◁◁◁◁◁◁◁◁◁◁◁◁◁◁▷▷▷▷▷▷▷▷▷▷▷▷▷▷▷▷▷▷▷▷▷▷▷▷

SQUASH BLOSSOMS (*FLORES DE CALABAZA*)

Mexican cooks adore squash blossoms as much as Italians do. Their flowery beauty is as appealing as their delicate flavour. In Mexico squash blossoms are most commonly used for soup, though you might like tossing them into Arroz con Elote (page 192) in place of the corn.

To clean, remove the stem and stalk, and cut the flowers roughly with scissors (a knife will crush the tender petals).

TOMATILLOS

A ripe, small, green tomato that is covered with a papery brown husk. Remove the husk and the skin underneath is slightly sticky, the tomatillo itself firm to the touch, unlike a ripe (red, yellow or green) eating tomato. Tomatillos add a distinctive, tart and bright flavour to dishes. I have heard that one can get similar results by adding some cooked unsweetened gooseberries to a sauce; I suspect it is true, though I would use gooseberries only in dishes in which the tomatillos were a small part, rather than the basis of the dish.

If you find fresh tomatillos, they must be cooked (though it has become quite fashionable recently in California to prepare salsas and relishes with uncooked ones; I don't think it suits them to their best advantage).

To cook: place in a saucepan, cover with water and bring to the boil. Simmer over a low-medium heat until the tomatillos change colour from a bright to a lighter, slightly browner green. Tomatillos are sometimes available in Britain sold in tins. They're good; drain before using.

SOURCES

La Mexicana
17 Farady Road
Rabans Lane
Aylesbury
Bucks HP19 3RY
Tel: (0296) 84243

Under the ownership of cookery writer Lourdes Nichols, La Mexicana supplies the widest variety of Mexican foods I have been able to find in the UK. Contact her directly or, if you live in London, call Mexicolore and they will collect what you need. You can stop in at their Battersea office or wait until the weekend when they will deliver to your home – for orders of £15 and over delivery is free within a ten-mile radius.

Here is a partial list of ingredients La Mexicana carries (less usual ones such as chipotles and tomatillos are not always available – telephone first and inquire): yellow and white tortilla chips; yellow and white corn tortillas, including an oval one for making *flautas*; flour tortillas (from 10 cm/4 in to 25 cm/10 in); sauces such as tomatillo, mole, and tomato-chilli salsas; nopales; tomatillos; dried chillies such as pasilla, ancho, chipotle; *mole* powder. A line of ready-prepared foods is also available.

Mexicolore
28 Warriner Gardens
London SW11 4EB
Tel: 071-622-9577

Basically, anything supplied through La Mexicana is also available from Mexicolore. They also carry a few other items, including *masa harina* (though at the time of writing they do not yet have the lovely white Quaker's *masa*) and tortilla presses. Walking into their tiny quarters is like a taste of Mexico

◁◁◁◁◁◁◁◁◁◁◁◁◁◁◁◁◁◁◁◁◁◁◁◁◁◁◁◁◁◁◁◁◁◁◁◁◁◁◁▷▷▷▷▷▷▷▷▷▷▷▷▷▷▷▷▷▷▷▷▷▷▷▷▷▷▷▷▷▷▷▷▷▷▷▷▷▷

in London – for they are a cultural organization devoted to bringing Mexican culture to Great Britain. Costumes, pinatas (decorated paper hanging shapes filled with sweets), slide shows, even a mariachi band – all are available through these people. They go into schools and share the music, dances and other aspects of Mexican culture with the students. If you are having a party, they will come out to your house and Mexicanize the place for you.

Garcia and Sons Spanish Delicatessen
248 Portobello Road
London W11 1LL
Tel: 071-221-6119
Black beans, corn and flour tortillas, mild chilli enchilada sauce.

Ridley Road Market (the West Indian stalls)
London E8
Fresh *nopales*, corn husks, hominy.

Panzers Delicatessen
13–19 Circus Road
St Johns Wood
London NW8 9TS
Tel: 071-722-8596
Quaker's *masa harina* (excellent for *tamales* and tortillas), good crisp tortilla chips, frozen flour and corn tortillas, pickled jalapeños.

Most Indian grocers sell fresh coriander, and white chapattis, sometimes even pita bread, may often be substituted for flour tortillas. The funny thing is one never knows where ingredients will turn up. I've found the most beautiful white *masa harina* in Penrith, Cumbria, for example. *Tostada* and *taco* shells are readily available throughout much of the UK, as are *frijoles refritos*, and even pickled jalapeños.

As for the salsas found in most supermarkets, give them a miss. Most are too sweet and tomatoey, not fresh and crisply chilli-tasting. Make your own – it's easy enough.

INDEX

⊲⊲⊲⊲⊲⊲⊲⊲⊲⊲⊲⊲⊲⊲⊲⊲⊲⊲⊲⊲⊲⊲⊲⊲⊲⊲⊲⊲⊲⊲⊲⊲⊲⊳⊳⊳⊳⊳⊳⊳⊳⊳⊳⊳⊳⊳⊳⊳⊳⊳⊳⊳⊳⊳⊳⊳⊳⊳⊳⊳⊳⊳